A HISTORY OF MIDDLE EUROPE

A History of Middle Europe

From the Earliest Times
to the Age of the World Wars

By LESLIE C. TIHANY

RUTGERS UNIVERSITY PRESS
New Brunswick   New Jersey

Library of Congress Cataloging in Publication Data

Tihany, Leslie Charles, 1911-
  A history of middle Europe.

  Includes index.
  I. Central Europe—History. I. Title.
DR36.T5   943   75-25945
ISBN: 0-8135-0814-2

This edition published by Dorset Press,
a division of Marboro Books Corporation,
by arrangement with Rutgers University Press.
1987 Dorset Press

Printed in the United States of America

M 9 8 7 6 5 4 3 2 1

TO MY FATHER AND MOTHER

in grateful and loving memory

"... it's all the same
If the wolves will eat us
Or if the devil eats us;
We will be eaten just the same.
Or if the bears will eat us,
That, too, will be just the same."
Endre Ady (1877–1919), in
"Partisans of Old Speak."

Contents

Foreword

History can be written in many ways, and each region of the world offers the historian its own set of choices and challenges. Since the time of the barbarian invasions the eastern marchlands of Europe, stretching from the Baltic to the Black, Aegean, and Adriatic seas, have been a battleground of nations and empires, their peoples buffeted by powerful forces beyond their control and set against each other by the ambitions of their leaders and the mutual antagonisms of different ethnic groups and social classes. In this age of nationalism ·each national state or ethnic group has developed a history of its own to fortify its existence, back its claims to territory, or assert its right to a place in the sun. The most talented historians of Eastern, Central, or Middle Europe rarely moved beyond this perspective; indeed, the imperatives of twentieth-century nationalism tend to be read backward into the past. The Marxist interpretations which the political fate of the region has made mandatory in the years since World War II, although now themselves attenuated by nationalism, have merely compounded the confusion, adding more distortion than clarification.

This is not to imply that national aspirations, ethnic conflict, and class struggle are not the stuff and substance of Middle European history. They are. The question is whether, in searching for broad political and social forces which give form to what otherwise appears as a chaotic series of events, one approaches the task with predetermined values and conclusions. No historian, of course, can be wholly free of the predilections of his time and of his personal philosophy and thus write only pure history "as it really was." The very choice of what events to include and how to relate them one to another, especially in a narrative covering a thousand years or more, presupposes a value system. But one of those values can be a conscious striving for a bias-free vision.

Leslie Tihany's great merit, in guiding his readers through the changing fortunes of dynasties and nations, is that he has no cause to plead, no preconceived theory to justify, no nation to exalt above its neighbors. His concern is to tell a human story, that of all the people, the silent peasants as well as the princes and the warriors. If there is a bias, it is a sympathy and understanding for all these nations and peoples whose destiny was rarely in their own hands.

The political map of Middle Europe, in whatever century, has been largely determined by the rise and fall of empires. Poland and Hungary built political institutions of their own and at times played a prominent part in the international politics of the day; and later the Balkan states, even as pawns, had some influence on the moves of the stronger pieces on the chessboard. Nevertheless, such unity as the region has known from time to time has been imposed from the outside. Such independence as parts of it have known has been the result of some temporary equilibrium among great powers, of occasional and unexpected periods of relaxation, or of a fierce will to resistance on the part of a people living on the more remote fringes of empire whose suppression, if possible, was not worth the cost. The overriding pattern has thus been one of dependence. The centers of ultimate authority were in distant places—Vienna, Constantinople, St. Petersburg, and later Berlin and Moscow—where the decisions to make war or peace, to shift boundaries, to raise armies, or to impose tribute were made. Peoples, like booty, go to the strong. Empires, of course, are neither static nor eternal. Generally they expand until they meet a stronger force and then retreat. Or they decay from within.

The unending series of kings and wars and shifts of territory may seem pointless in its confusion, but it has a human side, both in the character of the leaders, be they heroes or villains, strong or incompetent, and in the fate of the people. For underneath the surface there was a living history in the relations of landlord and serf, independent peasant and tax collector, artisan and merchant. And the lines of social division might coincide with or cross those of religion or language. For the great majority of individuals, politics did not go beyond solidarity with those of similar estate and defense against the immediate oppressor; international affairs might touch them only when an army on the march came through the local village.

Tihany gives us a multicolored canvas, often bewildering in its diversity. But he does not impose on this confusion an order which did not exist, just to make things easier for himself and the reader. He does, however, identify the forces at work and their relation to each other.

The ethnic map, as we have noted, at no time coincided with the political map, but there was great hope, as the age of nationalism made its appearance in the nineteenth century, that it would do so. As the great empires found it more and more difficult to cope with the revolt of nationalities inspired by that new religion, some of the latter began to make good their claim to independent nationhood: Greece, Serbia, Rumania, Bulgaria. The Habsburg Empire was shaken by the national question, and the national aspirations of the Poles had not died with the extinction of their country at the hands of three greedy and more powerful neighbors in the eighteenth century. The shattering effects of the First World War, which brought down the Russian, Austrian, and Ottoman empires, seemed to open a new era in which the self-determination of peoples would be recognized as the highest law. Woodrow Wilson was its prophet. The peace and the new world order were to be made on the basis of his principles.

The subsequent years, as we know, were years of disillusionment both for the peoples of Middle Europe and for their well-wishers elsewhere. The disillusionment would not have been so great if the illusions themselves had not grown to such large proportions. One was that the small independent nations could work out their relations among themselves in some semblance of order and equilibrium, a possibility gravely complicated by the fact that frontiers could not be drawn without leaving ethnic minorities under alien rule. A second illusion was that the international community, organized in the League of Nations, would guarantee security and keep the peace. A third, the illusion which proved fatal, was that the disappearance of predatory great powers on both sides of Middle Europe was more than a temporary phenomenon. When both Germany and Russia re-emerged as powerful empires, their decisions, whether in collusion or in conflict, determined the fate of the states lying between them. The democracies of Western Europe could not save them from Hitler; by the time they had mustered the will, they had lost the capability to do so.

Professor Tihany wisely concludes his narrative with the cataclysmic events of the two World Wars of this century. He is writing history, not contemporary world politics. Yet the perspective that he gives to his vast millennial panorama provides the key to an understanding of the controversies over Eastern Europe that have figured so prominently in American-Soviet relations and in American domestic politics since 1945. In brief, in a world which has not yet found its way to an order based on law or the restraint of power by moral principle, the dependent condition of Middle Europe remains as in former centuries. After the defeat of Hitler, with the balance of forces now global rather than European, the line between the two great agglomerations of power ran north and south through the middle of the European continent. As Winston Churchill reminded the world in his famous "iron curtain" speech at Fulton, Missouri, the ancient European capitals of Warsaw, Prague, and Budapest remained in bondage on the eastern side.

The Western world has deplored the fact of Soviet domination of peoples who aspire to self-determination and have a right to it, but sentiment and propaganda and diplomatic notes have not changed the facts of power which could only be challenged at the risk of general war. The Yugoslavs, by a happy combination of their own courage, Soviet miscalculation, and a favorable international situation, were able to make good their will to independence, but the Poles, Hungarians, and Czechoslovaks learned to their sorrow that they could neither win freedom for themselves nor expect to gain it through help from outside. There may be changes in degree. A Middle European state may find it possible to stray from total alignment in its foreign policy or to embark on unorthodox economic reforms, thanks to shifts in the tactics and the tolerance of the dominant power, in the temperature of the relations of the great powers, or in the character of the balance between them. But all will remain within the limits of the general pattern.

The history of Middle Europe is, in many ways, a chronicle of suffering, travail, and tragedy. Geography and history bestowed few favors on these peoples. Yet they have produced a remarkable record of individual and social achievement and a flowering of vital national cultures, even as they lived year after year, generation after generation, through domination, repression, conflict imposed by others, and conflict among themselves. These are people who have contributed mightily to world civilization and to the life of lands beyond their own, as we Americans, who number so many of them in the ranks of our nation, have good reason to know.

John C. Campbell

Acknowledgments

I should like to express my appreciation to the Rutgers University Library in New Brunswick, New Jersey, to Georgetown University Library in Washington, D.C., to the Library of the University of California at Los Angeles, and to the Department of Slavic Languages and Literatures of the Library of Congress, which graciously provided me with working facilities and with research assistance.

In libraries temporarily beyond my reach—the distant Bibliothèque Nationale in Paris and the nearby University of Cincinnati Library—I was able to research fine points vicariously thanks to the unstinting help of my lifelong friend M. Hugues—Jean de Dianoux, Consul Général de France; and to the resourceful probes of my research assistant, Mr. Dennis Hunter, a student at the University of Kentucky.

Help came from my family also. My wife Maria supplied the stimulus for the writing of the book and helped me with her knowledge of Eastern Europe and with translating Slavic-language texts. My son, Richard D. Tihany provided leads to new publications in his extracurricular field, the psychoanalytical approach to history. My stepson, Peter Dekom, generously contributed toward research costs.

To all the foregoing my deepest thanks.

A HISTORY OF MIDDLE EUROPE

Introduction

This book is about the pre-1918 history of European populations wedged in among Germans, Italians, and Russians. Gradually these peoples of Middle Europe evolved into nations and states with inconstant boundaries. But, unlike their Cro-Magnon kin in the coastal regions of the continent, most of these landlocked Middle Europeans came to experience dependence rather than independence as a recurrent form of political existence. On the foundations of their experience, accumulated traditions, and interlaced territories Wilson, Clemenceau, Hitler, Stalin, and Khrushchev built and rebuilt the middle zone of Europe as we know it today.

The concept of dependence is not easily grasped by Western readers, whose institutions and traditions are rooted in independence. Nor does the term lend itself to definition without difficulty. According to the Law of Nations *"quidquid est in territorio est etiam de territorio"* [1] (whoever inhabits the area is also master of the area). Dependence, therefore, is a state of political existence which involves denial, deprivation or limitation of mastery or sovereignty over one's own territory owing to the exercise or display of power by an external political authority.[2] It is in this basic sense that the term "dependent" is used here, with due attention to the various degrees and shades of the middle-zone dependent experience. In this part of the world variants of historical dependence include the complete subjugation of a people and the outright annexation of their territory, as for example was done to the Pannonians by the Romans in A.D. 8.[3] As another paradigm may be cited the case of Moldavia, incorporated in the Ottoman Empire and ruled through Greek hospodars (governors) after 1709.[4] Still another model of dependence is Transylvania, autonomous under its native princes from the middle of the sixteenth to the end of the seventeenth century though acknowledging the suzerainty of the sultan resident in Istanbul.[5] At the two ends of the dependent spectrum one may mention the Subcarpathian Ruthenes, who never exercised full mastery or sovereignty over their territory; and the Hungarians, who, even while *de facto* dependent from the sixteenth to the twentieth century, continued to consider themselves *de jure* independent in the terms of their constitutionality [6] and were able to improve their political status from dependence to interdependence with Austria between 1867 and 1918.[7]

Restlessness has characterized these dependent Middle Europeans since prehistory. Beginning with primitive times the immense area from the Baltic down to the Lower Danube has served as an inexhaustible reservoir of human material for the building of great civilizations, antique and modern, in the peninsular areas of southern Europe and eventually on other continents. Hordes of immigrants from Middle Europe became ancient Greeks, Romans, and modern Americans. Why did these restless tribes develop vertical north-to-south and horizontal east-west migratory patterns? Was their motivation simply a striving for easier living in more hospitable climates on the shores of a warm sea? Or was it also a flight from ample but indefensible territories used as a transiting corridor by hordes shut off from the Eurasian coast and peninsulas, sweeping from east to west and west to east in a perennially devastating shuttle?

In the following pages an attempt is made to submit plausible answers to such and other basic questions arising out of the middle-zone experience, in order to fill a gap for three categories of readers. First, for general historians, who know that history has not run the same course for the coastal and inland descendants of the Cro-Magnon Man and would perhaps like to read more about the reason why. Second, for inquisitive diplomats and businessmen who, for practical purposes, may wish to penetrate in depth, or at least scratch below the surface of, their areas of assignment. Third, for students and teachers in institutions of higher learning caught between a plethora of publications about modern dependent Eastern Europe and a paucity of books about its origins, formation, and peculiarities.

As from all history books, a philosophy of history and a thesis may be distilled from this monograph also. Its philosophy is the essentially pragmatic belief that history is the rapidly expanding totality of known human experience, which may at times supply evidence of past and forgotten errors to serve as present deterrents. The presentation based on this philosophy may be reduced to the thesis that human experience in landlocked Europe has in many respects paralleled the interplay between man and his environment in the continent's coastal regions but has deviated from it in other essential characteristics.

Parallels or similarities appear as the transformation of migratory barbarian societies into Christian, feudal, and dynastic states; crusades, hunts for heretics, and inquisitions; struggle between oligarchs and absolute monarchs; serfdom, peasant uprisings and nobles' revolts; romanesque, gothic, and baroque architecture; charters, golden bulls, and toleration edicts; universities, humanism, Renaissance, Reformation and Counter Reformation; enlightened despots; revolution and nationalism; industrialization, urban and rural social unrest, racism, and socialism.

In landlocked Middle Europe conditions peculiar to the area developed under the influence of factors not present in the coastal regions. In the west the Roman Empire was never fully replaced as a controlling agent either by the Carolingian or by the Holy Roman Empire. In the middle zone, on the other hand, there was an unceasing succession of controlling empires after the fall of Rome, not only Carolingian and Holy Roman, but also Byzantine, Ottoman, Habsburg, Romanov, and Hohenzollern. Three of these encroaching and expansionist superpowers—Byzantine, Ottoman, and Romanov— left only scant traces in the west after futile inroads of short duration as compared to the religious, cultural, and political imprint of their long rule which Middle Europe still bears. Additionally, in the west there were successful revolutions after the fiasco of the enlightened despots, and the "old regime" became a social and political anachronism by the opening of the nineteenth century. Not so in the middle zone, where it survived until and even beyond the age of the world wars, sheltering unattended and unmitigated sociopolitical evils crying for reform. Still further, in the coastal regions—as in Valois France encircled by Habsburg Spain—power vacuums could be successfully defended by renewed effort even after disastrous defeats. In Middle Europe there was never full recovery. In the oligarchic Hungary of the early sixteenth century and in the anarchic Poland of the late eighteenth, power vacuums were not detected until it was too late, beyond the hope of full recovery. All these historical peculiarities of the middle zone manifest themselves in three overriding themes: the impossibility of exercising durable self-determination, of transforming multinational realms into national states without violating the ethnic principle, and of integrating this landlocked theater of history as a major and viable component of world economy.

Some western and eastern historical realities became unrealities in the middle zone. In the west and in the east, native dynasties seized power from, rather than abandoned power to, oligarchies. These western and eastern ruling families were successful in organizing absolute monarchies, which later provided the foundations for modern nation states. In the middle zone, because of absentee monarchs, foreign dynasties, and the uncritical identification of aristocratic resistance with national interests, much-needed royal reforms were rejected as foreign machinations. The cohesion of fused states larger than small dynastic units could not be maintained even in the form of loose confederations, except by external overlords. Indigenous rulers failed in their counterattempts to capture the menacing imperial power centers. When these would-be emperor-kings disappeared after futile exertions, new power vacuums opened up to suck in alien intruders. When nationalism appeared in this multinational milieu, the historical role it played was not centripetal as in the west and the east, but rather centrifugal, culminating in a process of fragmentation and political erosion known as Balkanization.

During the pre-1918 phase of their history, the peoples of the middle zone became successively dependent on surrounding empires, first, in the southern tier below the Danube, before 1400. Dependence next reached the intermediate tier, the Carpathian basin, about the year 1500. The last tier to be reduced to dependence was the area of the Vistula plain in the north, during the seventeenth and eighteenth centuries.

When it came, the restoration of independence also proceeded in a northerly direction. It started with the southern tier in the early 1800s; progressed during the second half of the nineteenth century through the revolting but then compromising middle tier; and finally reached the northern tier during the early twentieth century.

By and large this book observes such a sequence of events in its attempt to present a needed [8] and continuously interrelated analytical narrative of modern middle-zone antecedents. The author tries to present in narrative form the main themes of the dependent Middle European existence from the prehistoric migrations to the collapse of the old order at the end of the First World War. At that point the reader may continue with Hugh Seton-Watson's classic *Eastern Europe between the Wars* (Cambridge, 1962) and with Joseph Rothschild's incisive *East Central Europe between the Two World Wars* (Seattle, 1974). Two controlling assumptions are used in bringing the reader to the age of the world wars. First, that no civilization may be properly understood without seeing its past in its present. Second, that in dealing with contemporary middle-zone structures we must not forget that the old underlies the modern, that the Old Testament is indispensable for understanding the New, and that the history of the United States would be incomprehensible without knowledge of the rise of Atlantic Europe. In the middle zone vast quantities of water had flowed under the bridges of the Vistula, the Moldau, the Danube, the Vardar, and the Maritsa before the appearance on the scene of Pilsudski, Masaryk, Horthy, Kings Alexander, Boris, and Carol, personages now half-forgotten and buried beneath enormous historical accumulations since Hitler and Stalin. The basic task is to sift in depth the inferior historical deposits of sediment which serve as foundations for the present.

In performing his analysis, the author tries to be responsive to the good advice that, in order to induce an understanding of the present by approaching it through the past,

the historian is not and cannot be concerned with all that did happen. He is and must be concerned with those particular events that did happen which turn out to be "basic" for his history. He is not concerned with the entire past, with all its infinitesimal detail; he is concerned only with the "basic" or significant past. And it is precisely this "basic" past, this meaning and significance of the past, that is continually changing, that is cumulative and progressive.[9]

To be progressive as well as cumulative the presentation must include the most recent research published in nonwestern languages. Such material has a tendency to remain long unincorporated in western publications. Additionally, the interpretation of the material, old and new, must have originality and provide new insights. This book has tried to keep abreast of recent research and attempts to provide new insights.

A presentation of facts and theories in a dispassionate, non-partisan, and nonaccusatory manner, avoiding ideological bias and a tendency to argue what middle-zone nationality suffered most at the hands of which, should be of some utility to American and other western readers. The common past is important in the common present of the middle-zone nations which are now dedicated to an ideology antagonistic to western socioeconomic ethics and belong, for the most part, to a formidable military alliance deployed in front of the western defense system. The key to an understanding of modern middle-zone comportment may be hidden among ignored antecedents.

1975

Fort Thomas, Kentucky   LCT

1

The Meeting of History
and Prehistory

For a fleeting moment in 335 B.C., probably along the present Bulgarian-Rumanian frontier, history crossed the Danube with Alexander the Great [1] into an immense and obscure domain still held by prehistory. The map of the Hellenistic geographer Eratosthenes [2] shows what Alexander thought lay before him beyond the horizontal west-to-east course of the great river: the dark interior of a world island extending to the northern shore of the encircling Ocean Stream. To the east, the Caspian was a vast inlet of the Stream. To the west, from the head of the Adriatic up to the Baltic Coast, roughly coinciding with the present military-ideological line of demarcation across Europe, ran the fabulous Amber Route,[3] along which intrepid Greek traders carried precious cargoes, risking their lives in a primeval wilderness inhabited by prehistoric hunters.

Before they embarked on the conquest of Persia, the Macedonians made their brief foray into the Danubian fringes of this unknown domain to cow the unruly frontier tribes. By the time they arrived, the upper neolithic settlements of the early hunters had long been covered under multiple strata of geological sediment. Some of the stone-age habitations, recently excavated in Hungary (at Pörgölhegy and Bodrogkeresztur), Czechoslovakia (at Kulna, Predmost, and Petrkovice), and Poland (at Maszycka),[4] link the vanished inland primitives to their coastal kinsmen of Lascaux and Altamira by a common bond of probably magic-oriented art.

The landlocked area in the heart of the continent had been inhabited for millennia. The oldest human fossils in Europe related to any archeological culture were found in 1965 near the Hungarian village of Vertesszölös.[5] The creature whose cranial fragments and teeth were excavated was of the same species as the million-year-old *Homo erectus* of Java, though of a more recent period. Outside the small Slovak town of Krapina have been found remains of a settlement of the Mousterian period, whose Neanderthal-type inhabitants hunted bears, wild horses, and rhinoceroses.[6] They were succeeded in the area by a reindeer-hunting population. The creators of the Vinkovici [7] culture in Yugoslavia were contemporaneous with the fifth excavated level of Troy (2000-1500 B.C.).[8] They were a warlike people who buried their dead flat on their backs in an east-west position. Their artifacts indicate vertical Balkan population movements toward the Aegean southeast. The Bell-Beaker culture [9] of the nineteenth century B.C. extended horizontally west to east along the Danube as far as Budapest. It memorializes a people who produced peculiar bell-shaped pottery and bowls standing on pediments. During the early Iron Age the aristocratic element of the southward moving population that occupied Yugoslavia's Drava riverbank lived on hills fortified by earthworks. Large tumuli marked their burial sites.[10]

These prehistoric cultures formed the great human reservoir which since time immemorial had been leaking population streams south into the peninsular appendages of the continent. By Alexander's time the peninsulas had been filled to the then-permissible demographic saturation point. The restless tribes between the Danube and the Baltic, finding the southern invasion route blocked, had begun pressing against one another along a horizontal east-west, rather than a downward, vertical north-south axis. For over half a millennium, until finally the Roman *limes* on the Lower Danube could be breached, the inland tribes had to be content with searching for better pastures to graze their flocks and for more defensible regions to assure group survival, to the east and to the west rather than to the south.

At the end of the fourth century B.C. the population reservoir dammed up by the Lower Danube was formed of residual pre-Indo-Europeans,[11] such as the Getae, who were probably proto-Dacians of indeterminate ethnic origin; and of western Indo-Europeans already differentiated into Slavic, Baltic, Celtic, and Germanic branches. Southward swarms of these Indo-Europeans had probably crossed the Danube barrier as early as 2250 B.C. and had evolved into Thracians, Illyrians, Macedonians, and Greeks after absorbing or destroying the indigenous Helladic populations of the Balkan peninsula. In the

twelfth century B.C.,[12] a second north-to-south wave of Dorian barbarians plunged the Mycenaean civilization of the earlier Indo-
European arrivals into one of the periodic dark ages of Europe. In
the meantime, beginning as early as the second millennium B.C., the
eastern Indo-Europeans had poured southeastward into the Anatolian
uplands from two directions.[13] From there, with herds of cattle driven
before them, they swept across the Iranian plateau into the distant
Indian subcontinent. During these movements, the Macedonians, Illyrians, Thracians, and Epirotes, who had crossed behind the proto-
Greeks from pre-history into history, from the north to the south side
of the great Danubian barrier, had become trapped in the mountain
valleys and high fastnesses of the north Balkans. These belated barbarian invaders were restrained from continuing their southward
march to the Peloponnesus, Crete, and Egypt beyond, by the earlier
swarms of invaders from the north who were turning into maritime
and civilized Greeks.

Though he did not know it, three layers of Indo-European populations faced Alexander in the vast spaces north of the Balkans
between the Danube and the Baltic: Celts, Slavs, and Balts. In the
North the Balts [14] still had a neolithic culture at the end of the fourth
century B.C. Their modern descendants, the Lithuanians and the Letts,
have the distinction of being probably the only Indo-Europeans who
have inhabited the same area from the time of Alexander until now
and also of remaining the last Europeans to be converted to Christianity.

Immediately to the south of the Balts, all the way down to the
northern Carpathian Mountains, the ancestors of the modern Slavic
nations lived in geographically contiguous ethnic and linguistic communities. West of the Pripet marshes were settlements of the Lausitz [15] folk. These were proto-Slavs noted by archeologists for the
urn-burial of their cremated dead. Artifacts found on the sixth and
seventh levels of Troy (fourteenth or thirteenth century B.C. resemble
Lausitz pottery.[16] Are these artifacts simply archeological evidence of
prehistoric trade connections or could they indicate vertical migrations in the course of which proto-Slavs became builders of the
Trojan civilization?

East of the marshes to the Dnieper were deployed the ancestors
of the modern eastern Slavs: Russians, Ukrainians, and White Russians. Unlike the Balts, the proto-Slavs, both east and west, were
situated within the prehistoric limits of bronze-working cultures by
1300 B.C. [17] About the time of the Greek-Persian wars in the early
fifth century B.C., the urn-burying Lausitz Slavs were adding an-

thropomorphic facial features to the receptacles containing the ashes of their dead.[18]

Astride the middle Danube, south of the Slavs, intruding into modern Czechoslovakia, Hungary, and Yugoslavia, the Celtic Indo-Europeans led a turbulent existence. Since the sixth century B.C. the Celts had lived in a culture known as La Tène,[19] which made use of the round millstone, the chariot, fire to clear forests for planting, piles to support dwellings built over water, and iron weapons. The Bohemian mountain bastion received its geographical name from the Boii, a Celtic tribe. Other Celtic groups persisted in attempting to penetrate peninsular Europe from the north, as far south as Rome (390 B.C.) and Delphi (279 B.C.), to modern Bulgaria in Hellenistic times, and beyond Europe into Asia Minor (279 B.C.).[20] Some of them crossed the Alps with Hannibal in 218 B.C.[21] Throughout the rest of north European prehistory the movements of the Celts typify the shift of the migration axis from a vertical north-south to a horizontal east-west direction, in shuttling movements propelled by increasing pressures from other Indo-Europeans. Archeologists are able to chart the pendulumlike horizontal swings of the Celtic tribes from inland as well as from coastal examples.[22]

The Celtic pressure down the Danube and across the Balkan Mountains toward Asia Minor may have appeared as a pincer movement to the Macedonians poised for an attack on the Persian Empire. It was perhaps for this reason that Alexander made a foray beyond the Danube before crossing the Hellespont. During the four centuries which elapsed between his death and the organization of the Roman colonies Dalmatia, Pannonia, and Dacia, stretching over most of modern Hungary, Yugoslavia, and Rumania, the horizontal Indo-European tribal gyrations had radically altered the ethnic composition of Danubian and Carpathian Europe. Iranian-affiliated Sarmatians, Roxolani, Quadi, and Jazygs had apparently arrived in the middle-zone plain in a rebound shuttle movement, having been as far east as Persia. Hard-to-identify Dacians, probably traceable to the Getae who had faced Alexander, then held the northern bank of the Lower Danube. Warlike Illyrian tribes known as Pannonii occupied the Sava Valley, western Hungary, Dalmatia, Bosnia, and Herzegovina. Hordes of Celtic Scordisci camped at the confluence of the Danube and the Sava, within the city limits of modern Belgrade.[23] These troublesome barbarians were defeated and scattered by the Dacian king Burebista [24] about the time of Caesar's assassination (44 B.C.). Had the dictator lived, there is some evidence that he might have campaigned on the Lower Danube. His death was avenged by

Octavius and Antony at Philippi in Macedonia, where Brutus fell on his sword in 42 B.C., and where a little over a century later St. Paul was to preach one of his first sermons before Europeans.

Achaea had been a Roman province since the end of the Third Punic War (146). Macedonia since the Fourth (148) Illyricum to the northwest had become a Roman dependency as early as 168 B.C. The problem facing the early emperors was the containment of the threat posed by the northern barbarians against the Balkan provinces. A solution was found in the organization of new provinces up to and beyond the Danube and its tributaries in order to block access to the peninsula of the north-south routes. Strategic salients were shoved into the land of the enemy to push him as far as possible from long-settled Roman territory. In accordance with this defensive concept were established the new Roman provinces of Dalmatia and Pannonia (A.D. 8), Moesia (A.D. 44), and Dacia (A.D. 106) in territories that now belong to Yugoslavia, Bulgaria, Hungary, and Rumania.

Under the Roman imperium the Roman style of life and the Latin language were gradually adopted in Dalmatia, Moesia, Pannonia, and in Dacia. These provinces were thoroughly Romanized by the stationing of legions, the introduction of colonists from other parts of the empire as far away as ·Syria and Libya, and by the building of provincial centers such as Sirmium (near Yugoslav Mitrovica) and Aquincum (on the outskirts of Budapest). The towns were equipped with all the amenities of the Roman way: palaces, amphitheatres, and luxurious baths. Dacia never fully lost its Latinity. Except for ruins of its Roman past, Pannonia on the other hand was later deprived of its Latin character. Its Romanized Illyrian population was swept away or submerged.

This is the course history had taken when, in the second century after Christ, the northernmost Indo-Europeans, the Germanic tribes, set themselves in motion along the prehistoric north-south migratory axis, down from their Baltic-Scandinavian ancestral homes toward the Carpathians and the Lower Danube.[25] The Marcomanni were beaten back in A.D. 160-180, but the Goths were in Dacia and on the Danube by A.D. 269-270. Charred remains of camps and settlements, buried hoards of coins, and evidence of hasty burials are memorials of this time of troubles.[26] By A.D. 271 Dacia had to be abandoned, and its population, except possibly for some of the hardiest mountain tribes, evacuated into Moesia.

The whole Carpathian basin took on the appearance of a disturbed anthill: Gepidae, Suebi, Visigoths, and Vandals battling each other for *Lebensraum,* survival, and plunder. In the midst of this pandemonium, having ridden their ponies across the Eurasian continent, the first horde of the Huns arrived on the Lower Volga in the early 370s.[27] The Huns dislodged the Ostrogoths settled there and pushed them westward into territories held by their kinsmen the Visigoths. Under irresistible pressure the Visigoths crossed the Lower Danube (376) into Roman Moesia without the required imperial permission. Emperor Valens himself marched against them but was slain in the great battle of Adrianople (378). Defeat set into motion the chain of events which nearly one hundred years later culminated in the deposition of Romulus Augustulus, the last of the Western Roman Emperors.

History, or rather prehistory, seemed to be repeating itself. The middle-European human reservoir was once again spilling over into the peninsular appendages of the continent, down toward and across the Mediterranean into Africa and then back again into Europe. To make matters worse, a second wave of Huns arrived from Asia in 425-427 and burst into the collapsing political status quo of both inland and coastal Europe. The old foundations—ethnic, linguistic, and cultural—were shattered. The new order bore no resemblance to the old. Even the placid Slavs who, surrounded by intolerable turmoil, had remained stationary north of the Carpathians, followed in the path of earlier Indo-Europeans southward into the Balkans, though some of them, ancestors of the Poles, seem to have migrated north along the Vistula. The Avars,[28] another race of mounted nomads, arrived from the confines of China during the middle years of the sixth century and proceeded to overrun what had been the Roman provinces of Dacia and Pannonia. They surrounded their settlements with ringlike earthen fortifications. The north Pannonian city of Arrabona the Romans had built on the Middle Danube became their capital under a new name which still survives as Györ, "the ringed city." During the seventh century the Avars were joined by the Tartar Bulgars [29] from the Volga. The two allies from the steppes crossed the Danube together in 679-680, advancing to the walls of Constantinople. An unexpected irruption from the south Russian steppe was made toward the end of the ninth century by the Magyars [30] or Hungarians, dislodged from their riparian homes in the Danube delta by another grassland tribe, the shifty Patzinaks.[31] As the Magyar conquerors of Pannonia rode past the ruins of the abandoned Roman amphitheater in the ghost town of Aquincum, they are said to have saluted the structure on the doubly erroneous assumption that it was the dilapidated palace of their supposed ancestor Attila the Hun.[32] The Cumanians,[33] last of the Eurasian inva-

ders, fled before the Mongol hordes of Batu Khan in the 1230s.
Like their Patzinak kinsmen, they later disappeared, melting into the
bloodstream of earlier arrivals. One more population movement took
place in the late twelfth or early thirteenth century, when the Romanized Dacians, evacuated in A.D. 271 to Moesia, began recrossing to
the north bank of the Danube and across the Transylvanian Alps
to rejoin their resolute kinsmen who for a millennium had clung to
their mountain redoubts and were lately fallen under the rule of
Hungarian kings.

The new ethnic foundations of Middle Europe were laid. Emerging populations, neither German nor Russian, of a mix distinct in its
composition from both east and west, set about their instinctive tasks
of developing cultures, evolving languages, and building states. The
Danube as a dividing line between history and prehistory disappeared during the Roman period. The middle-zone processes of forming cultures, languages, and states were henceforth recorded in
history.

2

The Landlocked
Territorial Imperative

Off the Atlantic coast of the continent, Nature built for herself what Shakespeare called an island fortress named England, girt by a moat defensive against the envy of less happier lands.[1] In landlocked Middle Europe, Nature built no fortresses either for herself or for the local breed of men as defense against the envy of human predators. Nor was there a sea-moat to provide prolonged security for peaceful domestic pursuits. The natural barriers to conquests and inroads were inadequate. The Danube line was repeatedly breached; the Carpathian passes were negotiated by successive waves of invaders; the Bohemian bastion could not be exclusively possessed by one ethnic group.

The plains, the river valleys, the mountain plateaus, and the swampland of the inland regions presented less desirable areas for settlement than did the coastal, peninsular, or insular territories. The latter, however, had already been occupied by Hellenic, Italic, Celtic, and Germanic populations, whose migrations had long preceded those of the Huns, the Avars, the Slavs, the Bulgars, and the Magyars. Some of these latecomers, the Huns for example, completely disappeared from Europe after penetrating as far west as Châlons-sur-Marne in France. The Bulgars remained on the approaches to Byzantium by entering into symbiosis with the Slavs. The Magyars, whose raids had taken them as far as the rivers Scheldt in the north and Rhone in the south, might have settled farther west had they found a power vacuum similar to that on the Pannonian plain and had they not been halted in their westward maraudings outside Augsburg by Otto the Great in 955. Nature in the east was thus of no great help to the exercise of the territorial imperative. If she favored any of the local breeds, it was in the early offensive rather than during the later defensive phases of their history. The land-locked Europeans therefore entered into a historical existence in which isolation from the outer world became a recurrent condition and independence often a patriotic goal.

Only those of the inland peoples who succeeded in reaching the sea, either in the far north or the far south, like the Finns and the Greeks, formed civilizations happily deviant from the middle-zone norm. The epics of both these peoples show primitive cognizance of group existence dominated, scourged, and redeemed by the sea. Not that Finnish and Greek independence were never lost. But even in a state of independence Greeks and Finns were singled out for priv-ileged treatment and accepted by the overlords as useful partners in power. In fact, the Romans built on Hellenic and Hellenistic foundations, the Russians, on Finnish. The Ottomans made the Phanariot Greeks of Constantinople agents of their diplomacy and ruled some of their Balkan subjects through them. Both the Swedes and the Russians preferred to have the Finns fighting with them rather than against them. The tsar, autocrat in the Russias, ruled as a constitutional monarch in nineteenth-century Finland. For this reason neither the Finns nor the Greeks except in their Byzantine variant can be treated as comakers of a common Middle European history.

That the familiar pattern set in the west by the Norman conquest of England was a far more intricate and complicated process in the east may be demonstrated by using examples of the Bulgarian and Hungarian conquests during the seventh and ninth centuries. Super-ficially, the Bulgarian example is closer to the Norman paradigm: the conqueror fuses with the conquered and takes over both the ethnic identity and the language (though not the name) of the latter. The Turkic Bulgars, who appeared in the Moesian areas of the Balkans during the seventh century, were absorbed racially and linguistically by the Slavs during the ensuing two centuries. What, however, makes the Bulgarian situation more complicated than the Norman pattern are the following details: the Bulgars crossed the Danube and invaded the south in 650-670 in politico-military partner-ship with the Avars. Among the populations the conquering partners found on the south bank and beyond the Balkan mountains were comparatively recent arrivals. These were Slavic settlers, who had come from the north during the fifth and sixth centuries. The terri-tories these Slavs inhabited belonged not to them but to the Byzantine Empire. The Slavs had already become Byzantium-oriented Christians. The gradual conversion of the heathen Bulgars took place later, in the course of a tug-of-war between Rome and Byzantium.[2] Christianization occurred against the violent opposition of the boyars, the land-amassing war chiefs; and, subsequently, under the threat of recurrent uprisings by landless pagan peasants. Barely had the processes of ethnic fusion, religious conversion, linguistic assimilation, and social adjustment been completed when, at the end of the fourteenth century, the Slav-Orthodox mix was overrun by the Moslem Turks. The new conquerors continued to rule over their Christian subjects for five hundred years. The Norman conquest is easily dated as 1066. The Bulgarian conquest took approximately two centuries, and then its final political effects were postponed by half a millennium by the suspension of sovereign national existence under the Ottoman occupation.

Infinitely more intricate was the Magyar conquest of Hungary. Prior to their arrival in the Carpathian basin, the pastoral Finno-Ugrian Magyars had already been subjugated, during their migratory existence on the steppe, by warlike Turkic tribes. The result was an ethnically and linguistically fused population.[3] The top social stratum adopted the Finno-Ugrian idiom of the subjugated, though liberally seeding it with the vocabulary of its own Chuvash-Turkic speech. Thus, at the moment of their invasion, the Magyar chiefs, like the Norman nobles, were linguistic assimilants speaking an acquired language. The populations they conquered spoke tongues foreign to them, Slavic in the west and probably Rumanian in the mountains of the east. Two deviations from the western norm then occurred. First the Magyars did not accept the language of the conquered but imposed their own on them in the central areas. Second, the absence of a "moat-defensive" enabled the preconquest languages in the Hungarian peripheral regions to resist linguistic imposition. This linguistic resistance was aided by uninterrupted communication with kinsmen across the political frontiers. The subsequent Ottoman conquest and occupation of nearly 175 years (1526-1699) separated the Magyar-speaking center from the bi- and trilingual peripheries in the south, occasioned an influx of Slavic speakers from the Balkans, and finally subjected the liberated Hungarians to a process of unwelcome Germanization. Hypothetically, a somewhat similar situation in England could be imagined only if the Normans, after 1066, had prevailed on the Saxons to adopt the French language; and if, due to a successful landing of the Spanish Armada in 1588, the Welsh had been able to establish linguistic colonies in and around London.

Historical events comparable to these hypothetical happenings took place in Hungary. There is still today a Serbian-speaking and Ortho-dox-rite enclave at Szentendre, just north of Budapest.

As a result of such ethnic combinations, the cultures which came into existence in historical times around Polish Maszycka, Czech Predmost, and Hungarian Bodrogkeresztur [4] lost whatever affinity they may originally have had to the prehistoric cultures around French Lascaux and Spanish Altamira. Furthermore, in the east, Latin did not become a linguistic mother stem, except in the case of Rumanian, to daughter languages, as it did in the west to Italian, Spanish, French, and Portuguese. Yet, the Slavic idioms were much closer to one another than tongues belonging to any other Indo-European subdivision. Cyril and Methodius, the Apostles of the Slavs were chosen in mid-ninth century by Byzantium to carry Christianity to distant Moravia because the native Slavic dialect these two brothers spoke around Salonika could be understood by the Slavs north of the Carpathians in the region of modern Brno. Unfortunately, for the future political cohesion of the area, a few years after the mission of the two Slavic apostles, the conquering Magyars (who would not become Slavs) annihilated the Moravian Empire and drove a wedge between the Slavs above the Middle Danube and their kin below the Drava. To make matters worse, the ethnic and cultural wedge separating west and South Slavs was extended on the east all the way to the Black Sea by the Orthodox Rumanians, antagonists of the Catholic Hungarians. The former saw their territories overrun by Turks in 1462 and 1504; the latter by both Turks and Germans in 1526. Division thus multiplied within division.

The absence of natural north-south barriers between the Baltic and the Aegean did not long prevent the middle zone from becoming a military transiting area for the new European powers rising in the west and in the east. Five major invasion routes developed through the early centuries between east and west, across territories held by the landlocked nations.[5] Earliest of these military routes was the one leading from the North German plain, from west of the River Elbe, above the Pripet marshes northeast of Kiev and southeast of Minsk, all the way to the Volga. This became the principal route of the *Drang nach Osten,* the German "push to the east," used by expan-sionist western empires both for attack and retreat. To the north of the main east-west invasion route, along the sandy dunes of the Baltic coast, from Pomerania in the southwest to the Gulf of Fin-land in the northeast, lay the route of eastward penetration used by the persistent Teutonic Knights and their related Livonian Brothers of the Sword. The effects were lasting in spite of crushing defeats the Teutons suffered at the hands of Alexander Nevski, a Kievan Russian, on the ice of Lake Peipus in 1242 and of the Poles between Grunwald and Tannenberg in 1410. A third major military road leading toward the east and into the Hungarian plain was the Danube valley. From the Magyar lowlands the road was open both to the southeast across either the Iron Gates or the Banat, and northeastward to the Russian steppe through the passes traversing the low-altitude Carpathians of Ruthenia. The Danubian route to the great Magyar plains was unsuccessfully tried by the Saxon and Franconian emperors during the late tenth century and the entire eleventh; successfully, by their Habsburg successors after 1683. The southeasterly extension of this route was a main military artery during the first, second, third, and fifth Crusades (1096, 1147, 1189, and 1217). The northeastern detour toward the Russias was successfully traversed by the kings of Hungary during their conquest of Galicia (1206-1208). It was also used in reverse direction by Kievan armies led by princely Arpad pretenders returning to Hungary from exile in 1046. Still later, 1242, the devastating Mongol hordes of the Great Khan poured through these mountain passes.

A fourth invasion route ran along the Black Sea littoral, across Rumanian territory, from the Ukraine down into the Balkans, utilized as early as 970 by Sviatoslav, Prince of Kiev, in the first Russian bid on land [6] to enable Russia to succeed Byzantium as a "Third Rome." The fifth, a heavily traveled military road connecting east and west, was the old crusading route down the Danube, the same as the third invasion path used upstream by the Ottomans in their two campaigns, which took them north to the gates of Vienna in 1529 and 1683. The liberating imperial armies under Prince Eugene of Savoy moved downstream along this same military road southward past Belgrade, at the juncture of the seventeenth and eighteenth centuries.

These five invasion routes of repeatedly proven military utility were historically instrumental in the rise of two basic themes peculiar to the middle zone. The first of these themes was the unceasing succession of dominating foreign empires; the second, the frustration of the native imperial dream. The Western Roman Empire fell in 476 and was not replaced by other imperial rule until that of the short-lived Carolingian Empire (800-911-987) and, later, by the loosely knit Holy Roman Empire of the German Nation (962-1806). This first Reich (as Voltaire remarked) was neither holy nor Roman and certainly not a centralized empire in the old Roman sense of the word. Still, the German founders and rulers of this federative power were able to capture and to hold the Eternal City and to have the imperial crown placed on their heads repeatedly by several popes.

In the eastern marches there was no respite between empires. First, Byzantium survived Rome by a millennium and continued to rule or culturally dominate the former Roman provinces in the northeast Balkans up to the Danube. Constantine's strategic concept of building an impregnable Second Rome at the convergence of the Bosporus, the Golden Horn, and the Sea of Marmara was fully justified—until the invention of gunpowder and the introduction of siege artillery which could open breaches in the famed Land Walls running from the sea to the inlet from the sea (1453). By this time, however, the Ottoman Empire had established itself in the Balkans, up to the Lower Danube, almost imperceptibly replacing its imperial Greek predecessor. The approaching end of this successor imperium became quite predictable by the second half of the eighteenth century. Before the "Sick Man" could breathe his last, however, his territorial legacy was being divided by its self-appointed heirs, the competing Habsburg and Romanov empires. In the north Prussia and Russia were slow in becoming imperial powers. But finally the rising empire of the Hohenzollerns, eventually ro reach its apogee as the Second Reich, joined the Habsburgs and the Romanovs at the end of the eighteenth century to divide the indefensible domains and the unwilling subjects of another Sick Man—Poland.

The second basic theme was the frustration of the imperial dream. No middle-zone sovereign ever became Byzantine Emperor ruling from the city of Constantine. Only one dynasty of midle-zone rulers, the Luxemburg kings of Hungary and Bohemia, was able to ascend the imperial throne of the Holy Roman Empire [7]—only partly because they were kings in Buda and Prague, but mostly because of family connections antedating their enthronement. Other Bulgarian, Serb, and Hungarian contenders for the imperial crowns, either of the east or of the west, failed. Never was there a Holy Byzantine Empire of the Bulgarian or of the Serb nation, as there was a Holy Roman Empire of the German Nation, although there were Bulgarian and Serb rulers who assumed imperial titles. Nor did political power generated in the middle zone ever dominate and shape the course of European history in the manner of the south, the west, and the east.

As the imperial dreams of the dynasts in Bulgaria, Serbia, and Hungary dissolved into thin air during the fourteenth and fifteenth centuries, the dynastic territories and subjects passed under foreign domination. The rule of the sultan was imposed in the Balkans and in central Hungary. This became the southern dependent tier. North of the Danube, the fortuitously marrying Habsburgs augmented their family domains. These territories became the central dependent tier. Still farther north, above the wreath of the Carpathians, the Bohemians, Moravians, Poles, and Lithuanians escaped the fate of being shifted from European civilization to conditions then customary in Asiatic empires, but sooner or later had to pay a price for the privilege of living in this temporarily independent tier: their national independence. Thus, as long as the Ottoman, Habsburg, Romanov, and Hohenzollern empires remained in existence, in other words, until the end of the First World War, freedom from foreign domination in dependent Europe was only a nostalgic memory or, sometimes, a foresighted dream. The majority of the populations probably accepted the dependent status quo as the normal state of affairs and lived out their lives generation after generation, their latent political and social discontent bursting forth in periodic revolts and uprisings. Until the rise of modern nationalism they remained on the whole passive masses inhabiting lands "less happier" than those of their neighbors to the west and to the east.

3

Between Rome
and Byzantium

Christianity had reached the middle zone long before it became a state religion in Rome. As we have noted, St. Paul stopped in the year 52 or 53 in Macedonia to preach the Gospel to the faithful of Philippi, to whom he later addressed one of his epistles.[1] From Macedonia to the north the earliest Christian missionary route led up the Vardar and Maritsa valleys, across present-day Yugoslavia, to the Pannonian plain. Funerary architecture shows, in accordance with the Acts of the Apostles, that in Moesia as well as in Pannonia and Dacia Christianity made its first sporadic appearances in colonies of Hellenistic and Jewish immigrants from Africa and Asia Minor.[2] The first Pannonian community of Christians was organized in 253-260 under Bishop Eusebius, who met a martyr's death in one of the waves of persecutions. There is evidence of other Christians, including several bishops, who were martyred for their faith in the quarries outside Sirmium (near Belgrade) under the Emperor Diocletian, during 293-294.[3] Half a century later yet another stream of early Christians poured into the area with the invading Visigoths, who had been converted to the heretical Arian creed by their apostle Ulfilas (311-383). It was for the purpose of extirpating this Arian heresy that a Church council was held in Sirmium in 378.[4]

How to prevent the spread of heresy was a problem for the Church to solve. Another problem that arose parallel with the emergence of the new monarchies was for the barbarian rulers to grapple with: which one of the two competing Christian variants, the Roman or the Byzantine, could be adopted with minimum danger to independence and sovereignty? The politics of medieval Roman Catholicism had as its main characteristic the division of powers between pope and emperor. If the Roman faith was to be embraced, it was preferable to ask the pope and not the emperor for missionaries and for a royal crown, because new Christians owing their conversion to the emperor were likely to become vassals of the Holy Roman Empire.

During the eleventh and twelfth centuries appeal to the pope was the preference of Hungarian, Polish, Croat, Serb, and Bulgarian rulers. In the case of Byzantine Christianity, the act of conversion was usually dictated by geographical proximity to Constantinople. There no choice had to be made between pope and emperor. The Byzantine ruler was Caesar as well as pope, head of both state and church, in a system known as caesaropapism. Indeed, the Greek Orthodox Church under its patriarch was of tremendous cultural-ideological potential but administratively little more than a religious department of the imperial state. Consequently, heathen rulers on the eastern fringes of the middle zone, from Bulgarian khans up to the Lithuanian dukes of Slavic subjects, looked on Byzantine Christianity with a jaundiced eye, knowing full well that baptism in it would have as its inevitable sequel a struggle to ward off Byzantine political imperium. One logical but not too practical way out of the dilemma was to capture Byzantium and assume the imperial dignity—a dream vainly pursued from the tenth century to the fourteenth by a succession of Bulgarian and Serb monarchs.

But whichever of the two competing Christian creeds was finally embraced, the transition from paganism to monotheism was seldom a smooth process. First, the ruler's decision to have himself and his people baptized usually ran into the violent opposition of the great war chiefs. Often these men would rather face death than see their tribally possessed territories reduced to royal fiefs in a Christian feudal system. Second, after the royal sword broke the desperate resistance of the tribal chiefs, a socioeconomic antagonism developed between the new feudal elite and the once-free tribal plebs who had become dependent tillers of the soil. Originally, while the memory of paganism and its institutions still lingered, the antagonism had an anti-Christian coloring. Later, as Christianity and feudalism established themselves on firmer foundations, the social antagonisms erupted in a heretical protest movement of the lower population strata against the *bene possessionati,* the propertied lords, of the official Christian establishment.

Internal turmoil accompanying the acceptance of Christianity will be dealt with in the following chapter. Externally, the shifting situation was mirrored in the continuing attempts of Byzantine diplomacy to make the best political use of the barbarian presence on or near imperial territory. The principal objective of this diplomacy was to win the invaders to eastern Christianity, thus bringing them under the imperial rule of Byzantium, against the pretensions of the pope and the western emperor.[5] The appearance of a formal, though as yet temporary, schism between Rome and Byzantium (863-868) gave the Greeks a free hand to spread their version of the faith among the Bulgarians settled on their territory. The Bulgarian khan, Boris I, an ally of the Carolingian emperors, was cajoled into submitting to an Eastern-rite baptism in 865. When once again he became a free agent, Boris reacted by asking the pope to send Catholic missionaries, and also a patriarch, to Bulgaria. The first request was immediately complied with. Granting the second demand would have meant raising the new Bulgarian Church to the time-honored rank of the five ancient sees headed by patriarchal princes of the Universal Church: Rome, Byzantium, Jerusalem, Antioch, and Alexandria. The request was therefore left unanswered.

It was at this time that the famous correspondence between Boris and Pope Nicholas I [6] took place, the former somewhat disingenuously ("how many are the patriarchs to be counted?") submitting a long list of questions about Christian doctrines and practices; the latter patiently and diplomatically giving replies befitting the importance of a barbarian ruler wavering between the Byzantine and the Roman churches. In the meantime, however, the schism between the two main churches proved to be ephemeral, being healed in 868. Immediately, preparations began for an ecumenical synod. This was held in Byzantium in 870, to decide the affiliation of the new Bulgarian Church. The Greeks won out. The Latin-rite representatives at the synod acquiesced in the decision that Bulgaria should be within the domain of the Eastern Church.[7] Obediently, the Latin missionaries withdrew from Bulgaria. But the Byzantines were no more inclined than the Romans to give the Bulgarians the patriarch they wanted. Under a compromise solution a metropolitan, nominally autonomous but *de facto* under the jurisdiction of the Patriarch of Constantinople, was placed at the head of the Bulgarian Church. The language of the liturgy was to be Greek. This, however, proved to be unpalatable to the Bulgarian faithful. Resistance to Hellenization provided a fertile ground for two great Bulgarian clerics to begin Bulgarization of the liturgy. These clerics were Sts. Clement and Naum, disciples of Sts. Cyril (827-869) and Methodius, (†884). The Slav vernacular foundations of Bulgarian Orthodoxy were their work.[8]

Boris's successor Symeon (893-927) was a devout Orthodox Christian educated in Byzantium and called "the half Greek." He was also a pretender to the imperial throne. To gain his objective, he laid siege to Byzantium in 913. It was an undertaking beyond his abilities. He had to desist and settle for a compromise solution, though it took him some time to find out that he had been tricked by the wily Greeks. The matrimonial arrangement under which he was allowed to take the emperor's sister to wife and assume the resounding title "Emperor of the Bulgarians" appeared to be genuine. But, while he knelt with his eyes piously closed, instead of the imperial crown only a sham substitute was placed on his head by the Patriarch of Constantinople in the great Basilica of St. Sophia.[9] The imperial title thus conferred was repudiated as invalid by the Byzantines as soon as Symeon had returned to his own country. To avenge himself, Symeon in 914 again attacked and inflicted a resounding defeat on the Byzantine army at Anchialus in 917. Then, in 925, he proclaimed himself "Emperor of the Bulgarians and the Romans". His son Peter (927-969) was appeased by Byzantine recognition as tsar (Caesar). This was not all. His archbishop got the coveted title of patriarch. His own social standing was raised by what had become the customary barbarian marriage into the imperial family.

When such appeasement ceased to keep the successors of Tsar Peter from militarily harassing the imperial city, the Byzantines decided to take sterner measures. Tsar Boris II was defeated, captured, and led through the streets of Byzantium shamefully tied to the emperor's chariot of triumph. Then, in 971, he was publicly degraded in the great Basilica of St. Sophia from Caesar to the rank of simple *Magister*. This humiliation failed to hold off the Bulgarians. It took the Macedonian Samuel, a self-styled successor to Symeon and Boris, only a few years to revive the imperial dream, proclaim himself tsar, and re-establish the Bulgarian Patriarchate. In the face of such irrepressible temerity Byzantium decided to end the Bulgarian menace once and for all. An all-out Bulgarian war began in 986. After he crushed and butchered the Bulgarian army in the battle of Kleidion in 1014, the victorious Emperor Basil II [10] assumed the title "Bulgar Slayer." Fourteen thousand Bulgarian captives were blinded, except for one in every one hundred to lead home the rest. These wretches were sent home to their Tsar Samuel to carry the emperor's compliments. The Bulgarian ruler died of an apopleptic fit at the terrible spectacle.

The fall of their first empire held back the Bulgarians for nearly two centuries, until the Latin capture of Byzantium during the Fourth

Crusade (1204). This seemed to provide a new opportunity for the Bulgarian ruler Ivan Asen II (1218-1241) to attempt to enthrone himself in Byzantium as emperor of a Slavo-Greek empire. But the Greeks themselves recaptured their capital from the Latins in 1261 and brought Tsar Ivan's dream to nought. Slav hegemony in the Balkans passed from the Bulgars to the Serbs after the battle of Velbuzhd in 1330. Although the Bulgarian rulers continued to bear an empty imperial title claiming dominion over Greeks as well as Bulgarians, their strategic goal ceased to be the capture of Byzantium. The new Bulgarian capital at Tirnovo, just north of the Balkan Mountains, was renamed Tsarigrad, the "City of the Caesars," to rule over the territories once belonging to the empire of the east. No new Bulgarian attack could be or was launched against Constantinople until 1913, during the First Balkan War. In the meantime Byzantium had fallen to the Turks rather than to the Slavs, and the "Third Rome" ultimately became a Russian instead of a Bulgarian reality. Still the Bulgarians remained steadfast in their Orthodox faith, their church a monument to the success of medieval Byzantine diplomacy.[11]

Byzantine diplomacy was successful in bringing barbarians into the Eastern Church and under the rule of the eastern emperor in inverse ratio to their distance from Byzantium. The militarily supported barbarian policy of capturing Byzantium and emulating in the east the Holy Roman Empire of the west was a complete failure. The Serbs, who had been baptized by Roman and not by Byzantine missionaries and who succeeded the Bulgarians in the pursuit of the imperial dream, eventually ended up in the eastern ecclesiastical orbit but never on the imperial throne. Pope Gregory VII of Canossa fame was the donor of royal crowns to the rulers of both Croatia and Serbia, to King Zvoinimir of the former in 1075 and to King Michael of the latter in 1077. The Serbian donation was no more than a gesture, but unlike Serbia, Croatia remained in the Roman orbit.

Serb medieval history reads like a repetition of Bulgarian history during the struggle for imperial hegemony. Under their Nemanya dynasty (1168-1371) the Serbs rose from histrionically humiliating defeat by the Byzantines (as, for example in 1172, when their prince Stephen had to pay homage to the emperor with a rope around his neck) to the glorious reigns of King Stephen Urosh II (1282-1321) and Emperor Stephen Dushan (1331-1355). The first of these rulers was satisfied to reign at home as a resplendent simulacrum of his imperial master in Constantinople, while intriguing with Frederick Barbarossa in 1189 against the Greek emperor. But the red-bearded German ruler's days of political usefulness were numbered: he was on his way not to fight the infidel, as he thought, but to accidental drowning in a muddy Cilician river. The second Stephen, surnamed Dushan, was more successful. First he decreed a Serbian Patriarchate, thus raising his realm to the same level as Rome, Byzantium, Jerusalem, Antioch, and Alexandria. Then, in 1346, he had his newly created patriarch crown him in the ancient Macedonian town of Skoplje as "Emperor of the Serbs and the Romans." Stephen Dushan's empire was an early Yugoslavia, larger in territorial extent than its twentieth-century successor. Yet even with all the south Slavs under his scepter, neither Stephen nor his son Urosh, the last in the Nemanya line, was able to capture the imperial city and mount the throne of Constantine's successors. Still, Byzantine diplomacy proved itself more than half successful. Although they failed to capture Byzantium, the Serbs entered and remained in the Byzantine religious-cultural orbit throughout their subsequent history.[12]

This was not the case with the Hungarians, whose royal crowns furnish visual evidence of the Roman-Byzantine contest for local dominance. St. Stephen, the first Hungarian king (1001-1038), received his famous crown directly from Pope Sylvester II in 1001. On close examination [13] only the upper part of the crown, consisting of two vertical golden bands resting on a red velvet base and bearing a slanting cross, is revealed to be of western origin. The lower part is a horizontal hooplike diadem, showing the recipient Hungarian King Geza I (1074-1077) in a subordinate position to the probable donor, Byzantine Emperor Michael VII Ducas. The two crowns were combined at a date subsequent to Stephen's reign. Together they indicate the struggle between Rome and Byzantium for Hungarian allegiance. Another reminder of this eleventh-century contest is the crown of Constantine Monomachus. This is a Byzantine regal ornament, sent between the reigns of Kings Stephen and Geza by the Emperor Constantine IX as a gift probably by Andrew I (1046-1060) or possibly to his queen.[14]

Medieval Hungary was situated astride the demarcation line between the western and eastern cultural domains. In the eastern, Transylvanian area of the kingdom, Byzantine influence was strong in the tenth century. The *gyula,* or territorial governor, who had his seat at the modern Alba Julia, became an early communicant in the Byzantine rite in 952.[15] So apparently did Bulcsu, one of the great tribal chieftains, captured and executed by Otto the Great at Augsburg in 955. Archeological evidence shows this Hungarian war chief to have been baptized in 948 in Byzantium, with the emperor himself standing as godfather.[16] The marriage of St. Stephen's son Prince

Emeric to a Byzantine princess around 1015 seemed to indicate a Hungarian policy of balancing western against eastern influence. In any event, the dynastic marriage was followed by the establishment of Greek Orthodox monasteries and convents as far west as Veszprem, near the Austrian border in Transdanubia.[17] Under succeeding Arpad kings Byzantine-Hungarian relations became so close that a possible swing by Hungary from the Latin to the eastern orbit could not be ruled out. The closeness of the relations was made apparent by dynastic marriages. Piroska, daughter of King St. Ladislas I (1077-1095) became empress in Byzantium in 1118 as the wife of John II Comnenus and mother of Emperor Manuel I surnamed Oungrikos ("the Hungarian"). After her death she was canonized as St. Irene in the Byzantine hagiology.[18] Yet, in spite of such close ties, Byzantine diplomacy was a loser in Hungary, except among the non-Magyar populations on the north- and southeast peripheries of the kingdom, where political boundaries could not prevent cultural symbiosis between neighboring Slav and Rumanian populations.

Among the Rumanian populations of Moldavia and Wallachia, two principalities bordering on the eastern bend of the Carpathians to the east and to the south, Bulgaro-Byzantine influence reigned supreme owing to conversion by missionaries from neighboring Bulgaria around 900. For this reason, the liturgical language of the Rumanian Church became, and remained until the end of the sixteenth century, the Old Church Slavonic created by the Apostles of the Slavs, Sts. Cyril and Methodius during the middle of the ninth. The Moldavian and Wallachian metropolitans (archbishops) were appointed by Byzantium during the last hundred years of its existence (1350-1450).[19]

In Poland to the north, the north-south dividing line between Roman and Byzantine cultural-religious affinities proved to be a deterrent to political homogeneity. The early Piast rulers of Poland did their best to navigate between the Roman Scylla and the Byzantine Charybdis. Prince Mieszko asked for and received the Roman Catholic sacrament of baptism in 966.[20] King Boleslav I had himself crowned with papal approval in 1025 but then proceeded forthwith to notify both the eastern and the western emperors that he would be independent of both.[21] In the far Lithuanian north, the chieftain Mindovg was baptized in 1251 and crowned in 1253 as a Latin Christian, also with the approval of the pope.[22] He took baptism lightly and reverted to paganism, but apostasy did not save him from assassination in 1263. When the mass conversion of the Lithuanians finally occurred in the fourteenth century, it took place under Roman and not Byzantine auspices. As in the case of Poland and Hungary, subject minority populations which had gravitated into the rival Byzantine orbit became a source of perennial political trouble.

In addition to bringing the emerging states of the middle zone into the Orthodox Church and under the rule of the eastern empire, Byzantine diplomacy had two subsidiary objectives. Byzantium wanted to neutralize the threat from the migratory barbarians by playing them off against each other and at the same time to keep the east-west frontier between the Byzantine and the western (first Carolingian, then Holy Roman) empires as far to the west as possible.[23]

The principal historical result of the Byzantine diplomatic ploy to divert barbarian attacks was the still remaining Hungarian wedge driven between the West Slavs (Czechs, Slovaks, and Poles) in the north and the South Slavs (Serbs, Croats, Slovenes, and Bulgarians) in the Balkans. By the time of Tsar Symeon's campaign against Byzantium in 895, the Byzantine tactic of raising a second hostile barbarian horde in the rear of an attacking barbarian host had been developed to a fine point. Thus, when the Bulgarian Symeon started marching against Byzantium, an embassy sent by Emperor Leo the Wise sought out the Magyars at their settlements in the Danube delta and enlisted them as auxiliary troops to cross the Danube and to attack the Bulgarians in the rear. Having no special liking for their distant Turkic kinsmen, who held the Danubian plain on which they already had their eyes, the Magyar chiefs readily consented. They stopped Symeon's march somewhere near Silistria. But the Bulgar tsar had not been observing Byzantine diplomacy without profiting from it. Now it was his turn, he felt, to send emissaries to the Patzinaks of ill fame, the Magyars' hostile neighbors between the Don and the Dnieper on the steppe, to negotiate a rear onslaught on the Byzantines' Hungarian auxiliaries. The Patzinaks executed this tactical task with relish and singular success, thus relieving the Bulgarians of Hungarian pressure.[24] They so enjoyed doing their job that, when it was over, they carried out a gratuitous attack on the Magyar settlements. They wiped them out to the extent of making the entire region uninhabitable. The Magyar war party returning from Bulgaria was forced to lead a general tribal migration to the Pannonian plain. Their scouts had already reconnoitered this former Roman province a few years previously and had reported it ripe for conquest. Magyar occupation of the Carpathian basin in 896 and the founding of the Hungarian kingdom in 1001 ensued. Henceforth the South Slavs were permanently separated from their northern kin by the new state.

The second Byzantine diplomatic maneuver, to keep the east-west dividing line as far west from Byzantine territory as possible, was only a partial success. After Charlemagne's destruction of the Avars in 791-796, the Carolingian border extended to the course of the Tisza River in present-day Hungary. When Boris I, whose domains extended north to the Tisza, began importing Frankish missionaries into Bulgaria, Byzantium riposted by organizing the Cyril and Methodius mission of lasting fame to carry Orthodox Christianity and Byzantine power in the Moravian borderlands of the Carolingian Empire (862-863). The brothers Cyril and Methodius [25] were Slavic-speaking subjects of the Byzantine Emperor, ideally suited to extending the influence of the eastern Orthodox Church by proselytizing among their distant West Slav kinsmen. The Moravians were then the leading element in a confederation of Slavic tribes which controlled the entire area from the Bohemian bastion down to the Drava and Sava rivers. Cyril and Methodius preached the Gospel to these tribes in their native Slavic vernacular. This provoked the antagonism of the Frankish Catholic missionaries from the west, whose mission was to extend the politico-religious influence of the residual Carolingian Empire eastward in the void left by the Avars. The pope, however, gave his approval to the Byzantine mission and even invested Methodius as archbishop of Sirmium in present-day northern Yugoslavia. Cyril died while on a visit to Rome with his brother in 869. Methodius continued the mission alone. It promised to be a success. The whole area from Byzantium up to the modern Czechoslovak-German border appeared to be consolidating as a north-westerly extension of Byzantine Christianity. A side result of the mission to the Moravians was the invention and spread of the Cyrillic alphabet, used to this day in the autocephalous Orthodox Slav churches of the east. Cyril and Methodius also established the permanent liturgical language of these churches by formulating the Old Church Slavonic (Old Bulgarian) religious idiom, which they based on and evolved from their native Salonika dialect.

It was at this time that Byzantium used military troop concentrations to force the Bulgarian Boris's baptism into the Orthodox faith in 865.[26] Five years later Byzantium scored another diplomatic victory when the Synod of Constantinople adjudicated Bulgaria to the Byzantine sphere.[27] This event sent the Latin (some of them Frankish) missionaries packing for their western homes. For the next quarter century the east-west line ran far to the north, in the area of modern Czechoslovakia, along the border of the Carolingian and Moravian empires, the latter having been turned into a Byzantine cultural outpost by the introduction of the Cyrillic alphabet, the Old Church Slavonic language, and of the vernacularized Greek Orthodox creed. But during the years 894-896 came disaster. One line of Byzantine diplomacy (the Bulgar-Magyar-Patzinak play) cancelled out another (the Cyril-Methodius apostolate). Moravia fell. The Magyar conquest of the Carpathian basin put an end to the Byzantine outposts in the far west. The ensuing Frankish-Hungarian alliance then brought Carolingian influence and the east-west line down to the Lower Danube.

Two and a half centuries later it became the diplomatic grand design of St. Irene's son, Manuel I Comnenus (1143-1180), surnamed Oungrikos, to push the east-west frontier up to the Ostmark (present-day Austria) by military means, if possible; or by the establishment of a Byzanto-Hungarian dual monarchy, if need be. Manuel's return to the ninth-century Byzantine diplomatic policy of distant western frontiers was occasioned by renewed German and Hungarian military inroads in the east. First Emperor Henry V in 1108 and then Margrave Leopold of the Ostmark in 1118 invaded Hungary. Then came a major Hungarian invasion of the empire, which reached as far south as Thrace and Macedonia (1127-1130). The suspicious Manuel interpreted these German and Hungarian military moves as indications of a Latin design on Byzantium (which, indeed, was captured by the Latins in 1204). He therefore counterattacked, carrying the war into the territory of his Magyar relations. The result was a military stalemate and then a compromise reached in 1167. Under it the Hungarian Prince Bela, educated in Byzantium in the Orthodox faith and engaged to a Byzantine princess, was to succeed Manuel on the imperial throne under the Hellenized name Alexius. At the same time or before, he would mount the royal throne of Hungary as King Bela III. But the birth of a son to the aging Manuel two years later filled him with so much paternal pride that he dropped his project of a dual Byzantine-Hungarian monarchy.[28] Had the project succeeded, the east-west frontier might have moved up north once again, to the modern Hungarian-Austrian border. When, after Manuel's death, his minor son Alexius was murdered in a palace revolution during 1182, Bela III (1172-1196), then king of Hungary, made an unsuccessful bid to link in his person the two crowns. There were too many diplomatic and ecclesiastical obstacles. By 1186 he lost interest in a personal union and switched to a westward orientation by marrying the Capetian Princess Margaret, daughter of Louis VII the Young of France. Hungary was thereafter lost to Byzantium.[29]

Over two and half centuries were yet to pass before the fall of the eastern empire. After that cataclysmic event in 1453, Orthodox Christianity remained without an effective political power base for another century, while the papacy was nearing exhaustion owing to its long struggle with the western emperors. The contest between Rome and Byzantium in the middle zone was over. The new struggle for men's immortal souls and perishable institutions north of the Danube was to be fought by Protestants and Catholics of future centuries.

4

Heathens and Heretics

The foresighted chiefs and princes who Christianized their subjects between the ninth and the fourteenth centuries, thus joining them to the western system, provoked a violent reaction, the like of which was not to be seen in Europe again for nearly a millennium. The external aspects of the change—from tribal confederation to Christian monarchy and from pagan practices to new forms of worship—were only visual manifestations of a radically provocative social and economic transformation. Opposition to the drastic metamorphosis came in its simplest form from ordinary human beings resisting change, as they always do. Both chiefs and masses joined in the resistance in the forlorn hope of warding off the imposition of an unaccustomed way of life in the place of a traditional life style. The chiefs resisted because they knew in their hearts that the substitution of a centralized monarchy for the old tribal order, of feudal fiefs for lands contractually divided among clans, would bring social and economic degradation. The masses were dead set against the new order because it augured the end of volatile pastoral freedom and the coming of immobile agricultural subordination. All resisters, chiefs as well as peasants, objected to the new Christian way of life because it tried to do away with ingrained and venerated pagan traditions and practices.

To all these objections and resentments was added a good dose of xenophobia. The coming of Christianity was accompanied by an influx of royally favored foreigners—priests, bishops, knights, courtiers, and new landowners. But even more reprehensible to the reactionary pagans than these outlanders was the conduct of some of the new

Christian monarchs of their blood, who at times did not disdain to
save their shaky new thrones by implied or open submission to either
the eastern or the western emperor. When such alienation of sovereignty took place, resistance to Christianization was likely to erupt
in a general heathen uprising.

Until hope for a pagan restoration was irretrievably lost, the old
pagan nobility, which went under the name of boyars in some of the
emerging states, acted as the prime agent of resistance. After this
intransigent class was wiped out and replaced by Christian feudal
lords, resistance was continued by the newly Christianized peasantry,
though not to the scriptural form of Christianity as such. The peasants
rejected the established church of the new barons. To downtrodden
and illiterate xenophobes the new church looked like a colonial intrusion of Byzantine or Latin imperialism. Heathens thus became
heretics with the passing of time, as Christianity gradually gained
acceptance as a permanent state of social existence. One could not
continue opposing Christianity, only forms of it.

Can we conjure up the pagans of old? What were their traditions,
cults, and practices which clashed with the new religion, to which
the majority of the populations clung so tenaciously?[1] Generations
of doomed pagans insisted on shaving their heads and on wearing
rustic leggings. Among those from the Eurasian steppe the horse
seemed to have played a totemistic role similar to the mystic position
assigned to cattle among the Indo-Europeans, except that horses were
not held in holy awe by the pagans of the steppe. They were used
as sacrificial animals. Their flesh was eaten, their entrails used for
divination, their tails borne aloft as war banners. Raw meat was
made edible without cooking during military expeditions by placing
it under the saddle for a good day's riding. The objects of worship
were trees, wells, rocks, heavenly bodies, fire, ancestors, and idols.
Inanimate things were believed to have inherently magic powers. If
of small size, they were carried about as charms, talismans, and amu-
lets. The shamans, or priests, were in charge of ceremonial dances,
oaths sworn on weapons, blood-mixing covenants, fertility rites, and
group singing. They performed magic, exorcised evil spirits, con-
jured up the spirits of the dead, cast and removed spells, served as
soothsayers, and were familiar with the black arts. These later went
under the collective name of witchcraft. Some of these practices were
so cherished and deeply rooted that the new faith could not afford
to divest its proselytes of them. On the other hand, the Christian
clergy found inadmissible the pagan institutions of polygamy and

certain forms of endogamy. The old order, or at least its hard core, had to yield to the new. But it did not yield easily.

Bulgaria, first of the new states to be Christianized, was also the first to see heathen uprisings. After the baptism of Boris I and his retinue in 865, the pagan boyars rose in revolt to restore the old ways, to drive out the foreigners, and to slay their ruler turned Christian. Egged on by his newly acquired Greek clergy, Boris showed no mercy in dealing with the vanquished tribal chiefs. Repentance could not save the life of the rebels and their families. Mass executions became the order of the day. Subsequently, the problem of how to disarm pagan resistance played an important role in the correspondence between Boris and Pope Nicholas I, the pontiff showing himself more conciliatory than the tsar. The effect of moderating papal wisdom was, however, negligible on Boris when in 893 he had to interrupt his monastic retreat to quell a second pagan uprising, which had broken out after his abdication. Still a third tribal revolt, led by crypto-pagan boyars against Tsar Peter in 928, was drowned in blood in order to secure the new establishment. By the middle of the tenth century tribal leadership had been liquidated and resistance to the religion of the Greeks shifted to the discontented peasants. These rustics had been reduced to starvation and misery during the first quarter of the century by plagues, wars, exceptionally severe winters, crop failures, and famines.[2]

Neighboring Serbia remained strongly pagan until the middle of the ninth century. Large-scale conversions occurred between 867 and 874, roughly coinciding with Boris's baptism in Bulgaria. But pockets of pagan resistance to Christianity remained, notably among the coastal Narentani tribe, known as *Pagani* to the Venetians, who were not loath to resort to arms to ward off conversion stubbornly for about a dozen years more.[3]

In Bohemia a particularly vicious pagan attack shook the new Christian establishment to its foundations during the closing years of the tenth century. The chain of violent events was set off in 995 by confrontation between Christian and heathen mores. Bishop Adalbert of Prague granted asylum in his cathedral to a woman claimed to be adulterous by pagan kinsmen of her husband, who pursued her to the main altar. There tribal justice was done by slaying the fugitive and then swearing a feud on the bloody weapons against the entire clan of her hapless Christian protector. Adalbert left for Rome. During his absence the pagan feudists besieged and captured his castle, putting all members of the household, women and children

included, to the avenging sword. Two years after this atrocity Bishop
Adalbert earned his sainthood by being martyred on the Baltic Coast
at the hands of the pagan Prussians, to whom he was bringing the
Gospel (997).[4]

Nowhere, however, was the socioeconomic background of the
heathen revolts revealed in greater clarity than in the four Hungarian pagan uprisings which accompanied and followed the establishment of a Christian monarchy by St. Stephen. The fuse of the
first great explosion was lighted upon the death of the ruling Christian Prince Geza in 997. Koppany, the eldest surviving male member
of the Arpad clan and tribal chieftain in southern Transdanubia,
presented two demands, both in accordance with pagan legality. His
first demand was to marry Sarolt, Geza's widow, by the pagan right of
the "younger husband." The Christian hierarchy had branded this
socially useful pagan custom (which provided for the continued welfare of the widow after her husband's death) as incest. Koppany's
second demand was political: elevation to the princely throne by right
of *senioritas,* the family law observed by the early Arpads, under
which the heir to the ruling prince was his oldest swordbearing kins-
man. Geza had broken with this rule as being dangerous to a Christian succession and adopted the Byzantine dynastic concept of *ido-
neitas* (suitability to rule). He had put the force of his supreme
authority behind the new Christian dynastic law by designating his
son, the future St. Stephen, as the suitable successor to the throne.
When Koppany attacked at the head of a heathen tribal army in
998, King Stephen crushed his revolt with the aid of German knights.
The pagan chief fell in battle. His dead body was quartered and
nailed to the gates of four cities. His estates were confiscated. Nor
did Stephen deal more gently with the participants in the Ajtony
rising in 1003, the second instance of large-scaled armed pagan resistance during his reign. Ajtony was probably the last of the Transylvanian *gyulas* (semiautonomous tribal governors), a Byzantine-rite
communicant, and a natural leader of the anti-Latin and anti-German
pagan Magyar tribes in the southeast. Stephen's victorious campaign
against Ajtony was an early phase of the destruction of the first
Bulgarian empire, which was completed by Emperor Basil II. After
the fall of Ajtony, his tribal lands were seized and transferred to the
royal domain.[5]

The two other Hungarian pagan revolts were touched off by the
deep humiliation inflicted on the warlike tribes when Peter Urseolo,
the half-Venetian successor of St. Stephen as king, swore a vassal's
oath to Emperor Henry III in 1045. Vata, last of the great tribal

leaders, placed himself at the head of the insurgents. Two Arpad princes, believed to be sympathetic to the pagan cause, were recalled from their Kievan exile. On their arrival the princes were naively petitioned to grant their people leave "to live according to the pagan faith, to kill the bishops and the priests, to destroy the churches, and to cast away the Christian religion." [6] Without waiting for permission, the rebels began acting on this agenda. Among the multitude of their victims was the Venetian Bishop and later St. Gellert, whose statue erected on the hill where he was martyred still dominates the Hungarian capital. Gellert had suspected Byzantine intrigues behind the uprising and in his correspondence used the terms "pagan" and "heretic" interchangeably. King Andrew I (1047-1060), one of the two returning Kievan exiles made king, dealt harshly with both Vata and his son Janus. The latter vainly attempted in 1061 a pagan putsch in the royal capital. This was the last pagan rising in Hungary. Following its failure, pagan practices were made punishable by decapitation.[7]

In Poland, as in Hungary, the entwined antecedents of pagan resistance and revolt were the introduction of a foreign religion, encroachment of the feudal system, and acceptance of the German emperor as suzerain overlord. Mieszko I, converted in 966, joined forces with the Holy Roman Emperor Otto II (973-983) to subjugate the still pagan Slav tribes of Polabians, Pomeranians, and Lusatian Sorbs. He also accepted imperial suzerainty and undertook to pay tribute. His successor Boleslav I allowed himself to be crowned king in 1025 by Conrad the Salian, about to become Holy Roman Emperor (1027). After such a series of humiliations, the death of Mieszko II in 1034 was a signal for a mass rising of the Polish pagans. It could not be put down for five years. This was a veritable revolution of regionalist peasant masses, both anti-German and anti-Christian.[8]

A direct and long-lasting consequence of the Christian-pagan rift in Poland was the effect of the appearance in 1228 of the crusading Order of the Teutonic Knights. These monastic mercenaries had been invited by the Polish ruler Conrad of Masovia to help in the subjugation and conversion of the heathen Prussians [9] on the Baltic. The Knights took half a century to carry out their Prussian crusade. During this time they sealed off the Poles from the Baltic Coast by establishing German colonies from Pomerania to Estonia.

In Lithuania it was the pagan rising of 1260 which temporarily overthrew the Christian monarchy and brought about the violent death of King Mindovg. Olgerd, last in the line of the pagan dukes, who died in 1377, ruled with the aid of the great tribal chiefs and seemed to consider worship of the sun as a politically unifying cult.[10] Prolonged resistance to Christianity was to a large extent due to its appearance in a crusading German garb. It was only in 1387 that the twilight of their tribal gods set in for the Lithuanians, though antipagan crusading continued until 1392, even after their official conversion to Christianity.

At the southern extremity of the middle zone, Christianity had triumphed over resisting pagans during the early tenth century. But the deep-seated social motivation of resistance had not been uprooted. Those strata of the population which found their lot worsening under the new order as the century progressed transferred their basic antagonism and xenophobia to the established religion of the aristocracy ministered by a foreign clergy. These population layers were ready to follow a heresiarch in a general assault on the creed of the high church. Such a leader of heretics was the priest Bogomil (Slavic for Theophil) who, around 950, began preaching to Bulgarian peasants and artisans a strange mixture of evangelical Christianity and Oriental dualism. Scriptural justification could be found for his doctrine in some of the epistles of St. Paul. The ultimate sources of the Bogomil heresy were probably Zoroastrianism and its offshoot Manichaeanism, both early Persian mystery religions, which saw the world as a battleground torn between good and evil, light and darkness. These beliefs, mixed with Gnostic Christian and Paulician aphorisms, first appeared in Europe in the Thracian camps of Byzantine troops brought in from Armenia.[11] Had not the Apostle Paul told the Corinthians that there were two worlds, one visible and temporary, the other invisible and eternal (2 Cor. 4:18); that the body and the soul were two separate entities, one to be rejected, the other to be resurrected, (Gal. 5:17; 1 Cor. 15:44). This scripturally authenticated dualism became the accepted creed of the Bogomils, who indeed saw two worlds around them, one for the overlords, the other for helots like themselves. The upper classes and their religion were thus identified with evil and darkness; the lower strata, with goodness and light. The analogies were carried deeper into the human being himself. The body was identified as a creation of the Devil; the soul, as the imperishable emanation of God. Such dichotomies were later reflected as civil disobedience in the political order and as puritanism in the religious sphere.[12]

As puritans the Bogomils bound themselves to abstinence from meat, wine, and nonreproductive sexual intercourse. Marriage itself was condemned in both its polygamous and monogamous variants as an abomination, though retained as a necessary evil. The other sacraments of the Church, however, were rejected, as were also the dogma of the incarnation, the veneration of the cross, the efficacy of icons and relics, and the obligation to attend church services.[13] In their relation with the authorities the Bogomils conveniently ignored the apostle's admonition to obey governments for they are ordained by God (Rom. 13:1-3; Titus 3:1). In their eyes, all laws made by men were evil and invalid and therefore not to be obeyed. Even such infractions of the criminal law as homicide and theft were to be excused on the grounds that they were directed against the Devil's creations in the visible world: the human body and material goods. Emperors, kings, princes, patriarchs, bishops, and landed proprietors were all creatures and servitors of the Devil. Their authority was therefore to be flouted. Like most self-righteous sectarians, the Bogomils finally reached the point where they proclaimed themselves the elect, the chosen of God, the only Christians, whose high priest was the only true pope.[14]

The movement gathered momentum during the eleventh century because it had found a mass following among the dispossessed. It also attracted members of the impoverished lower clergy. The first Bogomil revolt was joined even by the warlike pagan nomads circulating on the peripheries of the Byzantine empire and culminated in a victory over the Emperor Alexius Comnenus in 1087. When order was finally restored, inquisitorial persecutions followed. Yet the heresy continued to spread westward into the Serb-inhabitated areas and beyond. About 1200 the Serb ruler Stephen Nemanya I drove the trekking Bogomils into Catholic Bosnia, where they became the founders of prosperous artisans' communities. Some of the towns may still be archeologically placed by the adjoining cemeteries noted for the primitive art forms carved on the tombstones.[15] The basic symbol of the tombstones is not the cross but an upraised hand, disproportionately large, apparently reaching for God. Interestingly, the same motif appears on tombstones found in southern France which date back to the second half of the twelfth century.[16] These funerary monuments memorialize not only the uncompromisingly pious men and women over whom they were raised but also a possible historical east-west link between the Bogomil and the Albigensian heresies.[17] Three popes—Innocent III in 1203, Gregory IX in 1234, and Innocent VI in 1355—preached crusades against the Bogomils. Innocent III also preached a crusade against the Albigensians, which was successful in the extirpation of that heresy in 1213 through military and inquisitorial means. The Bogomils, on the other hand, held out in their Bosnian fastnesses and eventually welcomed as liberators the enemies of their persecutors when they came as invaders: the Serbs in 1349 and the Turks in 1391.

The other great Middle-European heresy, the Hussite movement,[18] also sprang from plebeian animosity to a foreign-sponsored religious establishment, led to internecine warfare, and overlapped national boundaries. Foreign inspiration came to the Czech Hussites from fourteenth-century England, where John Wyclif had been preaching a purification of the established church and a return to scriptural simplicity. Unlike Bogomilism, however, the Hussite movement displayed mysticism only on its extremist fringe and bore the high intellectual stamp of its founder, John Hus (1369?-1415), Rector Magnificus of the University of Prague. Martin Luther recognized him a hundred years later as one of the great precursors of the Protestant Reformation.[19] But Hus was born a century too soon, in a minor ethnic group, to succeed in his undertaking. His actions were nevertheless in clear response to the demand of contemporary historical conditions. As the fifteenth century dawned in Bohemia, latent hostility came to a head between the indigenous Czech-speaking peasants, artisans, craftsmen, townsfolk, students, and professors on one side; the penetrating German burghers, royal administrators, high Catholic clergy, and a native aristocracy in the process of being denationalized, on the other. Hus made himself an embodiment of the first faction's resistance to Germanization, its defense of Czech national interests, and its insistence on preserving the Czech character of the University of Prague. His theological teachings were noted for his doctrine of Utraquism (the communicant should receive the eucharist in both its components, bread as well as wine) and for a call to regulate the obstructionism of an unworthy clergy separating man from his God. Hus was summoned before the Synod of Constance to be examined for such teachings. He was provided with a safe-conduct by the German-Roman King (crowned Holy Roman Emperor in 1433) Sigismund. He went and, despite his safe-conduct, was burnt at the stake for heresy in 1415. Jerome of Prague, his closest collaborator, met with the same fate during the following year.

Within three years all of Bohemia was in the hands of the revolting Hussites. In 1419 the rebels won acceptance of their four demands, known as the Articles of Prague. First, there would have to be both bread and wine in the serving of the eucharist. Second, sermons would not be subject to censorship by the high hierarchy. Third, titles to church property would be examined and the right of land ownership limited. Fourth, there would be proper punishment for sin—in other words. offending, licentious, and corrupt priests and monks could not be exempt from civil jurisdiction by pleading clerical immunity.[20]

Soon the movement broke up into three factions: the conservative Calixtines, the moderate Taborites, and the radical chiliasts. The Calixtines consisted of upper and middle-class adherents and had as their symbol the communion chalice passed by the priest to the communicant. They called for compliance with the Articles of Prague and for an independent Bohemia outside the Holy Roman Empire. The Taborites (so called after their place of assembly on Mt. Tabor in Bohemia) were recruited from artisans, craftsmen, farmers, and some serfs. They went beyond the Calixtines in their rejection of the Church (since it was not in the Bible) and in their demand for the abolition of the hierarchy, the suppression of the monasteries, the prohibition of confession, the end of feudalism, the proclamation of a republic, and the emancipation of the serfs. The chiliasts came from the poorest segments of the population and expected a "paradise on earth" (primitive communism) after an imminent second coming of Christ. This radical wing was disavowed and expelled from the movement by the Taborites in 1421.[21]

The two crusades conducted by the King-Emperor Sigismund (1420-1422) and a third by the papal legate Cesarini in 1431 failed to cope with Hussite guerrilla tactics and field fortifications rapidly constructed by placing weapon-carrying wagons in a defensive circle. Diplomacy was resorted to. Through a compromise the Calixtines were brought back into the Church with the right to receive communion in both kinds. In return they became participants in the anti-Hussite crusade. After the great defeat inflicted on the Taborites in the battle of Lipany in 1434, hundreds of Hussite prisoners of war were said to have been slain by the victors.[22]

What were the effects of five hundred years of turmoil caused by fanatically embattled heathens and heretics? Externally, the consequences were widely felt. The Hussite heresy was the last revolt against Catholic orthodoxy that the waning strength of the Universal Church could cope with. Religious dissent continuing underground prepared the soil for the Protestant Reformation. The demonstrated existence of abuses and corruption in the Church provided stimulus for the Catholic Counter Reformation. The Hussites supplied a prototype for the great chain of revolutions, Dutch, English, American, French, and Russian, which altered the face of Western civilization. But internally in the middle zone, these civil wars weakened the potential resistance to imperial intruders, Turks in the south and Germans in the north. National hatreds were intensified, though revived contact during the Hussite wars between the Czechs of the empire and the Slovaks of Hungary was beneficial for future Czechoslovak unity.[23] Four hundred years later romantic nationalism found inspiration in the deeds of pagan, Bogomil, and Hussite freedom fighters.

5

The *Drang nach Osten*

The Germanic "push to the east" began while Rome was still at the height of its power. Restrained by imperial might and by population barriers from crossing the Rhine and the North Sea to the west, the Danube, the Alps, and the Pyrenees to the south, the coastal and riparian Germanic tribes could expand only in an easterly direction, toward the interior of the continent. More than a century and a half before the traditional 449 date of Hengest's and Horsa's landing in England, other Germanic tribes had migrated as far east as the Don River and subsequently became known to history as Ostrogoths or Eastern Goths.[1] This was the first phase of the Germanic push to the east. The visible weakening of Roman military power during the third and fourth centuries gradually emboldened the territorially restricted Germans to cross the Rhine, the North Sea, and the Danube. When the peninsular entrances were probed and found poorly defended, the prehistoric north-to-south rush resumed on a large scale. In this manner the traditional easterly direction of the Germanic push shifted temporarily toward both the west and the south.

The reoriented Germanic tribal movements gave newcomers from the Eurasian steppe, the Avars and later the Magyars, an opportunity to pour into and occupy the depopulated, wide-open spaces of the middle zone. The Avar empire, which ruled over sparsely settled and loosely organized Slavic tribes, was destroyed by Charlemagne in 796-803. So great was the impression made by the Frankish emperor on the Slavs that to this day the word for king in the various Slavic languages—*kralj*—is derived from and guards the memory of his name: Karl.

Thus, starting in the early ninth century, the Slavic peoples had to bear the brunt of the German push to the east. Again the southern peninsulas and the western islands were filled with organized states. Coastal raiding was still possible, but real territorial expansion was feasible only toward the east, where no states capable of offering resistance had yet come into existence north of the Danube. When an ill-defined and seemingly Byzantine-oriented Moravian empire of Slav peoples arose above the middle Danube and on the Pannonian plain, the later Carolingians found it relatively easy to destroy it in alliance with the newly arrived Magyars (862-896). This second phase of the *Drang*, the push into a stateless wilderness, continued until the coalescence of the heathen, tribal societies into Christian dynastic states.

Even before the arrival of the Magyars, the Frankish emperors and kings had begun driving into Slav territory east-west salients, which were then organized as marches or margraviates. One such march was the Ostmark, later to become Austria, which intruded between and separated the Czechs of Bohemia and the Slovenes at the head of the Adriatic. The Friul margraviate around modern Trieste and Rijeka (Fiume) was established as a gateway to the Balkans, an outlet to the sea, to provide military protection for the eastern border of the Western Empire and to promote the further eastward expansion of Latin Christianity.[2] Here, in the borderland of the Eastern Empire, Rome and Byzantium stood face to face, each proselytizing for its ideology and jockeying for a more favorable strategic position.

It was at this point that, in 892, the Frankish king Arnulf allied himself with the Magyars to bring about the ruin of the Moravian empire. He did this probably in the expectation that, having served their purpose, the Magyars would recede, or vanish like the Huns and the Avars. But, surprisingly, the Magyars set a historical precedent: they became the first nomads from the steppe to convert to the Latin Church and to organize a state as a permanent part of the European political system. Though this new state separated the Czechs, Slovaks, and Poles in the north from their Serb, Croat, and Bulgar kinsmen in the south, its successful organization on the western model gave an impetus to the formation of Christian monarchies throughout the middle zone. The second phase of the *Drang*, the intrusion of organized power into a politically unorganized wasteland, was now over. Henceforth, in the third phase, the Germans had to conduct their push to the east, except in the far Baltic north, with Christian states blocking their path.

Most dangerously exposed to the *Drang* at the beginning of the third phase was the fledgling Czech state in the Bohemian bastion. A more fitting, nonarchitectural metaphor to describe its predicament might be what a glance at the physical map reveals: the head of a man stuck in the mouth of a lion whose jaws are ready to snap closed. The early Czech rulers saw clearly this dangerously exposed geographical position and, after the disappearance of the Avars, had acquiesced in becoming Carolingian tributaries. The feudal relationship continued under succeeding German imperial dynasties. It was formalized in 962 after the coronation of Otto the Great as Holy Roman Emperor. According to S. H. Thomson,[3] there were twenty-two reigning Czech princes between 800 and 1125, of whom five swore a formal vassal's oath to German emperors. Vratislav, the first Czech king, received his royal crown in 1085 not from the pope but from Emperor Henry IV. The royal title of Vratislav's successors was confirmed in 1158 by Emperor Frederick I Barbarossa, who also managed to outflank Bohemia by turning its southeastern neighbor Moravia into a direct imperial fief. Frederick II, the last of the powerful Hohenstaufen emperors (who in the mid-1930s was to be hailed in Germany as a precursor of the Third Reich), issued a Golden Bull from his Sicilian capital in 1212 recognizing the Czech realm as a kingdom in perpetuity, linked to the Holy Roman Emperor in a liege-vassal relationship.[4] During the interregnum following the extinction of the Hohenstaufens, the proud and ambitious Czech King Ottokar II defied the empire. In skillful military campaigns he obliterated the Austro-Friuli salient by extending his rule from the Bohemian bastion down to the Adriatic Sea. But his success in re-establishing severed Slav communications and disrupted Slav unity was ephemeral. On the battlefield of Dürnkrut in 1278 the new Habsburg Emperor Rudolf and Ladislas IV of Hungary met as victors over his dead body. The real victor was Rudolf. Two and a half centuries later not only the imperial diadem but also both the Czech and the Hungarian crowns rested on the heads of his descendants.

Pagan Slavs outside the Bohemian bastion and heathen Prussians on the Baltic were dealt with less ceremoniously than the Czechs. They were forced by the sword to let the Germans push through their lands, often with the help of Bohemian and Polish rulers. German intrusion was also facilitated by divisiveness and internal imperialism between the new Polish and Bohemian states. The Czech Premyslid rulers coveted and in 1295 and 1300 temporarily obtained the throne of the Polish Piasts. During the fourteenth century, the Luxemburg successors of the Premyslid kings were also involved in pro-German and anti-Polish designs. Yet, Poland as well as Hungary managed to succeed where Bohemia had failed: in staying out of the Holy Roman Empire.

The resistance to the German eastward push increased in direct ratio to the centralization of power in the new states of the middle zone. Conversely, resistance weakened whenever feudal opposition absorbed the energies of the middle-zone kings. At times civil wars over disputed dynastic succession provided the advancing Germans with an opportunity to intervene militarily on the side of this or that faction. Military intervention became the Hungarian policy of the Salian Emperors Conrad II (1024-1039) and Henry III (1039-1056). Starting in 1030 and continuing until the temporary exhaustion of German imperial power at the end of the eleventh century, because of the investiture controversy with the Holy See, Hungary became the target of a series of German invasions.[5] Two of St. Stephen's short-reigning successors, Peter Urseolo (1038-1044) and Solomon (1063-1074), accepted German help against other Hungarian dynastic factions at the price of becoming imperial vassals. Both were driven from the throne by their subjects for this degradation. Their vassal's oaths to Henry III (1039-1056) and Henry IV (1056-1106) were repudiated and cancelled in open assembly (1051 and 1074).

When the emperors resorted to interstate warfare to enforce their claim to Hungary as an imperial fief, they were unable to do so. The years 1051-1052 proved especially disastrous for Henry III. During the summer of 1051 the wily Hungarians first cut his naval supply line down the Danube and then proceeded to put to flight his famished army when it reached the Vertes Mountains west of Buda. During the following year the German fleet besieging Pressburg (Pozsony, Bratislava) was sunk by Hungarian frogmen as it rested at anchor during the night.[6] The immediate consequence of these eleventh-century German-Hungarian wars was the Hungarian monarchy's alignment with the anti-imperial Guelph faction in the investiture controversy and its ramifications. After Henry IV's penance at Canossa (1077), St. Ladislas I of Hungary (1077-1095) fully exploited the continuing struggle between pope and emperor to embark on imperialist conquests of his own against Croatia and Slavonia, down to the Dalmatian coast, in complete disregard of both imperial and papal pretensions to serve as arbiters of European politics.[7]

It would be a mistake, however, to believe that the German eastward push was always warlike. It would be historically incorrect to claim that it was never welcomed by the rulers of the middle zone or that it failed to play a civilizing role in extending the limits of West-

ern culture. The Balkans were not immediately included in the
sphere of this cultural radiation. Because of the fact that Ottoman
power had overrun Byzantine territories even before the imperial
city itself fell in 1453, the road to the Balkans remained barred for
three centuries. The German civilizing mission was thus restricted to
the lands north of the Danube, with the exception of the Slovene area
of the former Friul march. In Poland, Bohemia, and Hungary,
peaceful German colonization had been going on apace since Carolingian times, usually at the invitation or at least with the tacit consent
of the local rulers. During the twelfth and thirteenth centuries pacific
German colonization of an almost autonomous character was in full
swing in Poland. The colonists from the west were granted royal and
ducal charters permitting them to live, to organize, to own and acquire
property, and to pursue trades under their own German law. The new
German settlements had a town-and-country character. German
burghers went about their business in the towns. Saxon, Silesian, and
Swabian peasants tilled fertile fields around meticulously clean, well-
laid-out farms and villages. Between towns and villages stood great
monasteries predominantly staffed with German monks under German abbots, sometimes to the irritating exclusion of native Poles.[8]
Consistently practiced intermarriages with princely German families
turned some Polish dynasts, such as the dukes of Wroclaw, for example, into strangers in their own land, surrounded by German courtiers
and employing German as a court language.[9] Sociologically such comportment seldom fails to stimulate xenophobia. Poland was no exception. The hatred of the foreigners was fanned by an ill-concealed contempt on the part of the Germans for their Polish hosts. The Poles, in
their turn, suspected the Germans of separatist tendencies, and not
without reason, as we shall see.

By establishing the Duchy of Silesia on the Upper Oder in 1327,
the Germans succeeded in driving a new salient into Slavic territory
between the Czechs and the Poles. Not that the ruling dynasties of
the two Slav neighbors had ever exhibited exceptionally common
tenacity to unite against German expansionism. As a member state of
the Holy Roman Empire, Bohemia seemed to attract German colonization even more than Poland. The three rims of the Bohemian bastion gradually took on the aspect of a Little Germany, with farms,
villages, towns, and monasteries with German customs, speech, and
culture. These settlements, as well as those further inland, came to be
known in history as the Sudetenland.[10] The native Czech idiom was
slowly relegated to the rank of a rustic dialect. By the end of the
fourteenth century even the University of Prague was beginning to

change from a Czech to a German character. As in Poland, a nativist reaction was not long in gathering. Along with other combustibles, it eventually flamed up in the great drama of the Bohemian pre-Reformation under John Hus.

In the meantime the Hungarian Arpads had been no more remiss in encouraging German colonization in their country than the Polish Piasts or the Czech Premyslids in theirs. The arrival of German monks, abbots, knights, farmers, and burghers had begun in the tenth century under Prince Geza (940-997), the father of St. Stephen. During the period of the German wars in the eleventh century, the pace of German immigration slackened, but it assumed large dimensions under Geza II (1141-1162). There were two principal reasons for the renewed influx. First, the crusading knights and campfollowers who had crossed Hungarian territory in 1096 under Peter of Amiens and Godfrey of Bouillon, or at least those of them who survived and returned to their native countries from the Holy Land, spread far and wide eyewitness stories of vast, fertile, and uninhabited areas in the land of the Magyars.[11] The familiar process of a low-density population area sucking in surplus populations from high-density regions began to operate. Second, as the new Hungarian monarchy entered the second century of its existence, the problem of the sparsely settled peripheral areas did not escape the attention of the royal councillors. These men were motivated not only by the desire to establish defensive outposts to control the passes through the mountain frontiers but also by the sociopolitical concept of creating an urban element of burghers as a counterweight to be used by the king in his perennial struggle against the oligarchically inclined great nobles. Transplanting Magyar populations from the western border to the Moldavian frontier in the eastern Carpathians was a partial answer to the problem of defense.[12] But the new class of burghers was an immediate necessity in the political balancing act. This sorely needed group could not be produced through nurtured growth; it had to be imported ready made. German colonists were the answer.

King Geza's invitations went out to Saxons, Swabians, Franks, and Flemings to settle under privileged conditions in two mountain-valley areas of his kingdom. The first of these regions was the inner rim of the Transylvanian Alps bordering on Wallachia and the adjacent basin of the Maros and Olt rivers. The second area was among the high Tatras on the present Polish-Slovak border, subsequently known as Zips (Szepes). The Tatra colonists went under the name of Zipsers; the Transylvanian German settlers received the collective name Saxons.[13] Both groups were granted extensive extraterritorial privileges as royal *hospes* (guests). For the Saxons of Transylvania a special territorial unit was established with the resounding title of *fundus regius* (royal ground). Self-government, freedom from taxation, and other privileges were bestowed on the settlers. The head of the Saxon self-government was an elected *comes* (count), directly responsible to the central royal government. The count ruled over an industrious population of German farmers, artisans, traders, and burghers. Attractive towns with Gothic cathedrals, gabled townhouses, and terraced beer gardens soon dotted the landscape. A similar way of life developed in the thirteen Zipser towns of the north.[14] It may not be without interest to note that the German migrations of the twelfth century to the mountainous regions of Hungary probably provided the historical background for the Pied Piper of Hamelin folk story.

The German idyl in Hungary took an ugly turn during the first quarter of the thirteenth century. The repercussions reached from the Lower Danube to the Gulf of Finland. The incident, which opened a new path to the German push, was produced by an interaction of the dying crusades with the renewed struggle between the Hungarian king and his recalcitrant barons. The flickering flame of the crusading spirit in the Holy Land left unemployed some of the knightly orders which had sprung up during the twelfth century for the double purpose of fighting the infidel and of carving out feudal domains for knights errant. Such an organization, looking for new fields to conquer, was the Order of the Teutonic Knights under their Grand Master Herman von Salza.[15] While the Grand Master was searching for greener fields, Andrew II of Hungary (1205-1235) was looking for allies in his fight against his barons. The oligarchs' resistance to royal power and its German aura culminated in the assassination of A: drew's German Queen Gertrude in 1213 and led to the issuance in 1222 of the Golden Bull, a feudal constitutional charter wrested by the magnates from the king in circumstances resembling the signing of the Magna Carta

To fortify himself for the gathering feudal storm, Andrew in 1211 hit upon the idea of inviting Herman von Salza and his Teutonic Knights to settle in the southeastern Barcza frontier region.[16] Here there was still an opportunity to crusade against heathen Tartars and Cumanians, who were harassing the border. Here the Knights might lead an autonomous existence as powerful vassals on a royal fief similar to the nearby *fundus regius* of the Saxons. To these latter, probably in an attempt further to strengthen his hand against the barons and to encourage more German immigration, Andrew granted in 1224 a generously permissive Golden Letter of Liberties.[17]

But then the lightning struck. Intercepted correspondence addressed by Herman von Salza to the Holy See revealed a proposal of the Grand Master to detach the Barcza fief from Hungary and to place it directly under the feudal lordship of the pope. Such base treachery King Andrew could not stomach. He marched against the Teutonic Knights in 1225 and drove them out of his kingdom into the neighboring northeastern Rumanian principality of Moldavia. It was in their Moldavian refuge during the following year that the discomfited Knights received a new letter of invitation, this time from the Polish duke, Conrad of Masovia,[18] to help him crusade against the pagan Prussians on the Baltic. Had Conrad not heard of the Barcza affair? Within four years the Teutonic Knights were firmly ensconced in their headquarters, the Castle of Torun (Thorn) on the banks of the Polish Vistula. Undaunted by his Hungarian experience, the incorrigible von Salza immediately began plotting, this time successfully, to detach his new fief from Polish suzerainty and to place it under papal feudal lordship.[19] Then he proceeded to obtain a charter confirming his audacious land-grab from the proto-Nazi Emperor Frederick II himself. From the base thus acquired, a new, fourth phase of the *Drang* opened, a crusade up the invasion route along the Baltic littoral,[20] which eventually resulted in the extension of German power, population, and culture as far north as Estonia and Finland.

The Knights' exploits on the Baltic began with the subjugation and extermination of the pagan Prussians, of whom nothing now remains except their name, and even that has been expropriated by their German successors. The Knights next turned against the port city of Danzig (Gdansk) and its adjacent Pomeranian area. By occupying the city and its hinterland in the 1250s they denied the Poles access to the sea. More *Lebensraum* and powerful help to obtain it beckoned from farther north. Another German crusading order, the Livonian Brothers of the Sword, who had followed in the footsteps of venturesome Bremen merchants to establish a bridgehead on the northern Baltic coast, which later became Latvia, joined forces with their Teutonic comrades in 1237 to pursue a common goal.[21] The result of the merger between the two orders was German encirclement of both Pomerania and Lithuania. Pomerania became a link between the territories of the Holy Roman Empire and the new German colony of Prussia. Lithuania embraced Christianity in 1251-1253, if only for a brief interlude, mainly to deprive the harassing Knights of their crusading excuse.

By the end of the thirteenth century the crusading Knights were not alone in carving out new German territories on the Baltic coast.

During the interregnum between the Hohenstaufens and Rudolf of Habsburg, which ended in 1273, the newly created margraves of Brandenburg began expanding into Polish territory along the Oder and Warta rivers. By 1307 these rapacious dynasts became so menacing that, to obtain help against their aggressive advance, the Poles had to turn again to the crusading Knights. With their accustomed *modus operandi,* the joined orders drove the Brandenburgs from Danzig and its Pomeranian hinterland and then in 1309 seized the conquered area for themselves. The Poles then sought the aid of another German dynasty, the Bavarian Wittelsbachs, to dislodge the Knights. To make the situation even more confused and ominous for the Poles, the new King of Bohemia, John of Luxemburg (1310-1346), renewed and continued to maintain for a quarter century the old Czech dynastic claim to the throne of Poland. If successfully pressed, the Bohemian claim would have meant the vicarious absorption of Poland in the Holy Roman Empire. A general German invasion of Poland in 1331-1332 seemed to have the force of a *coup de grâce* and was an ill augury of a possible partitioning. But through skillful diplomatic maneuvering and an appeal to the papacy, John of Luxemburg was brought to renounce his claim to the Polish crown in 1335 and the Teutonic Knights were canonically denounced as aggressors against Poland in 1339.[22] This did not move the Knights to restore any of the Polish territories they had seized, though they decided to bide their time before resuming their push for more land. The menace they continued to pose to both Poland and Lithuania continued well into the sixteenth century and was instrumental in bringing the two states into a political union.

None of the great historical tremors of the middle zone failed to provide an impetus for the German push to the east. The Mongolian invasions in the 1240s, the Ottoman conquest north of the Danube after 1526, the Turkish rollback starting with the relief of Vienna by the Poles in 1683, the subsequent gradual dilapidation of the Sublime Porte, and the hopeless decay of the Polish state at the end of the eighteenth century, all served as stimulants to the *Drang nach Osten,* either in its pacific form of colonization or in its martial form of aggression. But before these further developments could come to pass, an extraordinarily fortuitous political phenomenon of cohesion and unity, without precedent or sequel in the history of the middle zone, seemed to make up for the absence of natural frontiers in assuring temporary self-determination for landlocked Middle Europeans. This phenomenon was the Angevin-initiated, short-lived dynastic union of Poland, Hungary, and Lithuania. The union provided an outlet not to one but to three seas and generated political-military power in the immense territorial triangle delimited by the Baltic, the Adriatic, and the Black Sea.[23] Although the generation of this new power was not so much due to far-sighted statesmanship as to a fulfill-ment of dynastic ambitions, it made the middle zone, no longer land-locked, impervious to great-power imperialism for at least a century.

The Land Unlocked—
Monarchy of the Three Seas

The rise of a maritime middle-zone monarchy during the fourteenth century came about because of an exceptionally favorable set of historical interactions. The principal permissive factor was the simultaneous weakness of the imperialist potential in both west and east Such a joint appearance of circumstances propitious to the middle zone did not reoccur in European power relations until the end of World War I, and then with results similarly favorable to independence. The great difference lay in the fact that during the fourteenth century the inland political structure was not a function of other powers' victory or defeat in war as it was in 1918. It was self-created and filled with self-generated power.

The imperialist potential of the west had been greatly reduced during the first half of the fourteenth century because of the dynastic struggle among the Habsburg, Luxemburg, and Wittelsbach families ₍or the succession of the imperial Hohenstaufens. During the second half of the century, with the issuance of the German Golden Bull in 1356, the Holy Roman Empire became a loose federation of sovereignties and the emperor an elective though still prestigious presiding dignitary. The after-effects of the Black Death in 1348-1349, coupled with the coastal concentration of political-military energies required by the Hundred Years' War in 1338-1453, gave the middle zone a respite from western incursions other than privately conducted forays of crusading knights.

In the east, under the Tartar yoke during the early fourteenth century, Russia lay powerless, divided into a congeries of competing principalities and bereft of leadership. During the second half of the century began the struggle against the overlords of the Golden Horde; it lasted until the very end of the fifteenth century. A new Russia had to be built with Moscow as its center and with the prince of this city as the undisputed autocrat of the various Russias before the urgency of dealing with great domestic problems would permit action on the western marches. The middle zone was thus temporarily left to its own devices by both west and east.

An important factor which contributed to the organization of power in the landlocked middle zone was the continuing land-hunger of the princelings who, after the fiasco of the Crusades, could no longer hope to satiate their appetites outside Europe. With the death of St. Louis of France before the walls of Tunis in 1270, the Mediterranean once again became an intercultural moat between the northern and southern shores, such as it had not been since the years of rivalry between Rome and Carthage. The southern coast of the great inland sea was held by Moslem instead of Phoenician-Punic power. But history was repeating itself. The northern, Roman-type offensive to destroy power threatening from the south shore again resulted, as in the days of Hannibal, in a southern counteroffensive against Europe. This time the counterthrust was two-pronged: first by the Moors through Spain and then by their Turk coreligionists via the Balkans. During the fourteenth century most of the Iberian peninsula was Moorish. Before it ended, the Balkans became Turkish. Not only had the west been ejected from the Near East at the end of the Crusades, but it was being outflanked by Moslem salients driven into its own western and eastern territorial extremities.

Consequently, if any new realms were to be acquired by aspiring dynasties or their junior branches, the work of empire building would have to be carried out north of the Mediterranean, neither in the west nor in the east, but in the middle of Europe. One aspiring junior dynasty was the French Anjou family, descendants of Charles, younger brother of St. Louis IX (1226-1270). The Anjous or Angevins could trace their lineage without difficulty to Hugh Capet (987-996), founder of the third French dynastic line replacing the Carolingians; and, with some effort, to Charlemagne himself. Charles of Anjou laid the foundations for an Angevin penetration from the Mediterranean toward the Baltic into the Kingdom of the Two Sicilies, with its capital at Naples, which he had conquered from the last of the Hohenstaufens in 1268.[1] From this base Angevin power soon flowed in a northeasterly direction, through Greece and Albania, left vacuous by the ebbing of Byzantine influence; and still farther north, through Hungary and Poland, toward the still heathen Baltic shore. Since Charles of Anjou was an enemy of the Hohenstaufens, with whom the papacy had been carrying on a blood feud, his and his heirs' undertakings received unqualified papal blessing. Angevin support of the Holy See was so highly valued that, during the first half of the fourteenth century, no Anjou could do wrong, even when Queen Giovanna of Naples had her unwanted husband Andrea strangled and his body thrown from her bedroom balcony in the resort town of Aversa in 1345.[2]

The Angevin advance to the north was made possible by the convenient extinction of the principal reigning dynasties of the middle zone during the first three quarters of the fourteenth century. The Hungarian Arpads became extinct in 1301; the Czech Premyslids in 1306; the Polish Piasts in 1370; the Serb Nemanyas in 1371. The feudal oligarchs, who had been locked in a death struggle with some of these kings to prevent the rise of centralized power, became kingmakers. They favored foreign dynasties to replace the native kings of old. What the barons wanted was imported rulers unfamiliar with local conditions. The grateful newcomers, they reasoned, would gladly accept their tutelage and would be content to serve as Polichinelles manipulated by strings pulled from behind the throne. The Anjous looked like acceptable candidates to play such a role, though appearances eventually proved to be deceptive.

An urgent need for some kind of economic unity hastened the coalescence of the north-Danubian monarchies under princes, foreign or native. By the first quarter of the fourteenth century external commerce had become almost nonexistent in most of these lands, not only because they were landlocked and thus excluded from maritime trade, but also because goods to and from the west had to be transshipped at Vienna.[3] Duties collected and other charges payable at the Austrian transshipment point had become an unbearable increment in the selling and buying price of merchandise, both exported and imported. To avoid transshipment at Vienna was therefore a common interest of Bohemia's, Hungary's, and Poland's. Thus, as in the later formation of European empires, the need for economic unity, a customs union, or Zollverein, acted as a curtain-raiser to the spectacle of political coalescence.

The need for urgent action in the economic field, starting with the establishment of lower-duty trade arteries, was pressed by the rising bourgeoisie and the developing guilds, for which the German push to the east had been to a large extent responsible. The urban elements north of the Lower Danube became generally partisans of the Anjous, bred in the Italy of the fourteenth century, where the revival of interstate commerce, the rise of a new middle class, banking, capitalism, urban growth, and the birth of the limited-liability company had made rulers realize that the soundest foundations of princely power rested on the industry and prosperity of their humble and ignoble subjects. The Renaissance, with its emphasis on the free development of the human potential, was already in the air north of the Alps and of the Danube, though the full flowering did not come before the second half of the fifteenth century. But a new lay morality, ready to risk for earthly gains the penalty awaiting in the hereafter, was already motivating the creative energies and the acquisitive instincts not only of the newly risen great families, such as the Anjous and the Luxemburgs, but also those of the rapidly multiplying urbanites.

The revival of antiquity, which had started among the upper strata of society, was also filtering downward into the lower layers. One no longer had to serve in holy orders to be literate. Literacy was spreading among the upper classes. Princelings dreaming of greater realms could afford illuminated copies of the *Secretum secretorum* of the pseudo-Aristotle [4] in their castles. This was a medieval literary forgery, anachronistically mixing the ethos of the age of chivalry with the splendor of the Hellenistic period. It narrated, in the extravagant style of the medieval romances, the heroic deeds and irresistible conquests of Alexander the Great. In the minds of the future rulers the embellished, legendary past served up by the *Secretum secretorum* and by similar knightly tales became a powerful stimulus for future political expansion and dynastic glory.

The Franco-Flemish Luxemburgs, whose later fortunes were inextricably interwoven with the historical role of the Anjous, were closer to present than future dynastic glory. At the moment when the Angevin Charles Robert (1308-1342) of Naples was mounting the Hungarian throne as Charles I, the Luxemburg Henry VII (1308-1313) was being invested with the imperial power of the Holy Roman Empire. Three more Luxemburg emperors followed him on the German imperial throne: Charles IV (1346-1378), Wenceslas (1378-1419), and the Sigismund of anti-Hussite fame (1410-1437).[5] With the exception of Henry VII and with the addition of John the Blind (1310-1346), the Luxemburgs were also kings of Bohemia. Sigismund became king of both Hungary and Bohemia before he was elected King of the Romans and then Emperor of the Holy Roman Empire of the German Nation.

The Luxemburgs and Anjous had two things in common as far as the middle zone was concerned. They both traced their ancestry to the extinct Hungarian Arpad dynasty through the female line and they both represented the idea of regional unity superseding localized monarchy. On the other hand, the two families were dissimilar in two important respects: the Anjous rose from minor to major dynastic status with, the Luxemburgs without, papal support. To boot, the regional unity personified by the Anjous had a northern orientation, from the Balkans to the Baltic; while the Luxemburg pull was toward the west, into the parlous embrace of the Holy Roman Empire. The Anjou directional sweep proved to be stronger. Sigismund of Luxemburg, before he was elected ruler of Germany, in 1385, married Maria, the daughter of the Anjou Louis the Great of Hungary. The following year Louis's younger daughter Hedwig (St. Jadwiga) became the wife of the newly baptized Lithuanian Ladislas of Jagiello. Hungarian-Polish-Lithuanian, and eventually Bohemian, dynastic unity produced a power structure resting on common economic interests. It had outlets in the Baltic, Adriatic, and Black Seas, at long last permitting participation in maritime world commerce. A monarchy of three seas thus came into existence.[6]

The new outlet to the Baltic was limited to a narrow stretch on the coast between the Niemen and the Dvina rivers, north and south of which the Teutonic Knights were still in control of the littoral. Through this outlet, however, the cities of the Hanseatic League, the Flemish ports, and the great developing emporium of London itself could be reached. The Black Sea shore west of the Crimea, with the mouths of the Dniester, Bug, and Dnieper rivers, allowed fluvial traffic to be transshipped to Byzantine and Anatolian ports. The Adriatic stretch from Rijeka (Fiume) down to Dubrovnik (Ragusa) provided access to Levantine and other Mediterranean harbors. The vexing problem of overland commerce was solved at the Congress of Visegrad in 1335, where the kings of Hungary, Bohemia, and Poland eliminated Vienna as a transshipment stop for their countries, decreed commercial letters of guaranty for German and French exporters, and established new trade routes via Brno-Esztergom-Buda, Brno-Kosice, and Kosice-Lvov. Kosice was made a transshipment stop.[7] Not only did these gradually opened maritime outlets and overland trade routes enable the middle zone, for the first and last time in history, to have a proper share in world commerce but they also stimulated the growth of cities and the expansion of the incipient middle class.

Before he could devote his energies to the solution of the commercial problem at Visegrad, Charles Robert of Anjou had to spend the first decade of his reign restoring royal power over the rapacious, embittered, and unyielding oligarchs who had supported his candidacy in the hope that he would be a marionette in their hands. The decisive battle, in which mounted and infantry units sent by the Zipser cities made it possible for Charles to defeat the baronial army, was fought at Rozgony in 1312. The last of the great oligarchs, Mate Csak, lord of most of Slovakia, died in 1321, and with his death the new dynasty seemed secure and its throne stable.[8] But opposition among the feudal diehards secretly lingered on. On April 17, 1330, the entire royal family barely escaped assassination at the hands of the fanatical Felician Zach.[9] Charles's queen, Elizabeth, sister of Casimir the Great of Poland, lost four fingers when she raised her arm defensively between her husband and the would-be assassin. The sudden horror of the scene left an indelible impression of oligarchic power on the mind of the child Louis, who succeeded his father on the Hungarian throne in 1342 and his uncle Casimir as king of Poland in 1370. His double succession was the first step in the middle zone toward regional unity based on dynastic identity.

The second step was taken in 1385 when Louis's elder daughter Maria became the wife of Sigismund of Luxemburg.[10] He remained on the scene for over half a century, until his death in 1437. Sigismund was the personification of regionalism: after his coronation as King of Hungary in 1387 he successively became King of the Romans (1410), King of Bohemia (1419), and finally Holy Roman Emperor (1433). The western orientation of this Luxemburg king-emperor enabled him to collect in 1395-1396 a crusading army of French, English, and German nobles to join his Hungarian, Bohemian, and Wallachian effectives in a campaign to stop further Ottoman advance toward the southeastern marches of the empire. The military situation in the Balkans had become desperate by 1389, when the combined Serb, Bosnian, Wallachian, and Albanian armies were annihilated by the Turks in the great battle of Kossovo Field. Tirnovo, capital of the decayed Second Bulgarian Empire, was captured in 1393. The Turkish Hannibal was finally at the gates of western Christendom, on the Lower Danube.

The Christian forces led by Sigismund joined battle with the Ottoman armies under Sultan Bayazid I at Nicopolis, in Bulgarian territory south of the Danube. They suffered a disastrous defeat on September 28, 1396. The outcome was decided by the undisciplined bravery of the French knights, whose cavalry charge was launched independently of the central Christian command, and also by the timely arrival of a rested Serb army which, having been defeated seven years previous at Kossovo, was fighting on the Turkish side.[11] Sigismund fled by sea via Constantinople. The road was open into the Carpathian basin and catastrophe seemed imminent. Then the unforeseen came to the rescue. The Mongolian conqueror Tamerlane reached Asia Minor in the Ottoman rear and at the Battle of Ankara in 1402 defeated and captured Sultan Bayazid. Byzantium, besieged by the Turks, thus gained a respite of fifty-one years, until 1453. The Danubian peoples continued to enjoy immunity from southern imperialist penetration for nearly a century and a quarter, until 1526.

The most important step in dynastic regionalism, however, had already been taken by Louis the Great before his death in 1382. Louis permitted in advance a posthumus dissolution of the troubled Polish-Hungarian personal union by arranging for the elevation of the Polish throne of his younger daughter Hedwig (St. Jadwiga). Hedwig's marriage to Ladislas of Jagiello in 1386 resulted in the final Christianization of Lithuania and in the dynastic merger of the two realms formalized in 1413 and in 1569 by the Unions of Horodlo and Lublin.[12] The Polish-Lithuanian royal marriage and union brought about a regional federation which included not only the Kingdom of Poland and the Grand Duchy of Lithuania but also the rich Ruthenian-Ukrainian and other Russian provinces of the latter. The new regional unit extended eastward beyond the Dnieper River, past Smolensk, almost to the gates of Moscow. To round out the realm, Hedwig herself presided over the transfer to Polish sovereignty of the former Hungarian dependencies of Galicia and Lvov. Beyond the boundaries of the new dual monarchy, the Republic of Novgorod and the newly emerging Rumanian principality Moldavia entered as satellites into the Jagiello-Anjou orbit.[13]

What were the results of the joint Anjou-Piast-Jagiello-Luxemburg dynastic effort in unlocking the sealess land and in bringing into existence a universal middle-zone monarchy? We have already noted that the new regional unit, probably larger than any other European state then in existence, became impervious, for a while at least, to western, eastern, or southern imperialism, and that, temporarily, it participated on a large scale in world commerce. Mention has also been made of the fact that the Renaissance was already in the air in the north and that an intellectual fermentation seemed to be spreading over the land. Concrete symptoms of the intellectual quickening were the first three universities established east of Vienna: in Prague (1348) by the Luxemburg Charles IV; [14] in Cracow (1364) by the last Piast, Casimir the Great; [15] and in Pecs (1367) by the

Anjou Louis the Great.[16] The third of these academic foundations, conducted under Dominican auspices probably to combat the northward spread of Bogomilism from the Balkans, proved to be short-lived. But Prague and Cracow rose to international fame during the ensuing centuries, the first by preparing, with John Hus at its head, the intellectual climate for the Protestant Reformation; the second, by sheltering Copernicus, the genius who in mid-sixteenth century launched one of the greatest intellectual revolutions of humanity: the overthrow of the geocentric by the heliocentric concept of the universe.

But not all of the results were positive. The problem of the *Drang nach Osten* arose again both immediately and later on. Nor was the specter of oligarchy laid low. Indeed, the Polish, Lithuanian, and Hungarian oligarchs bore a resemblance to the Lernaean hydra of Greek mythology: two new heads seemed to sprout in the place of each decapitation. After the destruction of baronial power by each king, the recipients of new land grants evolved into a new *frondeur*, antiroyalist aristocracy. These stubborn feudal opponents of the rise of a centralized absolute monarchy had to be fought from realm to realm and from province to province. Hardly had Charles crushed the Hungarian oligarchic resistance at Rozgony (1312), when he had to march south to Dalmatia (1325-1326) to deal militarily with feudal anarchy and nobles' revolts in that dependency. As king of Poland Louis the Great proved to be less energetic than his father and timidly restrained, perhaps by memories of the assassination attempt against his parents in 1330, in curbing the great landowners. In Hungary also he permitted the disproportionate growth of latifundia. By the end of his reign baronial estates occupied 20 per cent of the realm as compared to only 15 per cent for royal estates.[17] It was while he was on the throne that the struggle between the high and the lower nobility, the latter supporting the king against the pretensions of the former, brought forth during the Hungarian parliament of 1351 the fatal political doctrine of *una et eadem libertas*,[18] the principle of aristocratic egalitarianism, an early form of the constitutional evil which also arose in Poland and eventually contributed to its partitions.

After Louis's death his kingdom and its dependencies were rent by the struggle of the rival baronial leagues. His widow Maria, born a Bosnian princess, ruled (1382-1386) with the support of only one of these leagues. Another baronial confederation exploited the ambitions of Sigismund, then the betrothed of Louis's elder daughter;

a third league in the Balkan provinces backed Charles the Little, an Anjou pretender from Naples. The political atrocities which accompanied the artistic brilliance of the Italian Renaissance began to occur in the northern Anjou lands also. In February 1386 Charles the Little was mortally wounded in the presence and probably with foreknowledge of the two queens, mother and daughter named, respectively, Elizabeth and Maria.[19] The instigator of the bloody deed was the Chancellor Garai, head of the league then acting as the power behind the throne. In July, during a trip of the queens to the south, under armed escort led by the chancellor himself, henchmen of the pro-Charles league waylaid the royal retinue, beheaded the chancellor, and tossed his severed head into the lap of the Queen Mother seated in her carriage. Both queens were imprisoned. Maria was released during the following summer to marry her fiancé Sigismund, but the Queen Mother was strangled in her prison.[20] Such political violence continued, as a result of the triangular struggle among royal power and mutually hostile baronial leagues.

Under the long rule of Sigismund (1387-1437) the sedition of the barons reached its highest intensity. The new Luxemburg king could mount the throne only by making common cause with the baronial Garai league. The early years of his reign were spent in battling rival leagues contesting the power of the Garais and meting out punishment intended as deterrent in its terrifying inhumanity to vanquished lords. In 1393 captured baronial rebels were executed by being tied to a horse's tail, dragged, and quartered.[21] During the parliament of 1397, dominated by the Garai league, Sigismund issued a safe-conduct to the chief of the Laczkfi league, which was anti-Garai, and, on arrival invited him to a conference in his private chambers, where he was set upon and slashed to ribbons by his concealed opponents.[22] Eighteen years later John Hus might have put less faith in the safe-conduct issued to him by Sigismund to attend the Synod of Constance had he known of this incident! Most recent historical research on the Hussite movement has produced no evidence of Hus's being aware of Sigismund's record of perfidy.[23] In 1401 Sigismund himself was arrested and imprisoned by one of the leagues for five months, during which his captors ruled as the Council of the Realm, in the name of the Holy Crown of St. Stephen. After his election to the German throne in 1410, Sigismund spent most of his time away from both Hungary and Bohemia.[24] His frequent and long absences set a pattern of political normality in both countries under baronial rule in the name of an absent king. Toward the end of his reign Sigismund ruled as a member of an oligarchic league camouflaged behind the façade of a knightly society of his creation under the name of the Order of the Dragon.

Another adverse result produced by the monarchy of the three seas was the engendering and hardening of national antipathies among neighboring peoples already filled with memories of an unhappy coexistence. Hungarian soldiery in Poland, Czech courtiers in Hungary, Polish magnates in the Ukraine seemed to provide substance for a new maxim that familiarity can breed not only contempt but hatred as well.

History at this juncture appeared to be teaching an important lesson: that imperialism is a two-way street and that the former victim of imperialist aggression will not hesitate to turn aggressor from a position of strength against a neighbor in a position of weakness. The dynastic imperialism of the northern Anjous was unsuccessful in its attempted conquest of Naples because, buttressed by papal support, the Kingdom of the Two Sicilies had not yet turned into a power vacuum. On the other hand, the northern Anjous were eminently successful in the Balkans, where Byzantine might was shriveling and where Serb-Bulgarian rivalry for hegemony over the South Slavs and the Greeks finally led to a transfer of the dominant role from Bulgarians to Serbs after the Bulgarian defeat in the Battle of Velbuzhd in 1330. A quarter century later, with the sudden death of the Serbian imperial conqueror Stephen Dushan (1331-1355), the area was left open to Hungarian penetration from the north and to the Ottoman advance from the southeast. The extinction of the Nemanyas in 1371 was followed by a period of anarchy caused by various pretenders to Stephen Dushan's mantle. In the circumstances Louis the Great had little difficulty in continuing and extending the Balkan imperialism of his Arpad predecessors down along the eastern Adriatic coast to Albania. Bulgaria, Serbia, Bosnia, Croatia, and Dalmatia thus became vassal states of Anjou Hungary. To the southeast, Louis was successful where his father Charles Robert had failed in reducing Moldavia and Cis-Oltania to satellite status. In the north, after the Anjou-Jagiello union in 1386, territorial and other forms of political expansion were pushing middle-zone power deep into areas—Novgorod, Smolensk, the Ukraine, Galicia, Lvov, Kiev—which regenerated Muscovite Russia eventually claimed as its own. The later Jagiellos, as we shall see, beheld themselves, for a fleeting moment at least, at the head of a universal empire, as saviors of Byzantium and of Christendom from the infidel.

In retrospect, the dynamics of the middle-zone monarchy during the fourteenth century appear to give great weight to the role of environment in the human behavior and experience which we record as history. Once in contact with the sea, the inland descendants of Cro-Magnon Man began acting much like their coastal cousins. While this thalassic contact lasted, history does not seem to run conspicuously different courses in the western continental area and in the formerly landlocked middle zone. Divergence set in once again, however, when the Moslem salient, driven north from Asia Minor, reached the Middle Danube and eliminated the Adriatic-Black Sea outlets.

In the following pages the approach, culmination, and receding of the Ottoman tide will be examined. In the meantime, three conclusions necessary for an understanding of the uninterrupted chain of ensuing action should be drawn. First, we should remember that middle-zone unity and power were only temporary. Second, it is obvious that Anjou-Luxemburg imperialism in the Balkans was detrimental to the much-needed creation of political-military cohesion among the peoples of southeastern Europe. Such cohesion might have resisted, or at least delayed until a strategically more propitious moment, the Turkish advance to the gates of Vienna. Finally, it should be noted that the inability of the Anjou-Jagiello rulers and their Luxemburg-Habsburg successors to deal with the leagues of their feudal oligarchs prevented the rise of absolute monarchy until it was imposed from the outside by foreign empires. A state of seditious feudal-oligarchic conditions, in which powerful landowners recurrently ruled with or without royal consent, unhindered by counterbalancing political alliance between king and people, became and remained for centuries a familiar political phenomenon. The most serious social consequence of this perpetuation of feudal oligarchy was a chronic state of peasant discontent which continued to manifest itself in successive revolts long after *Jacqueries* or peasant uprisings had become a historical memory in the west.

7

The Peasant Revolts

A steady worsening in the peasants' lot during the first half of the fifteenth century was a natural corollary of the unrestrained growth of feudal oligarchy. During the second half of the century, while in the key countries royal power was in the ascendant over baronial intransigence, the peasants continued to bear the weight of feudal obligations. In return, they received occasional protection from the throne against exactions beyond the limits set by law and custom. With the resurgence of oligarchic power and the decline of royal authority at the end of the century, these legal and traditional limits were no longer observed by the landowners. The existence of the peasants again began to deteriorate. It is interesting to note that the peasant uprisings—known as *Jacqueries* in the west—started and continued to flare up in the eastern part of the middle zone in ethnically mixed areas such as Transylvania, Moldavia, and the Ukraine. The fiercest struggles were usually fought in regions where the landlords and peasants were of different nationality and religion.

The consequences of internal divisiveness were made serious by the increasing military threat from the south. After the fall of the Balkans, which was nearly complete by the early fifteenth century, Ottoman expansion farther north could have been blocked at the southern barrier only by a general crusade or by Hungarian military power. The first never materialized except in a limited, regional sense. The second was dissipated by a spreading internal anarchy. There can be little doubt that the peasant revolts and wars that took place between Sigismund's death in 1437 and the great Hungarian peasant war of 1514 contributed to the withering of the military potential which might have contained or delayed the Turkish rush of power across the Lower Danube into Central Europe. For this reason, Hungarian internal developments during the late fifteenth and early sixteenth centuries were of prime importance for the whole area.

In a sense the peasant uprisings were a continuation of the earlier revolts of heretics, Bogomils and Hussites, against their landlords of a high-church persuasion. For example, the Hussite translation of the Bible into the various middle-zone vernaculars was used during the fifteenth century as a manifesto against those who collected rents and taxes, whose greed for money made them unworthy of the Kingdom of God. Some of the early revolts took place on estates owned by the Church or in areas where the ecclesiastical authorities were particularly remorseless in collecting the tithe during hard times. To leave no doubt in the minds of the peasants listening to a reading of the Hussite Bible, the diatribe against high priests in the Gospel according to St. John employed the word "bishops." The Hussite sermons made frequent use of the Book of Amos and its prophecies concerning the punishment awaiting the rich. A favorite topic for sermons was the close relationship between the role of the prophet and the vocation of the biblical shepherd—updated as the contemporary peasant.[1] If indeed the early religious heresies had contained a socioeconomic element, it is also true that in the origins of the later peasant revolts the motivating force of religious dissent was distinctly present. The connection was clearly felt by the rulers as early as 1487, a date which marks the introduction of serfdom in Bohemia in consequence of the Hussite risings.[2]

Connected with the religious and ethnic factors influencing the rising discontent of the peasants was the role of economics in the case of the landowners. In the wake of the commercial revolution of the fourteenth century and its attendant migrations of rural populations toward the new urban centers came a rising Europe-wide demand for grain at constantly increasing prices.[3] In response to this lucrative need for cereals in the commercializing and urbanizing west, the owners of the vast landed estates of the middle zone recognized their economic interest in having "coerced cash-crop labor"[4] geared to maximum production at a minimum cost of maintenance. The net result of this recognition of the barons' economic interest was their increasingly high-handed imposition and exaction of feudal obligations.

The most onerous of these feudal obligations were the *robota,* the gratuitous labor due to the landowner up to four days a week (known as the *corvée* in the west); the tithe payable not in produce but in money to the Church; and the surrender to the owner of the *nona,* one-ninth of the produce raised on rented land.[5] Still, beyond the limits of legal feudal obligations during the fifteenth century, though sometimes illegally restrained or legally suspended in times of regional labor shortage, was the peasants' right to move and change employment from one estate to another in pursuit of their own likes and interests. Though this freedom was guaranteed by law, mass kidnappings of peasant families to return them by force to their abandoned residences occurred during periods of baronial power unrestrained by royal authority. Such occurrences had a tendency to turn into violent clashes not only between peasants and armed overseers but also between the feudal militia of rival landlords. Other unpopular burdens provoking peasant resentment were the prohibitions on hunting, trapping, and fowling, as well as recurrent bans on cattle exporting except by royal permission. Such permission was seldom granted without the kind of *quid pro quo* only a powerful landowner could provide. A side result of cattle export bans was sudden mass unemployment and misery among herdsmen and armed guards, whose yearly subsistence depended on seasonal cattle drives scheduled once or twice a year.[6]

Another grievance was provoked by the approach of the Turks. From the end of the fourteenth century, following the apparent imminence of an Ottoman onslaught after the Battle of Nicopolis in 1396, a defense force known as the "parcel militia" [7] had been in existence in Hungary and its dependencies. The financial obligation to equip this force was laid on nobles possessing more than twenty "parcels" of land. They were required to arm and send to the royal army one light cavalryman for each twenty parcels of land owned. The actual military obligation to take up arms and to serve in campaigns far from home rested on the peasants dispatched in units to fight under the banners of the king. True, the use of the parcel militia beyond the frontiers of the realm was prohibited. On the other hand, Turkish incursions across the border had been occurring since 1371 and were not unusual at the turn of the century. For a while the military draft was not universally felt by the peasants because, during the second half of the fifteenth century, standing armies composed of professional mercenaries had come into existence in some of the middle-zone countries. These professional forces were, however, disbanded after 1490, on the eve of the impending Ottoman invasion, because of financial chaos due to the weakening of royal authority. As far as the peasants were concerned, the end of the standing army meant the involuntary acceptance of a greater military burden. Thenceforth they served not only as effectives for the parcel militia but also as "crusaders" (*kuruc,* corrupted from *crux,* cross) against the infidel.

Clashes between peasants and their masters were still unknown or rare under the Anjous. The great French *Jacquerie* of 1358 set no precedent for the middle zone; at least none immediately followed it. But, during the reign of Sigismund, with the spreading of the oligarchic anarchy, peasant discontent began to turn into localized outbursts of violence. While the Hussite wars of the king-emperor were in progress, it was at times difficult to distinguish between embattled Taborites and marauding peasants.

The first distinctly recognizable middle-zone peasant uprising took place during the year of Sigismund's death, in the spring of 1437, in Transylvania. It appears to have been smoldering since 1415, when Pope John XXIII [8] exempted the nobility of certain regions, including Transylvania, from paying the tithe. As a result local ecclesiastical authorities began resorting to greater severity in collecting this unpopular Church tax from the peasants. A complexity of grievances and resentments, social, economic, and racial as well as ecclesiastic, interacted to set off the uprising twenty-two years later. A cardinal grievance appears to have been temporary suspension of the right of free displacement. A charismatic leader was found in the person of Janos Kardos, a peasant veteran of the parcel militia.[9] After driving their landlords from their estates, the rebels turned against the prosperous neighboring Saxons and, in an apparent outburst of economic and xenophobic resentment, invaded in force their autonomous region, the *fundus regius* or the "royal ground." The quickly raised army of the Transylvanian voivode (governor), which rushed to the rescue of the despoiled landowners and beleaguered Saxons, had little difficulty defeating and dispersing Kardos's motley army. But victory over the peasants did not lead to the re-establishment of law and order. It acted, on the contrary, as a new grievance to the peasants, who had by then seen in practice the possibility of collective armed resistance. The historical role of the Kardos rising was a prelude to a much greater peasant revolt in Transylvania, which broke out three months later and quickly spread beyond regional limits (1437-1438).

Antal Nagy of Buda, another veteran of the Turkish campaigns, set himself at the head of a mixed Hungarian-Rumanian army of peasants and then naively sent a delegation of his followers directly to the king to obtain redress against the landlords for long-standing grievances. The three principal peasant complaints carried to the king were the remorseless collection of the tithe, the surrender of one-ninth of the produce, the *nona,* as rent to the landlord, and the denial of the right to move about freely. The Rumanian peasants were additionally protesting against forced conversions from Ortho-doxy to Catholicism. The list of grievances never reached the mon-arch. The members of the peasant embassy carrying it were arrested and executed by the voivodal authorities. The peasant encampment was then attacked and a pitched battle followed. Unexpectedly the peasants defeated the feudal army of the landlords and the bishop. During the negotiations that followed, the rustics scored a point by obtaining the abolition of the *nona.* But before the other points concerning the tithe and free displacement could be taken up the landowners launched a second attack. They suffered a second defeat. New parleys followed, again interrupted by the resumption of sud-den baronial attacks. Finally the tactic of dispersing, scattering, iso-lating, and attacking the armed peasants was successful. Antal Nagy was killed in battle in mid-December. His followers made their last stand inside Kolozsvar (Cluj), which fell to the besieging baronial army in February 1438. No mercy was shown. The captured leaders of the insurgents were impaled on stakes erected at the gates of the city. Concessions granted to the peasants during the uprising were annulled.[10]

In the meantime rebellion appeared to be spreading from the countryside to the towns. Artisans and craftsmen helped the peasants defend Cluj in February 1438. In May 1439 the poor people of Buda rose against the German, Italian, and Hungarian patricians, sacked their shops, and broke into the royal treasury, from which a large gold hoard was removed. According to a contemporary chronicle, the reason for the outbreak was "Hungarian envy of German riches." [11] The chronicler also claims that the actual rioters set on the German and other foreign burghers were peasants stealthily brought into the city by Hungarian elements.

The Renaissance rulers of Hungary, Bohemia, and Poland-Lithuania dealt summarily with unruly barons, even if they hap-pened to be related to the ruling families. But the kings did not change the feudal system. They simply saw to it that it was func-tioning according to its own rules and not at the whimsy of the participants. The peasants' right to free movement was defended, partly because the influx of rural populations into the towns was in line with the royal policy of encouraging urbanization. By 1490, how-ever, coinciding with the decline of royal authority, a legal concept of perpetual peasant servility began making its appearance. From the simple juridical definition of *rusticitas* (the condition of being a peasant) developed the legal person of the *servus* (servant) and his status *servilis conditio* (the condition of being a servant.)[12]

In sociological terms this meant the development of a caste system binding successive generations to the same vocation. It did not yet mean serfdom, not even the denial of the right of free displacement, except as a temporary emergency measure. Yet, by the last decade of the fifteenth century, Hungarian, Slovak, Ruthenian, Ukrainian, and Rumanian peasants began to react adversely and violently to the perpetuation of their servile status. The reaction was manifested in sporadic rural riots touched off by the appearance of tax collectors, especially when the purpose was to collect a newly enacted tax. Such was the case in one of the Szekely frontier-post settlements on the western slope of the Eastern Carpathians, hitherto tax-exempt, when in 1506 an attempt was made to collect a new impost assessed according to head of cattle.[13] Other symptoms were the increase in the number of runaway peasant-servants, who became outlaws headquartered in inaccessible mountain fastnesses; armed resistance at harvest time to surrendering one-ninth of the produce to the bailiffs of the landowner; and formal strikes by peasants employed in the salt mines. The tinder of rural discontent was accumulating, awaiting only a spark set off by a parallel historical process to be kindled into leaping flames.

The conflagration came in 1514 and was set ablaze by the preaching of a "crusade" against the Turk at the order of the newly elected Medici Pope Leo X. The countries called upon to participate were Hungary, Poland, Sweden, and Denmark. The organizing work was entrusted to the Hungarian Cardinal Bakocz, an unsuccessful candidate in the recent conclave for the throne of St. Peter. The clergy under Bakocz began assembling a crusading host, which soon reached a strength of about a hundred thousand and was encamped outside the Hungarian capital. It was composed of servile peasants, shepherds, cattle drivers, salt miners, discharged veterans of mercenary armies, urban slum dwellers, wandering students, priests of the lower clergy, and even some members of the impoverished petty nobility. Economically most of these men were probably at the end of their tether. Their behavior was undisciplined and menacing. Soon the authorities began to doubt their own judgment in having armed them. The obscure cavalry officer of probably petty noble origin and low grade whom Bakocz in April 1514 had placed in command was named George Dozsa (1472-1514).[14] The leader had an unblemished military record. He had distinguished himself in skirmishes against the Turk under the walls of Belgrade. Bakocz must have known that he was from the Transylvanian region of seething peasant discontent. The cardinal could not have known, however, that ideologically Dozsa had been indoctrinated with heretical ideas of social leveling during idle hours whiled away around campfires discussing the social content of the Scriptures with malcontent priests. Such clerical companions of radical views were present in the camp at the moment of the mutiny. This came when the crusading host, refusing to disband and to surrender its arms at the order of the apprehensive authorities, transformed itself into a peasant army and began marching not against the Turks but the peasants' sworn enemies, the lords of the great estates.

The rearguard of the peasant army was destroyed by troops of the cardinal, but Dozsa had already moved south with about thirty or forty thousand men. In a proclamation issued to the people of the whole kingdom, he called for a general rising, convoked a peasant assembly, and stressed that he was acting as a loyal subject of the king, who rejected the tyranny of the landowners. At the mass peasant gathering, where some three thousand more joined his army, he delivered a memorable speech. The oration showed political acumen and gave an insight into the peasants' social motivation. Dozsa explained to them that the opportunity they had seized to rise against the lords was exceptional, unique, and might never return, because their army as it then stood had been assembled by the authorities themselves with the blessing of the Church. He went on to say that there was a connection between bonded labor conditions on the great estates and inadequate defense against the Turk. He charged that the barons placed the security of the kingdom in jeopardy by giving vent to their greed at home while ignoring the danger from abroad. He ended by demanding equality among nobles, peasants, and townsfolk.[15] In a simultaneous manifesto circulated in the countryside among rustics who had not yet taken up arms, immunity from the law was promised to those who kill tax collectors who extort money from the people. A form of general mobilization was then ordered and enforced in areas under peasant control.[16] Dozsa next marched on Temesvar (Timisoara) held by the great oligarch Stephen Bathori, chief of one of the two principal baronial leagues. In the extreme danger Bathori appealed for help to his greatest rival, John Zapolya, head of the other powerful confederation of magnates. Temesvar was relieved by Zapolya's army in mid-July. The peasant army was defeated and its leaders captured. The punishment meted out to them was unprecedented in its cruelty. Dozsa was crowned King of the Peasants with a red-hot iron hoop while being roasted alive on a fiery throne. His lieutenants were forced to gnaw at his burning flesh before being put to death.[17]

It took until September to mop up the other peasant forces which had been operating in isolation from the main army in Transdanubia, Slovakia, Transylvania, and the Maramaros region in the northeast. But the final chapter was written during the meeting of the Estates held in October 1514. The assembly declared perpetual serfdom for the peasants by abolishing the right of free movement and "tying them to the soil" (*ad glebam adstrictum*). Serfs were forbidden to bear arms, were consigned to everlasting servitude as tillers of the soil (*perpetua rusticitas*), subject to the *robota,* or gratuitous forced labor one day a week on the lands of the nobles, had to pay a head tax of one forint, had to surrender one-ninth of their produce as rent, and were assigned a host of other feudal obligations.

The three-volume code of laws embodying these draconic decrees, known as the *Tripartitum,*[18] was accepted though never ratified either by the king or the Estates. Nevertheless, it remained in effect in Hungary until the revolution of 1848. Because it was printed and published in Vienna in 1517, it served as a model for other countries of the middle zone and may have been instrumental in the further development of serfdom. In Bohemia serfdom had been in existence, in an originally milder but subsequently more severe form, since 1487. In Poland it became institutionalized in 1511.

In the meantime, the inexorable advance of Ottoman power had reduced the Monarchy of the Three Seas to a Baltic coastline extending from Gdansk (Danzig) to the Gulf of Riga. The outlet to the Adriatic had been lost before 1500 when the Turks occupied the Balkans. By 1478 the Turkish vanguard was ravaging the outskirts of Venice. The Jagiello-held shore of the Black Sea was seized by the sultan between 1475 and 1484. After 1492 there was no Hungarian standing army on the Lower Danube. Victory over the revolting peasants in 1514 left the Hungarian barons intoxicated with power in a powerless land, oblivious to the approaching doom. The twelve additional years which elapsed before the strategic Hungarian gateway to the west and to the north was forced by the Turks were a period of respite granted by domestic complications among the Ottomans.

8

The Ottoman Breakthrough

By bursting into the center of the Carpathian basin in 1526 and skirting it to the east to ravage as far north as the Ukrainian city of Lvov (in 1498 and again in 1675), the Turks destroyed not only middle-zone regional unity and aspirations, the imperial dreams of the rulers, the maritime links to the oceanic world via the Adriatic and the Black Sea, but also the flowering of the Renaissance south of Poland and Bohemia. Their presence probably helped the Protestant Reformation to strike deep roots. Conversely, Ottoman occupation east of Vienna may well have been prolonged because of the unhealing and murderous divisions in the ranks of western Christendom.

The civilization of the Italian Renaissance had entered the middle zone in the train of the Anjous of Naples during the 1300s and made its first stirrings in Hungary. In this country, still undisturbed by religious strife, the unfolding of the new way of life was faster and fuller than in neighboring Bohemia, where its creative energies were consumed in the flames of theological controversy.[1] In Poland, where the intellectual predominance of the Roman Catholic clergy had not yet been challenged either by clerical heretics or by literate laymen, the first manifestations of the humanistic outlook were less secular and "pagan" than in Italy.[2] The masterpieces of the local humanists, whether in Latin or in the various vernaculars, rarely managed to reach or to impress the west. During the late northern Renaissance the Polish cosmologist Nicholas Copernicus (1473-1543) and the Moravian pedagogue John Comenius (1592-1670) proved to be illustrious exceptions. But architecture constitutes the lasting monument of the middle-zone Renaissance; it still serves as a visible reminder of a great cultural unity in which the spread of new ideas and novel art forms could not be stopped even at distant political frontiers. Plastic Renaissance art survives in Hungary in small gems like the red-marble Bakocz Chapel of the Basilica of Esztergom.[3] The monumental royal palaces can now impress the viewer only in contemporary pictures, having been destroyed during centuries of conquest and reconquest. The great statuary which once adorned the palaces was floated down the Danube in Turkish barges to add more majesty to the sultan's new capital. In Bohemia, perhaps because of the Catholic victory over the Hussites, the Gothic style of the high Middle Ages remained the preferred architectural form, until it merged into the Baroque of the Counter Reformation, almost without an intermediate Renaissance stage. The Vladislav Hall of the Hradcany Palace in Prague, however, preserves the late fifteenth-century Czech Renaissance style.[4] In Poland the great altar of Our Lady in the Cathedral of Cracow, together with the Florentine-built palace and chapel of Sigismund I (1506-1548) on the Wawel Hill of the same city, are reminders that the Renaissance had been there.[5]

It was a Jagiello king, Vladislav VI, who began his rule over Poland-Lithuania in 1434 and over Hungary in 1440, whose tragic death on the battlefield of Varna in 1444 epitomizes the transition from the Age of Chivalry to the Renaissance. The young king was fired by the militant Christian idea of driving the Turk from Europe, saving Byzantium, and perhaps becoming the crowned head of a new universal Christian empire. As a Christian knight he swore sacred oaths on the altar to carry out his noble resolve. As a Renaissance king he negotiated and signed documents of truce with the sultan. Also as a Renaissance ruler, he broke the truce and violated the sanctity of treaties when the interests of his states demanded a resumption of hostilities.

Byzantium was still in Christian hands. A combined Papal-Venetian-Burgundian fleet—so the Papal Legate Cesarini had assured the king—would prevent Murad II from ferrying his troops from Asia Minor to the European side of the Hellespont. But, inexplicably, the Christian naval units watched the Ottoman crossing without firing a cannon. The sultan quickly merged his Asian and European hosts. Then he appeared with an army of 100,000 men, where he was not expected, in the rear of the 20,000 crusading Christians at Varna on the Black Sea Coast. The outcome of the battle was decided by Vladislav's heroic but foolhardy charge at the head of five

hundred Polish and Hungarian horsemen into the palisaded en-
closure of the janissaries guarding the sultan's tent. The king was
never again seen, alive or dead. The crusading army broke and fled
in panic.[6] Nothing could have saved Byzantium, though it took nine
more years before Turkish artillery made a breach in the famous
Land Walls and, with Turkish ships hauled overland attacking from
the Golden Horn, the city of Constantine became the Sublime Porte.[7]

If the end of the Middle Ages was symbolized by the Jagiellonian
king's quixotic cavalry charge at Varna, the spirit of the Renaissance
found its highest expression, higher than the palaces and chapels of
hewn stone, in the careers of great men of obscure origin, in the
rise of dynasties without royal ancestors, and in the alliance between
the despot and the scholar. In the middle zone, however, the humanistic mix was slightly different. In Italy both parties to the alliance were Italians. In the north native rulers surrounded themselves
with foreign, mostly Italian and German, artists and erudites. This
influx of humanists from abroad was a force in creating a new
European cultural unity, in blotting out the dividing line between
coastal and inland subcultures. But the new homogeneity lasted only
eighty-two years, the length of time that elapsed between the battles
of Varna (1444) and Mohacs (1526). Nine years after Varna, during the
faetful year of 1453, Byzantium fell and the Hundred Years' War
ended. Thus Christian power disappeared in the east and had become too exhausted in the west to permit a return to the crusading
spirit of 1096, which might have stemmed the tide at a lower latitude,
below the Danube. But night was not yet ready to fall. During the
Varna-Mohacs span of less than three generations, the statecraft of
the Italian Renaissance, even before it could be formulated by
Machiavelli, was being used by the rulers of Hungary, Bohemia,
and Poland-Lithuania to continue the task of regional empire building begun by the Anjous, the Luxemburgs, and the Jagiellos. Their
task was made possible by military geniuses sprung from nowhere,
who fought a delaying action against the Turk, prolonging the
middle-zone Renaissance into the sixteenth century in the south and
into the seventeenth in the north.

One such military genius of obscure origins was the Hungarian
John Hunyadi (1407-1456) who, three years after the fall of Byzantium, stopped the conquering Mohammed II at Belgrade in 1456
and then died of the plague which broke out among his victorious
troops.[8] In a book published in 1934, the conservative Hungarian
historian Szekfü presented evidence for the hypothesis that Hunyadi
was an illegitimate offspring of the King-Emperor Sigismund.[9] Be that

as it may, Hunyadi was a *condottiere* in the noblest sense, a man who rose from being leader of six hired horsemen in the 1420s to become an officer in Sigismund's bodyguard at the Ecumenical Council of Basel in 1434. In the meantime he had been to Lombardy with the king-emperor in 1431 and spent the two following years as a captain of mercenaries in the court of Philip Visconti, Duke of Milan. By 1441 he was voivode of Transylvania, commander-in-chief of the armies of the Danube, and Hungary's greatest landowner. His strategic concept, offense is the best defense, failed at Varna but proved workable in a series of Balkan campaigns, in the course of which he liberated Bulgaria, Serbia, and Bosnia, pushing the Turks south from the Danube, down to the mountains of Albania. His triumph and death at Belgrade in 1456 were followed by a new but brief outbreak of oligarchic chaos in his country. The disorders were ended by the rise of the long-overdue but short-lived absolute monarchy under his younger son Matthias Corvinus as king.

Another great leader who seemed to appear from nowhere was the Albanian George Castriota, better known as Scanderbeg (1403-1468).[10] His princely origins are clearer than Hunyadi's, but like the great Hungarian, he had basic training as a *condottiere,* some exposure to Italian domestic affairs; and, in historical perspective, the military merit of having fought a delaying action to postpone and divert the Ottoman rush of power. Financial backing to keep up Castriota's struggle against the Turk came from Naples, Venice, the papacy, and Hungary, with whose Hunyadi-led armies he tried to unite across Serb territory. In a sense, his career was reminiscent of those early Balkan princelings who, after being educated in Constantinople, became thorns in the flesh of the sultan. Scanderbeg spent his early youth in the Ottoman court. There he learned the military art of the Turks and was converted to Islam. The year before Varna (1443), however, he fled Adrianople, then the Turkish capital, and returned to his mountain-dwelling people to raise the tribes against the sultan. Once home, he reverted to his original Christian faith. Next he entered into correspondence with King Vladislav, the future hero of Varna, and attempted to join the crusading army on its way to the Black Sea, but was prevented from reaching the Belgrade assembly point by the Serb ruler George Brankovich (1427?-1456). This probably saved his life, or at least the military potential he commanded.

The sultan could not fit an Albanian campaign into his overall strategy until after the great reverse his armies had suffered under the walls of Belgrade in 1456. It was then, after the death of Hunyadi, that Scanderbeg became the Turk-beating Balkan hero, who held off the invading Ottomans for seven long years while Europe applauded. During the early phase of this resistance the Albanian leader received considerable financial assistance from Alfonso V, the Aragonese King of Naples (1416-1458), who had remembered the empire-building of his Anjou predecessors and had been negotiating with Hunyadi about becoming King of Hungary. After death took Alfonso, the Doge of Venice became Scanderbeg's financial mentor, with the result that the wrath of the sultan turned against the city of the lagoons. The Venetian war which followed lasted sixteen years. In 1468, before it ended, Scanderbeg died, Albania was conquered, Moldavia was attacked (1475) and Turkish horsemen were plundering the suburbs of Venice (1478). The Albanian diversion, which kept the Ottomans occupied, coincided with the strong, centralized rule of Matthias Corvinus in Hungary and George Podiebrad in Bohemia. It was the historical role of George Castriota to lure the Turk away from the Danube and to permit the organization of defense at the gateway into the northern middle zone. In a fortuitous coincidence, the power of the aristocratic leagues and confederations, which were primarily responsible for military debility north of the Danube, went into a temporary eclipse in both Hungary and Bohemia with the rise of powerful centralized monarchies in these two countries during the same year (1458).

In several respects the two new kings, Matthias Corvinus [11] of Hungary (1458-1490) and George Podiebrad [12] of Bohemia (1458-1471), resembled each other. Both were newcomers without royal antecedents. Both were national kings, the kind not seen in their homelands since the extinction of the Arpads and of the Premyslids in the fourteenth century. They were both Renaissance rulers, ambitious, crafty, and amoral when it came to the pursuit of state interests, but magnanimous in patronizing the humanists. Both were regionalists. Podiebrad was willing to sacrifice even his hope of founding a dynasty to bring about a Bohemian-Polish personal union. Corvinus, in pursuit of the imperial dream of wearing the crown of his putative grandfather, the King-Emperor Sigismund, was successful, though only during his lifetime, in bringing about a regional union of Hungary, Austria, Moravia, Silesia, and Lusatia. The core of this dynastic federation was Hungary and Austria. It was an early, reversed form of the Austro-Hungarian Dual Monarchy of the nineteenth century. Under the first two Habsburgs to sit briefly on the Hungarian throne, Sigismund's son-in-law Albert (1437-1439) and the latter's son Ladislas V (1444-1457), there had been a brief precedent for a regional union

of Austria and Hungary. Under Ladislas V Bohemia was added to
the regional grouping in the guise of a personal union, making it
look even more like the Habsburg monarchy on the eve of the first
World War. Matthias eventually clashed with George Podiebrad over
the crown of Bohemia, the wearer of which was one of the seven
imperial electors. Matthias, therefore, needed it in his drive to prepare
his own election as Holy Roman Emperor. Death stopped him in the
captured city of Vienna from realizing this ambition. Neither he nor
George Podiebrad could leave their thrones to their sons. But from
1490 until 1918, Bohemia and Hungary never ceased to be members
of the same regional unit.

The two kings were dissimilar in many respects. Podiebrad was
twenty years older than Corvinus. He did not have the glorious family
prestige Matthias enjoyed as the only surviving son of the victor of
Belgrade. Nor did Podiebrad, who bore a Hussite taint (though he
was only a conservative utraquist and an enemy of the Taborites),
enjoy papal support. The Holy See chose to give its backing to
Corvinus, partly because the son of John Hunyadi was the logical
choice to lead an eventual great crusade to drive the Turk from
Europe, and partly because papal aspirations and Corvinus's dynastic
interests coincided in Bohemia. With Matthias on the throne in
Prague, Hussitism in both its Calixtine-utraquist and Taborite forms
would be eradicated, while Matthias's progress toward the Holy Roman imperial throne would be speeded. None of these things came
to pass. Corvinus survived Podiebrad by nineteen years; both were
succeeded by a member of the Jagiello junior line, Vladislas II (1471-
1516 in Bohemia and 1490-1516 in Hungary). The new Jagiello ruler
was a weak king, elected for that very reason in Hungary by the
revived oligarchic confederations. The barons needed relief from the
strong-handed absolutism of the dead Matthias.

Matthias's foreign policy has remained enigmatic to this day because of its preoccupation with acquisitions and objectives in the
west instead of the organization and launching of a great counteroffensive in the southeast to end the Ottoman menace. The papacy
was urging this latter objective.[18] Corvinus never fully complied. He
conducted several campaigns in the Balkans between 1463 and 1483,
in the course of which he repeated some of his father's feats of arms.
He conquered Bosnia in 1463 and captured the strategic Turkish
fortresses of Sabac and Smenderovo in 1475, respectively on the south
banks of the Sava and the Danube. When the Turkish war with
Venice ended and the sultan attempted an invasion of Hungary,
his troops were defeated by Matthias's standing army, the Black Host,

at Kenyermezö in 1479. But after restoring Christian control of the Straits of Otranto between Italy and Albania during the following year, a curious inertia began to manifest itself in Matthias's southeastern policy. The lack of military action against the Turks, which marked Matthias's last ten years may be explained by the Turco-Hungarian truce signed in 1483 and renewed in 1486. Corvinus needed a respite in the east to pursue his imperial ambitions. The intriguing episode of Djem,[14] a pretender to the Ottoman throne, whom Matthias demonstrably but vainly sought to associate with his planned crusade to expel the Turk from Europe, may also have been a part of the grand design.

Djem was the younger son of Mohammed the Conqueror and governor of the Ottoman provinces in Asia. On his father's death in 1481, he revolted against his older half-brother Bayazid II. After defeat by the forces of his brother, Djem fled to Rhodes in 1482 and remained in western hands until his unexpected death in 1495. He died a month after a joint audience granted him in Rome by Pope Alexander VI, of the House of Borgia, and King Charles VIII of France. During the last eight years of his life Matthias Corvinus appears to have made repeated attempts, all frustrated, to bring Djem to his court.[15] Perhaps he thought that, with the help of the son of the conqueror of Byzantium, who might be content to rule only the larger, Asian part of the Ottoman Empire, without Constantinople and the Balkans, he could realize the Christian grand design of driving the infidel from Europe. In the absence of any concrete evidence to prove that such was indeed Matthias's southeastern policy, it is more likely to assume that the Hungarian king was trying, unsuccessfully, to get hold of Djem's person as a subtle ploy to lead the insistent pope to believe that his real and supreme objective remained the great crusade against the Turk, while actually he was concentrating his diplomatic and military effort in the west in a forlorn attempt to reach the Holy Roman throne. In the newly excavated garden walks of the Renaissance royal palace in Buda, the so-called Beatrix Fountain shows the imperial crown topping the entwined escutcheons of Matthias and of his Aragonese-Italian wife.[16] Perhaps the king thought that his descent from the King-Emperor Sigismund (of which, according to contemporaries, he "made no secret")[17] entitled him to make heraldic use of the imperial diadem. Or, perhaps, he had all too confidently assigned himself the armorial bearings for which he was striving. In either interpretation, the fact that stands out is the dynastic fixation of Hungarian policy on a western objective at a time when great danger lay in the east.

The northern domains of Poland and Lithuania remained immune to, though not untouched by, the rising Turkish danger. The old troubles and evils had not ceased. The oligarchs continued to defy centralization, especially in Little Poland around Cracow. Sigismund, Duke of Lithuania, was assassinated in 1440 by his aristocratic opposition. After the death of Casimir IV (1447-1492), baronial power seemed to grow unchecked in the direction of that peculiarly paradoxical Polish institution, the aristocratic-egalitarian parliamentary royal republic,[18] which stifled political movement and eventually led to Poland's disappearance from the map. Another old trouble which continued to bedevil the Poles was the aggressive presence of the Teutonic Knights, against whom a new war was fought in 1453-1466. No final solution came from the fighting, though a longer stretch of the Baltic coast fell under Polish control. A drastic turn of events, which benefited Poland, came about in 1525. The Order accepted the new faith of Luther. It callously gave up the pretense of crusading for Catholicism in return for being allowed to retain control of vast territorial domains on the condition of accepting Polish suzerainty.[19] This secularization of the Order marked the end of the Knights' institutional menace. But the presence of great German landowners, descendants of the laicized crusaders, known as "Baltic barons," continued until the end of the First World War and even beyond. The headaches of dynastic combinations also continued. For a while it even seemed that a Polish-Lithuanian-Bohemian-Hungarian regional unit might revive the old Monarchy of the Three Seas. As the first quarter of the sixteenth century came to an end, Jagiellos ruled in all these countries. In Poland and Lithuania they reigned with, in Bohemia and Hungary without, the political federation of their realms.

In Hungary the sudden death of Matthias Corvinus in captured Vienna (1490) was followed by the reappearance of oligarchic anarchy unrestrained by the last two Jagiellos, the weak, do-nothing Vladislas II (1490-1516) and his son, the young, inexperienced Louis II (1516-1526). During the second year of Vladislas's reign, the royal standing army established by Corvinus was attacked by baronial hosts at the southern border. It was hacked to pieces and scattered practically within sight of Turkish units watching from their vantage points across the river. The Ottoman strategic position had been steadily improving. The buffer principality of Wallachia had fallen to the Turks in 1462.[20] With the reduction of Moldavia in 1504,[21] an outflanking invasion route was opened to the Polish north. The great Peasant War of 1514 was, for any would-be attacker, an inviting and vivid display of internal disintegration and chaos in Hungary. There were further complications favoring the Turks. In the west, war broke out between the French king Francis I (1515-1547) and the Habsburg emperor Charles V (1519-1556) in 1522. The king of France was defeated and captured in the Battle of Pavia (February 24, 1525). The Habsburgs and the Bohemian-Hungarian Jagiellos were linked by a double set of marriages. Louis II of Hungary-Bohemia was married to Maria, a sister of Emperor Charles V. Austrian Archduke Ferdinand, the emperor's brother, was the husband of Louis's sister Anna. To turn the tables on the emperor, Francis I from his prison in Madrid was secretly encouraging the energetic new sultan, Suleiman II (1520-1566),[22] to attack the Habsburgs from the east, through the domains of their Hungarian relatives.[23]

The new Ottoman ruler, the greatest since Mohammed the Conqueror, needed no encouragement. In 1521 he had already taken Belgrade, the key fortress guarding the entry into Hungary and the middle zone. The German imperial diets held between 1521 and 1526 at Worms, Speyer, and Nuremberg, listened to, but were too occupied with internal troubles—the spreading Protestant Reformation and the German Peasants' War (1524-1525)—to be able to comply with Hungarian requests for troops and money.[24] On April 23, 1526, Suleiman the Magnificent left Constantinople for his conquest of Hungary. He reached Belgrade on July 2. The Ottoman forces which crossed the Drava into the Jagiello realm, consisted of 70,000 regulars and 40,000 irregulars. On July 20, the twenty-year-old Louis II marched off to war from Buda with only 3,000 men to give an example to his reluctant barons, who had refused to enter the field unless the king did. By the time King Louis reached Mohacs, near the confluence of the Danube and the Drava rivers, he had about 25,000 effectives with him. Of these approximately 16,000-17,000 were Hungarians; the rest were Polish, German, and Czech mercenaries. The king's artillery consisted of 85 cannon, of which, however, only 53 could be landed in time from the barges which had brought them down the Danube. The greatest of the barons, John Zapolya, never reached the battlefield, though he had sent word to the king not to give battle until his arrival. His advice was disregarded. Supreme command was entrusted to Paul Tomori, the Archbishop of Kalocsa, who had a bold offensive strategy, which unfortunately misfired. On August 29, 1526, the attacking Christians were stopped by the murderous fire of the concentrated Turkish artillery, took flight, and were slaughtered by the pursuing Turkish cavalry. Fifteen thousand Christians were left dead on the battlefield, including Archbishop

Tomori, five bishops, the Chief Justice, and many members of the Royal Privy Council. King Louis, in heavy armor, mounted on a wounded horse, was led away from the carnage by his bodyguard through the marshlands of the flooded Danube. He and his mount sank while crossing a swamp and were drowned.[25]

The battle of Mohacs was not one of the decisive battles of the world. Its historical effect beyond the Balkan and Danubian areas was small. For the Danubian peoples, however, it signalled the end of an epoch and the onset of dependence in one form or another until the end of the nineteenth century. It was one of those few battles in world history from which there is never recovery for the vanquished, like the defeat at Chaeronea in 338 B.C. for the Greeks, the rout at Zama in 202 B.C. for the Carthaginians, or the destruction of their infantry at Rocroi in 1643 for the Spanish. As one of their poets put it, the battlefield of Mohacs became for Middle Europeans an immense cemetery of national grandeur.[26]

9

The Politics of Dependence: Patterns of Collaboration and Resistance

The Ottoman victors of Mohacs first set foot on European soil in 1346 as Byzantine mercenaries on a punitive expedition against the Greek emperor's unruly Serb subjects.[1] Oblivious to their landing on the north shore of the Hellespont, the Hungarian Louis the Great was waging war that year against the Venetians for possession of the Dalmatian coast. He was also busy preparing a campaign against Naples in pursuit of large dynastic chimeras. The year after Louis added the Polish crown to the Hungarian regalia that had become his in 1370, Turkish armies first raided the territory of his Danubian realm.[2] The same year that saw the union of Poland and Lithuania under his daughter Jadwiga and Vladislav of Jagiello (1386) also witnessed the Turkish capture of the Greek port of Salonika.[3] The Ottoman nemesis which eventually overtook it was thus already present at the cradle of the Monarchy of the Three Seas. Directly in the south and indirectly in the north, the Ottoman intrusion into Europe was responsible for the disintegration of this one and only self-ruled middle-zone federation. The onset of political dependence in the area followed.

The origins of the conquering Turks are somewhat obscure. Their language belongs to the Altaic family, which also includes the idioms of the Mongols and the Tungus (ancestors of the Manchus).[4] According to the geneticist historian Darlington, the Turkish ethnic identity is the result of a westward migration during which Asiatic nomads "hybridized and mixed with the Aryan tribes moving east into Persia and India." [5]

The Turkish trek into Asia Minor from the confines of the Chinese Empire was probably set and kept in motion by Mongol pressure in the rear. The simultaneous decay of Persian, Arab, and Byzantine power was a coincidental incentive for conquest. From the Persians the Turks first received the Moslem faith at the beginning of the tenth century. From the Abbasid caliphs of Baghdad, which they took in 1055, they absorbed the conquering zeal of Islam. From the Byzantines, whom they first defeated in 1071 at Manzikert and whose imperial city they captured in 1453, they inherited the institutions, the statecraft, and a territorial theater for European expansion. The composite Ottoman Turkish organization, which eventually extended its power from Constantinople to the walls of Vienna, was built on foundations laid by the earlier Seljuk Turkish conquerors who had preceded the Ottomans and had first fought their way into the Byzantine Empire at Manzikert. But both Seljuk and Ottoman were merely dynastic names. The warlike Islamic subjects of the Seljuk as well as the later Ottoman rulers were the same people: the Turks.[6]

The Ottoman breakthrough into the Carpathian basin was delayed by probably a century. It took place at Mohacs in 1526 instead of after Nicopolis in 1396 because of several unforeseen developments. The first of the unexpected events was the irruption of Tamerlane's Mongols into the Ottoman rear in 1402. The Mongol onslaught was followed by internal troubles lasting half a century: struggles among pretenders for succession to the Ottoman throne, destruction of the Turkish navy by the Venetians in 1416, and a revolt of the army's elite corps in 1447. The renewal of the momentum under Mohammed the Conqueror (1451-1481), the high point of which was the taking of Byzantium, was slowed down from the mid-forties until 1490 by the military and political revival of central ruling power in Hungary under Hunyadi and his son Corvinus. The final breakthrough across the Danube awaited the leadership and the indomitable will to conquer of Suleiman the Magnificent (1520-1566).[7]

The organization of the Ottoman Empire under Suleiman, his immediate predecessors, and his successors may be understood only in the light of a demographic reality. The Turks were a conquering minority for whom the collaboration of the conquered majority was an indispensable administrative, governmental, and military necessity.[8] Territorial expansion called for a constantly increasing number of collaborators, willing or forced, in order to rule and defend newly conquered territories. Bureaucratic and military proliferation quantitatively increased personal ambitions to rise in the administration and defense of enlarged territories. Conquest and collaboration thus acted as a vicious circle. Conversion to the Islamic faith was required only if the collaborator was to rule or command over Moslems. No conversion was required if the collaborator was to rule or to command for the sultan his own ethnic or religious community or another ethnic community with which he had some religious affinity. Conversion could take place either as the voluntary act of an adult or as premeditated, systematic assimilation through the schooling of Christian children in Turkish ways. The latter method was used to fill, on reaching adulthood, positions in the bureaucracy and in the ranks of the army. Voluntary assimilation was most frequent and most enduring in areas closest to the Ottoman power center, in Bulgaria, Rumelia, and Thrace. It diminished along an east-to-northwest axis with the drop of the percentage of Turkish occupiers in the conquered Christian populations. Bulgarians of the Islamic faith, called Pomaks, survive to this day near the Turkish-Bulgarian frontier. Special types of willing converts and assimilants were persecuted minorities. Such were the heretical Bogomils of Bosnia, secret sympathizers with the Turkish foes of their high-church oppressors before and open auxiliaries, openly sharing the conquerors' faith during and after the occupation.

Prototypes of nonconverted collaborators employed to govern their own ethnic and religious community were the Greeks of Constantinople. Though Emperor Constantine XI died fighting on the walls of Byzantium on May 29, 1453, there was no discontinuity in the office and person of the capital's Greek eparch. A change took place only in the person of the Greek patriarch. On June 1 George Scholarios (Gennadios) swore loyalty to the sultan and was installed as religious head of the Greek community.[9] The new masters of Byzantium found their Greek subjects especially helpful, because of their linguistic skills, in staffing clerical positions in the diplomatic service and in organizing the various palace schools,[10] in which the curriculum included not only law and religion but also European industrial and military arts. These vocational colleges enrolled captured Christian slaves as well as sons of illustrious Christian families, Greek, Armenian, Slav, and Albanian. The Greek organizers and preceptors of the Ottoman system of higher vocational education thus presided over the systematic Turkicization of future generations of collaborators.[11]

A memorable pattern in collaboration without conversion was established by the so-called Phanariots, Greek inhabitants of the lighthouse area (Phanar) of the Ottoman capital. The late conservative Rumanian historian Jorga described this special breed of col-

laborators as a "closed caste, from which came *dragomans* (inter-
preters), Grand Dragomans, diplomatic agents, spies, bishops, metropolitans, patriarchs, high dignitaries of the 'Great Church' of Constantinople . . . and finally Princes of Wallachia and Moldavia." [12]
Banking and commerce remained also largely in Greek hands, especially the lucrative trade of importing wheat from the plains of
Wallachia and Moldavia via the Danube and the Black Sea, to feed
the teeming population of the Turkish capital.

The lives of some eminent Greek collaborators make astounding
reading. The Despot Jacob Basilic [13] rose to be ruler of Moldavia
(1561-1563) for the sultan, only to be killed by the trusting boyars
he had mulcted. Michael Cantacuzene,[14] of Byzantine imperial descent, enriched by the family business of discreet white slavery on
behalf of the sultan's harem, made a gift to his imperial master of
fifteen ships built and outfitted at his own expense to compensate
in a small way for the destruction of the Turkish fleet at Lepanto
by Don Juan of Austria in 1571.[15] Panayataki,[16] a native of the island of Chios, became in 1669 Grand Dragoman—by then a sort of
head interpreter, chief of protocol, and political undersecretary in
the emerging Ottoman Foreign Office—the most important point of
personal contact between foreign ambassadors and the Sublime Porte.
The same office, with greatly enlarged functions and prestige, was
held for two decades, beginning in 1673, by another famous Phanariot, Alexander Mavrocordato,[17] who guided Ottoman diplomacy during the melancholy years following the second Turkish failure to
capture Vienna in 1683. The Phanariots proved themselves so adept
in statecraft that for over a century (1711-1821) the Sublime Porte
used them as vassal ruling princes to govern the Danubian provinces
of Wallachia and Moldavia.

Two of these Phanariot ruling princes, Constantine Brancoveanu [18] (1688-1714) and Constantine Hangerli [19] (1797-1799) would be
fit subjects for the medieval tragic concept of fall from a high estate.
Brancoveanu had the misfortune of being engaged in an intrigue
with Peter the Great of Russia at a time when the Sublime Porte
was extremely sensitive over its declining fortunes between the
humiliating treaties of Karlowitz (1699) and Passarowitz (1718). Brancoveanu was deposed without warning in 1714 and spirited to Constantinople. There was executed at the palace with his two sons
and his son-in-law in a pleasant garden spot overlooking the Bosporus,
before the eyes of the sultan. When his younger son, only sixteen
years old, tearfully offered to embrace Islam if only his life were

spared, Brancoveanu told the boy "to die a thousand times rather than deny Jesus Christ"; and then, turning to the executioner, tersely said: "I wish to die a Christian. Strike!"[20]

Less noble was the figure and less heroic the death of Hangerli, a shrewd and wily Greek from the Cyclades. This collaborator made a speciality of collecting double taxes for his own coffers, bribing the highest Church authorities, including the Ecumenical Patriarch in Constantinople, and acting as a secret informer to the Seraglio on Turkish military leaders in the field. His fatal mistake was to squeal on a pasha whose wife happened to be the sultan's mistress. A contemporary western traveler describes the sequel to this deadly error in judgment. Hangerli submitted his report as winter was ending. On March 1, 1799, an emissary from Istanbul arrived in Bucharest accompanied by a gigantic black executioner, in his pocket a firman signed by Selim III ordering Hangerli's execution. The two unexpected guests made their way into the palace and entered the prince's private chambers, where the executioner summarily strangled Hangerli in the presence of his court nobles. The head of the corpse was then chopped off and the naked body was thrown into the street below.[21] *Sic semper tyrannis!*—if they collaborated well but not too wisely with the Turks.

Among the elite of collaborators who kept their Christian religion while ruling their own people for the sultan, was the great Hungarian oligarch John Zapolya (1487-1541), victor over the rebellious peasants in 1514 and one of the two rival kings of Hungary after Mohacs. To hold his own against his royal adversary, Ferdinand of Habsburg (1503-1564), Zapolya accepted Turkish troops from Suleiman. He appeared in a histrionically staged spectacle held on the field of Mohacs (August 18, 1529) to kiss as vassal the hand of his liege lord the sultan.[22] With Zapolya's son John Sigismund (1540-1571) begins the long line of Transylvanian princes ending with Mihály Apafi (1632-1690), tributaries to the sultan, who ruled this former Hungarian province as an autonomous principality under Ottoman suzerainty. Another famous Christian collaborator of the period is Alvisio Gritti,[23] an illegitimate son of the Doge of Venice and diplomatic agent between the sultan and the Zapolyas, slain in 1534 while engaged in an intrigue to supplant King John on the Hungarian throne with Turkish help.

The civil war in Hungary after 1526 between the national party and the pro-Habsburg faction set the tone for the special type of nationalist, anti-German collaborator, who enters into a dependent relationship with the Porte in return for military help, because he would rather see Hungary as a vassal state of the Turkish sultan than of the German emperor. An outstanding representative of this type was Imre Thököli [24] (1657-1705), appointed King of Hungary (though he declined the title) by Mohammed IV (1648-1687). Thököli fought the Habsburg armies in alliance with the Turks. Contemporary German engravings erroneously show him in the Turkish camp besieging Vienna in 1683. Actually, Thököli and his army did march with the Turks against Vienna but were defeated by the Habsburg General Charles of Lorraine at Bratislava (Pressburg, Pozsony), a few miles from Vienna, six weeks before the relief of the city by John III Sobieski's Poles and Charles of Lorraine's Germans.

The Hungarian Zapolya and Thököli were not unique and unprecedented military collaborators. The use of Christian auxiliaries fighting in the Ottoman armies under their own leaders and own banners dates back to the fourteenth century. Greeks, Macedonians, and Albanians fought in the Turkish ranks against the Serbs on Kossovo Field in 1389. The Serbs fought on the Turkish side against the Mongols of Tamerlane at Ankara in 1402 and against the Christians of Vladislas Jagiello at Varna in 1444. The great cannon which breached the walls of Byzantium in 1453 were the work of Christian engineers, variously described as Albanian or Hungarian. The Turkish army besieging Vienna in 1529 included several thousand German irregulars, remnants of the revolting peasant army beaten with Luther's blessing in 1525.

Conversion to Islam opened the way for the ambitious to the highest places in the Ottoman army and government. Ten years after the capture of Byzantium we find Mahmoud Pasha,[25] a renegade descendant of the Emperor Alexios Angelos, serving as Grand Vizier under Mohammed the Conqueror. The three Grand Viziers who brought the Ottoman Empire to its apogee—Ibrahim, Rustem, and Sokolli—were born Christians.[26] The civil service and the military forces were headed by European Christians converted to Islam. This included the Divan—the sultan's cabinet—where the government of the empire resided. Between 1453 and 1623 the imperial administration was directed by twenty-one Grand Viziers, of whom eleven are said to have been South Slavs, five Albanians, and only three ethnic Turks born in the Islamic faith.[27] Under Suleiman the Magnificent the Divan consisted of eight viziers, of whom three were Croatians, two Albanians, one Hungarian, and only two Moslem at birth.[28]

The excellent palace schools of Istanbul were the training ground of the great Turkicized leaders of the empire. The Köpörülli Grand Viziers [29] of Albanian Christian origin, who presided over the destinies of the declining empire, are said to have been products and graduates of these colleges. Mohammed Ali (1769-1849), another converted Albanian born in Rumelia, became the founder of an Egyptian royal dynasty which lasted from 1811 to 1952. The greatest of Albanian national heroes, Scanderbeg (1403-1468), had also become a convert to Islam during his youth while a hostage in Adrianople, but returned to the Christian faith of his forefathers after his flight from the Turks.

A form of institutionalized collaboration peculiar to the Ottoman Empire was systematically prepared by the *devshirme*,[30] or recruitment by forced levies of Christian boys. These children were brought up and rigorously trained as Moslems and Turks to serve in the army as janissaries [31] (recruits) or at the court as ichoglans [32] (palace pages). The janissaries were the elite army infantry corps founded by Murad I (1359-1389), the slain victor of Kossovo. Over the centuries the janissaries metamorphosed from a disciplined group of military celibates into a troublesome hereditary caste, into an Oriental Praetorian Guard, who murdered and replaced sultans at will in swift palace revolutions. When, under Murad III (1574-1595) the janissaries were permitted to marry, a fatal blow was dealt to their discipline.[33] The decay of this once elite corps, which had been primarily responsible for the greatest Ottoman military victories, paralleled the decline of the empire. The end came under Mahmud II (1808-1839), during the critical days of the Greek War of Independence. The janissaries mutinied over the formation of a new military corps. They were surrounded in their Constantinople barracks, raked by artillery fire, and wiped out of existence in 1826. Though politically this was a blessing, the further martial misfortunes of the Ottomans during their campaigns were probably not unconnected with the gradual vanishing of these professionally trained and fully assimilated military collaborators.

Resistance as well as collaboration is a function of a state of political dependence. Collaboration is immediate accommodation to externally imposed political change. Resistance is active refusal to accept such change. In examining these two behavioral functions it is well to keep in mind that the smaller incidence of resistance and the more frequent occurrence of collaboration were undoubtedly influenced by the time element. South of the Danube, Ottoman overlordship lasted 500 years; north of the Danube, 150. It becomes more prudent to accommodate and collaborate than to refuse and resist as the years eat into the lifespans of persons and generations. In retrospect, under the microscopes of the sociologist and the political scientist, it would seem that, both south and north of the Danube, the collaborationist behavior was prevalent among those who had much to keep and a great deal more to gain; while resistance had a tendency to manifest itself in population groups which had nothing to lose and something to gain. In the western Danubian areas, such as Hungary and Croatia, where there was a choice between German and Turkish overlordship, an anti-German bias could motivate collaboration with the Turks. Conversely, resistance to the death could often spring from deeply ingrained Turcophobia or simply from loyalty to higher authority and from patriotism. The bitter realization of being caught "between two heathens"—Turks on one side, Germans on the other—in a hopeless defense of one's own country, dates back to this period of encirclement. So does the middle-zone political tendency to shift and balance, to play off both ends against each other, so noticeable in this and later historical situations. It is also true that, with the diminution of Ottoman power from about 1700 on, resistance as a political and military attitude slowly began gaining over collaborationist behavior.

South of the Danube, where mountains and valleys traditionally favor the defender, resistance had been going on since the fourteenth century. The Montenegrins never stopped fighting the invaders and by the early eighteenth century were left in peace under their Njegosh prince-bishops. The earliest sporadic, guerrilla-type Balkan resisters were the Serb Haiduks.[34] These were defiant and poverty-stricken village youths who preferred a life of romantic banditry and freebooting centered in some inaccessible mountain cave to obeying the whims of a petty Turkish tyrant bossing the home community in the valley. The Haiduks started out as isolated bands of outlaws, Balkan Robin Hoods who robbed the rich and gave to the poor, refugees from the consequences of some minor crime, avengers of cruel Turkish deeds visited on kinsmen, patriots in a regional rather than in a national sense, deeply resentful of the conquerors' and occupiers' cultural and religious peculiarities.

As the defense line holding back the Turks moved up to the Lower Danube and from there, after 1526, up to the middle course of the river, the Haiduks, coalesced into larger groups of irregular partisans, overflowed into Hungary. There they were gradually integrated into the armies of both the anti- and pro-German factions. The first anti-Habsburg Hungarian uprising under Stephen Bocskai [35] (1557-1606) scored its initial successes in 1604 with the aid of a Haiduk army of 3,000 freebooters and deserters from the imperial armies. Bocskai showed his gratitude by providing homesteads for his troops, beginning in 1605. In that year alone he settled 9,250 Haiduks on his own estates.[36] He further rewarded the deserving by collective patents of nobility. During the imperial campaigns of the late seventeenth and early eighteenth centuries, which rolled the Ottomans back below the Lower Danube, many Haiduks reverted to their role of anti-Turkish partisans by fighting as irregulars in the ranks of the Habsburg armies.

Another form of resistance began among the Serbs south of the Danube and gradually spread north into Hungary and Transylvania. This was the peasant uprising, which had been in temporary abeyance since Zapolya made short and brutal shrift of Dozsa in 1514. The new uprisings were stimulated by the collapse of the established order and by civil war. Circumstances were so unsettled that the possibility of improving the peasants' wretched lot could not be overlooked. The new disorders followed the pattern set by Dozsa's army. They started as self-styled crusades against the Moslem infidel, then turned into *Jacqueries* against feudal landowners. The difference lay in the fact that the post-1526 uprisings were not officially proclaimed crusades under an appointed commander, but rather spontaneous movements gathered around a self-proclaimed charismatic leader. Such a leader appeared during the winter following the battle of Mohacs among the fluctuating Serb populations straddling the Danube in the person of Ivan Cherny, the "Black Tsar" of the peasants. "Tsar" Ivan was able through sheer personal magnetism to collect around him more than 12,000 South Slav rustics. He fired their fighting spirit by promising to lead them to victory over the Turks. This never happened, in spite of the joint approval of the two rival kings, John Zapolya and Ferdinand of Habsburg. When, finally Ivan Cherny moved north instead of south and sacked Szabadka (Subotica), Temesvar (Timisoara), and Szeged, Zapolya's army closed in on him during the summer of 1527 and put an end to the rebellion with the public beheading of the leader.[37]

Two other peasant risings of the sixteenth century started out as anti-Turkish resistance movements and ended as rebellions against the feudal order. During 1569 the charismatic Rumanian serf George Karacsony, who seems to have been under the influence of anti-Trinitarian religious teachings, easily collected 5,000 peasant followers to fight the Turkish occupiers. No weapons would be needed, Karacsony told his men, because the Lord's glance would melt the might of the infidel unsmitten by the sword. Early in 1570, 600 of his unarmed and fanaticized followers attacked a nearby Turkish fort. They were slaughtered to a man. In the meantime, other members of Karacsony's army had been pillaging estates and castles of local landowners. The end was hastened by the disaster of the 600. An army sent by the patricians of the city of Debrecen defeated Karacsony's remaining forces and executed the leaders.[38] Still the movement spread and again erupted in the uprising of the Croatian serfs under Mathias Gubecz (1572-1573), who led an army of 12,000, not against the Turks, but in a vengeful attack on castles, tollhouses, and churches. The end was the same: defeat at the hands of the forces of law and order, followed by mass executions resembling in their cruelty those of 1514.[39]

Serfdom during the sixteenth century was still new and yet unbridled in the Danubian lands. The establishment which maintained it was unable to enforce the "tied to the soil" clause of the 1514 law, because it was faced with the problems of the Ottoman occupation and was also in the throes of a civil war. Consequently, it became increasingly easy for serfs, especially young swains, to run away and get lost in a troop fighting the Turks. A soldier's life in the field was far preferable to tilling the soil at home under some heavy-handed landowner. For the peasants, beating plowshares into swords became an attractive possibility. The number of runaway serfs rose to new heights by the middle of the sixteenth century. At the royal and imperial army recruiting stations in the towns, quotas had to be filled to man the ramparts of the border fortresses, and no questions were asked.[40]

Life in and around these fortresses, which constituted the new line of defense, roughly along the present Czechoslovak-Hungarian and Austrian-Hungarian frontiers, was both invigorating and rewarding. Winters were spent in good fellowship, in drinking, dice-rolling, and wenching, with some military drilling. Fighting began in the spring and included not only clashes with Turkish regulars but, as diversions, raids on groups of Ottoman tax collectors and the waylaying of richly laden trains of Turkish provincial beys and agas moving between their administrative centers. There were also public duels between Christians and Moslems, in the manner of medieval tournaments though with more up-to-date weapons. In the course of these paired combats military valor did not go unrewarded. A young runaway serf could even receive patents of nobility. Death, of course, was always a possibility, either at the end of the duel or by getting caught after or during a raid. In the latter case captives not likely to be ransomed were meted out the accepted penalties of Ottoman justice: impaling, dismemberment, mutilation, cutting off noses and ears, or, as a special favor, beheading. But there were risks worth taking for the sake of social mobility. Starting in 1544, peasants in Habsburg-ruled territory had to be prepared to fight the Turks anyway. The new military obligation was established by a new law which required every owner of more than four oxen to be armed with swords and guns to serve in military campaigns in case of need.[41]

The runaway serfs and peasant recruits who manned the fortresses guarding the new defense line could never complain that their lives were dreary and uneventful. Fortress warfare [42] continued between the defenders and the invaders almost without interruption from the fall of Buda in 1541 until its recapture by the Christians in 1686. It was in these fortresses that the noblest deeds of resistance and self-sacrifice took place, motivated by loyalty, a sense of duty, and patriotism. In 1552 the fortress of Temesvar, defended against a besieging Turkish army of 80,000 men by 2,300 Spanish, German, Czech, and Hungarian soldiers, held out for four weeks. It then capitulated on the promise of safe passage. When the trusting defenders laid down their arms and began marching through the gates, they were put to the sword. In the same year it took 10,000 Turks three days to capture the small fort of Dregely, whose 150 defenders fell to the last man. A few months later it was the turn of the fortress of Eger, defended by 1,900 Christians against 100,000 Turks. The walls successfully withstood a siege of one month (September 15–October 18, 1552). In 1566 Suleiman the Magnificent besieged and died before the fortress of Szigetvar, whose equally magnificent defender Nicholas Zrinyi followed the sultan into death three days later during a suicidal sortie at the head of his remaining troops.[43] In 1594 the Christian defenders surrendered the fortress of Györ and in 1660 the city of Nagyvarad (Oradea-Mare). When the fortress of Szigetvar was rebuilt almost a century after its fall, the Turks returned to besiege it, and having succeeded in their undertaking, destroyed its walls and bastions with gunpowder.

While providing posterity with glorious examples of valor, resistance as well as collaboration left a legacy of psychological dependence among succeeding generations. The military cost of conducting fortress warfare for 145 years could not be borne by the local economy and became the responsibility of a line of Habsburg emperor-kings. They shouldered it by laying a special form of tax (*Türkenhilfe,*[44] "help against the Turks") on their German subjects. Since the defense funds and forces were increasingly of German provenance, a permanent situation arose in which the local populations had to make adjustments to the reality and presence of foreign command, foreign soldiery, foreign administration, and foreign colonizers, even in those areas of their national territory which had escaped Ottoman conquest and occupation. This inevitably led to a gradual weakening of the sense of state sovereignty and to acquiescence in political dependence as the normal and accustomed form of existence.[45] At the same time, the various patterns of collaboration fixed in the historical memory the successful figures of the quisling and the renegade, who rise to power and amass riches by carrying out the orders of a foreign occupying power in their own country.

10

The Cultural Effects—the
Turks and the Reformation

The diary of Johann Ferdinand Auer,[1] or at least the section of it which describes the diarist's journey in 1663 from Bratislava (Pressburg, Pozsony) to Belgrade, should be required reading for medical personnel preparing a clinical study of cultural shock. Although he belonged to the fourth generation after Mohacs, young Auer was apparently still traumatized by the territorial coexistence of two antithetical cultures.

The narrator, captured in a skirmish with the Turks, was taken in irons with other POW's, to be interrogated by a *subashi,* an officer of the Ottoman field gendarmerie, who camped in a tent with his family. The children derided the prisoners and spat upon them. Three hundred men were then taken and locked up for the night in a dungeon. Two of them died before dawn. Next morning, as they were being led across a drawbridge, fifteen on a chain fastened to iron collars around their necks, they were cursed in several languages by elderly, white-bearded Ottoman dignitaries seated on carpets spread on the parapets. After a forced march on the double, the prisoners arrived before an elaborate tent hung with Oriental rugs and curtains woven of silver threads. At the entrance, cross-legged on a red-velvet divan, sat an imposing turbaned figure clad in the finest satin damask garments, his manicured fingers covered with huge diamond rings. With a half-concealed ironic smile on his lips, stroking his curled black beard, the vizier listened to the prisoners identify themselves in halting Latin. In the background executioners could be seen at their gruesome work on the greensward. Apparently bored, the chief contemptuously waved the group on to its next stop. This was a tower which served as a collecting prison and was under the command of a Turkish-speaking Christian. Food was provided, one pound of meat for ten men. To get the rest of their fare the prisoners were let loose on the countryside to scavenge, beg, or steal. Out of forty prisoners twenty died during the three weeks spent in the tower. The bodies had to be left lying on the ground at the main gate for two or three days, until a Turkish *chauss* (noncommissioned officer) came to cut off the ears, which had monetary value. Burial was left for the surviving prisoners. These were finally loaded into river barges for a twelve-day voyage to Belgrade, during which six men died of dysentery. At the end of the trip the prisoners, among them Auer, were assigned to work in an arsenal, under the supervision of a band of Gypsies, to await ransoming.[2]

Apparently, as the years of the occupation continued, the sharpness of the cultural shock did not lessen. But its imprint deepened. Turkish-occupied Europe was not the same after as it had been before Ottoman rule, no more than Spain emerged unchanged after eight centuries of Moorish occupation. The differences between the Moorish and Turkish cultural effects were, however, more important than the similarities. The Arabs were civilization makers; the Turks, civilization absorbers. As Pushkin said of the Tartars, the Turks brought their subjects neither Aristotle nor algebra. When they finally receded, they left behind devastation, backwardness, and underdevelopment. The net cultural effect of their centuries-long presence was the redrawing of the dividing line between the coastal and inland descendants of the Cro-Magnon Man.

The positive cultural traces left behind by the Turks were insignificant. Ethnically they left only a superficial imprint because there could be no intermarriage between Moslems and Christians without conversion. Also, because, in the army and in the bureaucracy at least, non-Turk Moslems usually outnumbered Turkish Moslems. The subject populations probably left more of an ethnic stamp on the conquerors than the conquerors left on the conquered. Religiously their influence was felt mostly among a minority in the top stratum. Even there occasionally it was strong enough to draw individuals but not whole families. A noted example of this phenomenon were the South Slav Sokolovich brothers in the 1550s. The Islamic convert Medmed became Grand Vizier. He made his unconverted Christian brother Macarius *igumen* (abbot) of the Monastery of Hilendar and later Patriarch of Ipek.[3] To the Turks the great masses of Christian peasantry were raia (cattle), to be left alone to graze peacefully in their pastures as long as they provided taxes and recruits.[4] If Christian religious observance showed a tendency to become politicized, it would be dealt with energetically. Thus, after the shrine of the Serb patron Saint Sava in the monastery of Mileseva became a center of budding nationalistic resistance, in 1595 the Turks secretly removed the body from its crypt and burned it.[5]

No direct attempt was made to impose the Islamic faith on the Christian masses. The Bogomils of Bosnia were willing converts. The Pomaks of Bulgaria may have been pressured into embracing Islam. Beyond these two still extant groups, about the only Islamic reminders in the once Ottoman-occupied countries are the slender minarets the traveler sees preserved in places from Eger in northern Hungary to Sarajevo and Nish in southern Yugoslavia; also a few curiosities in ecclesiastical architecture—Byzantine basilicas converted into mosques and then reconverted into Christian churches, with the cross superimposed over the crescent on the top of a massive dome. North of the Danube, where the occupation lasted only 150 years, the linguistic traces of the conquest are insignificant. In the Hungarian vocabulary there are approximately thirty Ottoman Turkish words.[6] South of the Danube 500 years of Turkish presence left more copious linguistic reminders: 8,742 Ottoman Turkish borrowings in Serbo-Croatian[7] and "several thousand Turkicisms" in Bulgarian.[8]

The Orientalizing cultural influence was more noticeable, while it lasted, in the Balkans than north of the Danube. For example, even in the Dalmatian city-state of Dubrovnik (Ragusa), the only piece of land between Hungary and Yemen that escaped incorporation in the Ottoman Empire (because, like modern Hong Kong, it was useful as a maritime commercial outlet), western travelers at the end of the sixteenth century noted that women were often veiled and sequestered and that the groom did not see his bride till their wedding day.[9]

North of the Danube the Turkish presence was responsible for demographically induced cultural changes. South Slav refugees fleeing the Turks began crossing into Hungarian territory north of the Danube as early as the beginning of the fifteenth century. They eventually Slavicized the south-Hungarian Banat, Bachka, Syrmia, and south Baranya areas. After the fall of independent Serbia in 1459, the number of South Slav displaced persons crossing into Hungary is said to have doubled.[10] Between 1483 and 1486, 200,000 Serbs entered what is today the Yugoslav autonomous province of the Voyvodina.[11] As late as 1690 the northward movement of the Serbs continued. In that year alone 37,000 Serb families crossed the Danube under the leadership of Arsene III Chernojevich, Patriarch of Ipek.[12] The refugees received privileges and were granted a charter for an autonomous Orthodox Church at Sremski Karlovici in 1716.[13]

In addition to changing the ethnic character of the lands they overran north of the Danube, the Turks indirectly stimulated the growth of vernacular literatures among the South Slavs and also among the Hungarians. South of the Danube, the heroic deeds of the Haiduks and the Uskoks gave rise to a genre of orally transmitted folk ballads and lyrics, recited by a rustic bard accompanying himself on a guitarlike native instrument called a *guzla*.[14] This vernacular poetry served as a means of cultural cohesion during the nineteenth-century period of national awakening. In Croatia Nicholas Zrinyi (1620-1664), great-grandson and namesake of the hero of Szigetvar (1566), was the author of the neoclassic epic *The Fall of Sziget* [15] (1646) and also of technical works on military strategy in Hungarian. His younger brother Peter treated the same subject in the Croatian language. Hungarian resistance against the Turkish invader and the life of the soldiers in the border fortresses inspired the narrative poetry of Sebastian Tinodi [16] (1510-1556) and the patriotic lyrics of Balint Balassa [17] (1554-1594), who saw his embattled country as a "school for heroes" and the "shield of Christendom." The spread of this vernacular poetry north of the Danube was facilitated by the expansion of the new printing industry. The Protestant Reformation played an important role in encouraging pamphleteering in the vernacular. In the area now occupied by Hungary, Yugoslavia, Rumania, and Slovakia there were, during the sixteenth century, in Protestant hands alone, seven permanent and sixteen intinerant printing press establishments,[18] specializing in anti-Catholic brochures printed in the native idioms.

The Turks also stimulated a culinary revival by bringing into the conquered lands unknown spices, cereals, and plants from the Near East. Thanks to their presence, the local cuisines became more palatable and more highly seasoned. They introduced into their European possessions paprika, sesame, tobacco, coffee, rice, corn, and cotton. They brought and planted the attar-yielding damask rose, which still remains the source and basic raw material of the perfume industry of Bulgaria.[19] They left behind as a permanent cultural legacy the coffee-house, that leisurely male hangout and public business office, as an enduring monument of their presence from Vidin to Vienna. They also built, popularized, and bequeathed to posterity sybaritically elaborate baths, some of which are still open to the public in cities once held by Ottoman armies.

Quite circumstantially, the Turkish presence also fostered the growth and naturalization of a subculture considered characteristic of the middle zone: that of the Gypsies. These nomadic arrivals from far-away India were swept into the Danubian lands from the Balkans by the invading Turks, whose camp followers they may have been through the Indus-Bosporus-Danube area. The presence of the Gypsies is signalled in Byzantine territory as early as 1322. By 1348 bands of them were noted as far north as Serbia. In 1386 they were mentioned as slaves in Moldavia and Wallachia. One of their earliest appearances north of the Danube, inside the southeastern Carpathian basin, was recorded in the Transylvanian city of Brashov (Kronstadt) in 1416, in a contemporary reference to the arrival of 150 "Egyptians" under a leader named Emaus. Eleven years later a group of Gypsies was first observed as far west as Paris.[20]

The synchronism between Turkish military movements and the appearance of Gypsy groups near the theaters of war is noticeable. The Gypsies were in Serbia two years after the Turks crossed the Hellespont into Europe; in Moldavia and Wallachia ten years before Sigismund's army was annihilated at Nicopolis; in Transylvania a year after a Turkish raid into the Banat of Temesvar. Were they refugees from or advance scouts for the advancing Turkish armies? Why did they conceal their true identity and misrepresent themselves as Egyptians? Some of the sources, like Auer's diary, indicate that they held low positions of trust under the Turks. Other evidence seems to place them in a state of peaceful symbiosis with the conquerors during periods which saw mass flights of South Slavs into territory already liberated from the Ottomans. For example, when the Banat was ceded by the Porte to the Habsburgs in 1718, the populations of the newly reconquered territory included a large number of nomadic Gypsies.[21]

Why had these strange people remained with the Turks? There is a likely explanation for the roughly coinciding movements of Turks and Gypsies into the middle zone. The latter had moved into the Byzantine Empire during an early period when the westward surge of the Turks and the Mongols, between the tenth and the fifteenth century, turned the territories between the Indus and the Aegean into a turbulent corridor of migrations. The Sanskrit-descended Indo-European language of the Gypsies and the large number of medieval Greek words in their vocabulary show that they used this corridor and that, having traversed it, they spent some time under Byzantine imperium.[22] Their northward spread in the Balkans, across the Danube and toward the west, is probably an indication that as nomads they made use of the westward extension by the Turks of the migratory corridor, sometimes as refugees, occasionally perhaps as scouts and spies. A corollary and permanent cultural result of their presence was Gypsy orchestration of the ethnic folk music of the Ottoman-ruled populations into a gaudily baroque style, which was then passed on to the west by Liszt's rhapsodies and Brahms's dances as an unadulterated form of folk art. It remained for twentieth-century musicologists like Bela Bartok and Zoltan Kodaly to penetrate below the Gypsy superstratum and to bring to the surface specimens of the less melodious, less capricious, less passionate, but indigenous musical substratum.

The irruption of the Turks into the middle-Danube plain was contemporaneous with the appearance of Protestantism east of Vienna. The present cartographic distribution of the various Protestant denominations east of Germany is a reminder of Turkish presence in middle-zone Catholic lands. Protestantism has now all but disappeared from countries like Poland, which escaped Ottoman conquest. On the other hand, it has been preserved in lands like Hungary and Transylvania, which were Turkish-ruled or Turkish-dominated for a century and a half. Where Protestantism survived, the Lutheran form prevailed in areas under Habsburg control and among German populations; Calvinism and Unitarianism in those dominated by the Turks. It should be recalled that the Calvinists did not receive the recognition and the privileges accorded to the Lutherans at the religious peace of Augsburg in 1555 [23] and remained in opposition to the emperor until they won recognition at Westphalia in 1648.[24] In the meantime, in an attempt to gain the privileges already possessed by the Lutherans, they did not disdain from using the *Türkenhilfe*, the military appropriations asked by the emperor to raise armies against the Turks, as leverage to improve their status. Thus, at the imperial Diet of 1576 the Wittelsbach Elector Palatine, political leader of the German Calvinists, openly stated that he would vote for the *Türkenhilfe* only in return for recognition by the Diet of the Helvetic (Calvinist) Confession.[25]

Modern confessional maps of the Carpathian basin show a heavy concentration of Reformed (Calvinist) populations in the central plains area and in the Magyar-Szekely ethnic areas of Transylvania. These territories were once under the rule or protection of the sultan. The Unitarians also became and remained strong in Transylvania, especially after their exodus from Poland. Lutheranism, on the other hand, struck deep roots in areas beyond Turkish penetration: in Slovakia, in the Saxon and Zipser areas, and in the urban middle classes. The Counter Reformation, which in Habsburg-held lands and in other Turk-free countries began immediately after the Council of Trent (1545-1564), had to be delayed in the Ottoman-ruled Danubian lands until after the rollback around 1700. By that late date both Calvinism and Unitarianism had struck deep roots in Hungary and Transylvania and had become amalgamated with the spirit of nascent anti-German nationalism. The fact that the easternmost limits of Reformation-created Protestantism lie today in mid-Rumania, along the Transylvanian border with Wallachia and Moldavia, is due to a prolongation of Ottoman suzerainty until the end of the seventeenth century in this part of Europe. An interesting surviving monument of this Moslem-Protestant symbiosis is the famous Black Church of Brashov, a Gothic-style Lutheran cathedral, the interior of which is heavily hung with Turkish and other Oriental prayer rugs.

There may have been several reasons for Turkish preference for the Protestant form of Christianity, in addition to the obvious facts that the early Protestants were anti-imperial and had no religious international center beyond the Ottoman Empire to give them political guidance. The Moslem Turk probably felt more at home in a whitewashed, unornamented Calvinist church than he did in a Catholic cathedral decorated with what he considered sacrilegiously painted and graven images. Islam and the Calvinistic wing of the Reformation resembled each other in their iconoclastic proclivities and also in their austerity toward the plastic arts. Doctrinally as well there was a coincidental affinity between the Calvinist dogma of predestination and the kismet (predetermined fate) professed by the Moslems. With Unitarianism, the Turkish point of contact was the acceptance of Christ as a great moral leader, as a prophet, but not as a divinity. There was also an important economic reason. The Roman Catholic Church continued to own *de jure* immense landed properties in the occupied areas, even though these estates had passed into the *de facto* ownership of the Ottoman treasury after the disappearance of the Catholic hierarchy. Ottoman economic interests thus called for the replacement of the old possessor-church establishment by a new, nonpossessing, Protestant church organization, without legal claims against the Ottoman treasury.

The preferential Ottoman sympathy evoked by all these Protestant affinities is probably responsible for the emancipation of Calvinists and Unitarians in Turkish-occupied Europe earlier than in the west. The Dutch Calvinist Reformed Church was established in the German town of Emden in 1571 by self-exiled Protestant divines [26] denied freedom of religion and conscience in their home provinces held by the troops of Philip II of Spain. The Hungarian Calvinist Reformed Church at this time had been in organized existence for nearly a decade, having been established as an autonomous ecclesiastical body during 1562-1567, with a Presbyterian form of church government, in the Turkish-controlled town of Debrecen,[27] known to this day as the "Calvinist Rome." Calvinism, tolerated by the Turks, became known as the "Magyar religion." Religious tolerance under the Ottomans also preceded the acceptance of "heresy" as a recognized confession of faith under western monarchs. The Transylvanian Diet in 1571 placed both Calvinists and Unitarians on an equal footing with Catholics and Lutherans.[28] At this time in France anti-Calvinist sentiment was about to culminate in the massacre of St. Bartholomew's Day (1572), while in Germany the Helvetic (Calvinist) Confession was refused recognition until the Peace of Westphalia in 1648. As for the Unitarians, their Spanish apostle Michael Servetus was burnt at the stake in Calvin's Geneva in 1553 for his denial of the divinity of Christ. This was an act of Protestant intolerance which had an influence on the Transylvanian divine Ferenc David (1510?-1579).[29] He broke with Calvinism in 1567 and became the first bishop of a Unitarian church, which still survives in Transylvania, with a splendid cathedral in the city of Cluj (Kolozsvar).

Calvinist and Unitarian communities of the east developed, until the end of the seventeenth century, if not exactly in isolation from, then at least without close organizational ties to their sister churches in the west. The lack of close contact probably explained why Calvinism and Unitarianism in the Danubian lands did not become puritanical, rigidly moralistic, and ascetically inclined. American, Scottish, Dutch, and Swiss Calvinist divines would be well advised, if they wish to understand their middle-zone coreligionists, to read in translation the nineteenth-century Hungarian poet Alexander Petöfi's comic poem "Csokonai," [30] which describes the ludicrous adventures of a Calvinist pastor and a Reformed Church theological student in a wine cellar of the "Calvinist Rome," Debrecen.

The Lutherans, the oldest and politically most pliant of the Protestant denominations, also profited from the Turkish presence. The law passed in 1523-1524 by the Hungarian Estates, which condemned them to death in the flames of the pyre (*Lutherani autem comburantur*),[31] remained a dead letter after Mohacs, with a few early exceptions. Thus, two Lutheran pastors were executed by the national king Zapolya in 1527, probably because of their participation in a miners' revolt rather than as heretics.[32] In 1528 two German ex-monks, accused of being Anabaptists (a sect equally abhorred by both Catholics and Lutherans), were burnt at the stake in Habsburg-held Pressburg.[33] On the whole, however, Protestantism spread in and near Ottoman-occupied territories without martyrs and without wars of religion. The Lutherans, following the example of their founder, ranged themselves on the side of the temporal authorities, Habsburg or Ottoman. Under neither did they have anything to fear from the Roman Church. All but six of the Catholic bishops of Hungary were killed on the battlefield of Mohacs. The power and wealth of the Catholic Church in Hungary and Transylvania, based on immense landed estates, was crumbling because of the reduction of the hierarchy and property seizures by both sides in the civil war of the two kings, John and Ferdinand. There was a general climate of chaos and anarchy in which a badly fragmented establishment was unable to apply force, as in Germany and France, to stop the spread of the Lutheran Reformation from the towns into the countryside. Consequently, during the two generations following the battle of Mohacs, the majority of the populations inhabiting both Ottoman and nearby Habsburg-held territories turned Protestant.

Immediately after Mohacs, Luther took a stand more anti-Rome than anti-Turk. In his correspondence [34] with the widowed Hungarian Queen Maria (sister of the Emperor Charles V), he blamed the Church of Rome for the prevalence of Turkish power. His followers further developed this theme and charged that the successes of the Turks were indeed God's punishment for the sins of the Catholics in persecuting the Protestants. Between 1528 and 1529, however, Luther had partially changed his views. While still ascribing Turkish triumph both at Varna and at Mohacs to the faulty leadership of corrupt Catholic prelates, he proposed a general German offensive against the Ottomans under the personal leadership of Charles V. But Germany as well as France was entering a long period of religious wars, which did not end until 1648 and left both countries in a state of debility. There could be no general offensive such as proposed by Luther. Charles V was interested in fighting the Turks only near home, in the western basin of the Mediterranean.[35] At the end of the sixteenth century and during the Thirty Years' War (1618-1648), Germany may well have been saved from Turkish encroachment only because of concurrent internal troubles in the Ottoman Empire. The Turks were at a low stage of vitality due to the incipient decay and revolts of the janissaries and to the fratricidal anarchy through the reigns of Osman II to Murad IV (1618-1640).

It is interesting to note that in the Balkans, where the absence of a Catholic-Protestant antithesis deprived the Ottomans of the opportunity to keep on conquering by dividing their Christian enemies and where the division between Rome and Byzantium had crystallized

into an Orthodox preponderance, the Porte granted the same tolerance to Catholic missionaries as it did in Catholic areas to Protestant
proselytizers. The Franciscans were not prevented from spreading
the Roman faith, though the Jesuits were abhorred and excluded,[36]
probably because of their special fifth vow of obedience to the pope.
A few Jesuits were admitted sporadically after 1612, mostly because of
their medical reputation, but they could come in large numbers only
around 1700, in the wake of the liberating imperial armies. Obviously
the Ottoman political objective was the same in both Orthodox and
Catholic countries: to diminish the influence of the politically dominant form of Christianity by letting its own Christian opposition un-
dermine its power base without let or hindrance. Sir Thomas More,
awaiting execution during 1534 in the Tower of London and writing
his last book about the progress of the Turks, saw the situation clearly:

> If the Princes of Christendom everywhere about would . . . have set
> their hands in time, the Turk had never taken any one place. . . . But partly
> because dissensions have fallen among ourself, partly because no man careth
> what harm other folk feel . . . the Turk is in a very few years wonderfully
> increased, and Christendom on the other side is sore decayed.[37]

To More, "decayed" meant fragmented, fallen away from Rome.
Christian fragmentation and Turkish presence were simultaneous phe-
nomena in the Catholic Danubian lands. The modern traveler still
sees the results of this fragmentation on a trip east of Vienna, all the
way to the Predeal Pass in the Carpathians, even if he has time to
watch only the identifying emblems on the church steeples. In the
Orthodox lands south of the Danube he will see more religious uni-
formity, though less cultural affinity with the west than in the mixed
Catholic-Protestant territories to the north. A cultural comparison
with conquered and religiously more homogeneous Poland, where the
Reformation faded away while it was still in its period of militancy
in the south, gives support to the hypothesis that in Hungary and
Transylvania Protestant survival and differentiation were functions of
Turkish domination. The reasons for the continuation and ramifica-
tion of Protestantism in the unconquered northern Czech, Moravian,
and Slovak lands are to be sought retrospectively in the Hussite up-
heaval and, later, in Bohemian involvement in the Thirty Years'
War.[38]

11

Free Middle Europe— What Price Freedom?

By the early 1540s a prototypal iron curtain made its appearance across the middle zone, separating territories occupied, annexed, or "protected" by the intruding eastern power from areas contiguous to the west defended either by the Habsburg emperor or by the Polish king. The line of demarcation ran somewhat east of the present Austrian-Hungarian frontier, slightly north of the now existing border between Hungary and Czechoslovakia, and extending eastward beyond the Carpathian Mountains north and east of the boundaries of modern Rumania, across the ill-defined, no-man's land of the Ukraine. North and west of this early iron curtain lay what remained of the Monarchy of the Three Seas: Habsburg Hungary, Slovakia, Bohemia, and Jagiello Poland-Lithuania. This was free Middle Europe, or at least Middle Europe free from the Turks. The Turk-free rump paid for its freedom either by immediate or eventual incorporation into the Habsburg empire, as did Bohemia and Hungary, including Slovakia; or by gradual decay, self-destruction, and partitioning among neighbors no less imperialistically inclined than the Turks, as in the case of Poland-Lithuania. There was, however, a consolation prize for the Turk-free, Habsburg-ruled or multipartitioned areas of the middle zone: they remained a part of European civilization and, on liberation, had to contend with a shorter cultural lag behind the west than did the less fortunate European subjects of the Ottoman Empire.

Immediately north of the line of demarcation, the Slovak population was rather acted upon than acting during the sixteenth and seventeenth centuries. The importance of their area—now Slovakia, then ten northern counties of Hungary—increased after Mohacs. Since the

Turks occupied central Hungary, the Hungarian capital and the seat of the Hungarian Estates were moved to Bratislava on the Danube, a short distance east of Vienna. With Ferdinand of Habsburg as the sole king after 1540 in both Hungary and Bohemia, the German influence in Slovakia became stronger, not only politically but also religiously. The Reformation and the Counter Reformation became almost simultaneous processes. The second half of the sixteenth century saw not only the spread of Lutheranism from the German burghers of the cities into the countryside inhabited by Slovaks, but also the coming of the Jesuits. Hungarian influence also increased, not only because of the shifting of the Magyar administrative-legislative center from the south to the Slovak-inhabited northern counties, but in consequence of several other developments as well. The great landowning families which gradually replaced the older pre-Mohacs aristocracy—the Illeshazys, the Esterhazys, and the Rakoczis—became the socially dominant force in Slovakia. Here alone was the Habsburg king-emperor able to make donations of land or to pawn estates to raise funds needed for defense against the Turks. It was also via the unoccupied northern counties that the Turkish-sponsored, anti-Habsburg Hungarian princes marched from Transylvania against the imperial forces. Stephen Bocskai (1557-1606), Gabriel Bethlen (1580-1629), Imre Thököli (1657-1705), and later the Rakoczis, deployed their forces of Haiduks and *kuruc* in the north; convoked assemblies of anti-German Estates in the towns of Kosice (Kassa), Banska Bystrica (Besztercebanya), Krapina (Korpona); and maintained contact with the anti-Habsburg Protestant Bohemian Estates before and during the Thirty Years' War (1618-1648).[1] Sociologically, the main effect of this strategic utilization of northern Habsburg Hungary was the Magyarization of the socially more ambitious elements of the Slovak population and, to a lesser extent, the enhancement of the German character of the cities and towns. Both the Habsburg monarchs and the Hungarian princely commanders in the area issued patents of Hungarian nobility to their deserving partisans. Thus a new Hungarian elite of Slovak origin came into existence north of the Turkish battle zone. The Diet in Bratislava and the local county assemblies provided an arena for the talents and ambitions of the new gentry, which showed its origins by tending to be Lutheran. As usual, the assimilants found their newly acquired nationality a greater source of pride than was the case with the older nobility. With the rise of nationalism in the late eighteenth and early nineteenth centuries, the new gentry played an important political role.

Farther to the north, in Turk-free Bohemia and Moravia, a great expending of political and religious energies preceded the later period of indifferent inertia after 1620. Immediately after Mohacs, Bohemia assumed a key role in European politics because, with the Bohemian crown on his head, the Habsburg ruler and claimant to the Holy Roman imperial throne himself became one of the seven electoral princes who chose emperors. It was for this reason that, in 1547, even before the abdication of his brother Charles V as emperor in 1556, Ferdinand of Austria (1526-1564), since 1526 elected king of both Hungary and Bohemia, proclaimed the Bohemian crown hereditary in the Habsburg family. Under Ferdinand's grandson Rudolf II (1576-1612) even the seat of the emperor was moved from Vienna to Prague. Indeed, the Habsburg hold on Bohemia became indispensable for the retention of the imperial dignity. When it was challenged in 1618 by the defenestration from the Hradcany Castle heights of the emperor's emissaries and by the ascension to the Bohemian throne of the Calvinist Frederick of Wittelsbach, son-in-law of King James I of England, the result was the Thirty Years' War. This seemingly interminable conflict left Bohemia and Moravia exhausted, depleted, and inert for the next two centuries. The origins of the terrible and devastating war [2] derived not only from the reciprocal religious insecurity and intolerance of Catholic and Protestant German princes and the determination of the Habsburg dynasty to retain the imperial crown at any cost, but also, directly, from the situation which had developed in Bohemia-Moravia after the Hussite wars. The emperor's emissaries were thrown out of the Hradcany windows by the outraged Czechs in a denominational dispute over certain Protestant churches which had been destroyed or turned over to the Catholics in 1617 in violation of the Letter of Majesty, a document of religious toleration, issued by Emperor Rudolf in 1609. A great deal had happened during those eight years. The Jesuits, who first went to Prague in 1556, had gone on the offensive. In Moravia, for example, where there had been only fifty Roman Catholic parishes in 1560, there were 280 by 1619.[3] Proportionately with the increase of the Protestant German challenge to Catholic Habsburg hegemony in the empire, a threat backed by the Protestant Czech Estates, rose the intensity and intransigence of the Jesuit-directed and Habsburg-sponsored Counter Reformation in Bohemia-Moravia.

The real losers of the Thirty Years' War were the Czech Protestants, who fought with the militant fervor of their Hussite forebears in the Battle of the White Mountain in 1620. For the Czechs, White Mountain proved to be a partial Mohacs in the sense that there was no recovery from the lost battle, not at least for two centuries. But, in contrast to the psychological effects in Hungary, where warfare continued during and after the Turkish occupation, in Bohemia a great stillness seems to have fallen on the land after 1620. Even the national character appeared to have undergone a change in the incessant wars and defeats suffered in the face of overwhelming odds since 1415. Saved from the Turks, the Czechs were taken by the Austro-Germans. Bohemia was pacified. Its cities and rural areas showed a Czech-German ethnic ambivalence. The high nobility turned German-Austrian in speech, culture, and manners. The land eventually began to serve as a theater of war for the battles of other nations, at which the natives were only interested spectators. The French troops of Louis XV took Prague from the Austrians in 1741. Frederick the Great of Prussia fought Maria Theresa of Austria intermittently on Bohemian soil from 1744 to 1758. Napoleon defeated the emperors of Austria and Russia near the Czech village of Austerlitz in 1805. Bismarck humbled the Habsburgs in 1866 at the Czech hamlet of Königgrätz (Sadova).

Poland and her associated Grand Duchy of Lithuania were particularly fortunate. They had, unlike Bohemia, avoided incorporation in the Holy Roman Empire and, unlike Muscovy, escaped subjection to Tartar rule. Later, unlike Hungary, these two countries were spared Turkish occupation. The Polish-Lithuanian state also succeeded where Hungary and Bohemia both failed after Mohacs: in warding off Habsburg attempts to secure the royal crown, and, during the seventeenth century, in staying out of the Thirty Years' War. The destruction of statehood and the detachment from the west in the southern areas of the middle zone were contrastingly paralleled in Poland by a "Golden Age," during which the Renaissance, the Reformation, and the Counter Reformation were telescoped historical processes.[4] With the secularization of the Teutonic Knights in 1525 and their acceptance of Polish suzerainty, the menace of the *Drang nach Osten* also seemed to have ended. Territorially, in mid-sixteenth century, the Polish-Lithuanian union constituted the second largest state in Europe and ranked sixth in population (six million). Moreover, while Germany and France were in the throes of internecine religious wars, both the Reformation and the Counter Reformation ran their course in Poland-Lithuania without armed conflicts between Catholics and Protestants.

In spite of these propitious beginnings, however, Poland was, in historical retrospect, a country doomed for several reasons to disappear from the map of Europe. First, geography, which had saved her from the Turks, exposed her to the imperialism of more conveniently located powers, not only German and Ottoman, but Russian and Swedish as well. Second, she had not even weak natural frontiers comparable to the Danube, the Carpathian Wreath, or the Bohemian bastion, but was in fact a wide-open plain impossible to defend against superior outside powers. Third, the power balance between defenders and would-be invaders gradually tipped in favor of the latter, because of the continuation and aggravation of apparently incurable internal weaknesses endemic to the middle zone. These weaknesses were the oligarchic resistance to the establishment of a strong centralized monarchy, the introduction and expansion of serfdom, and the increasing incidence in the eastern part of the country of ethnically and religiously compounded peasant revolts. To these endemic weaknesses were added peculiarly Polish social and political debilities: the evolution of an aristocratic parliamentary democracy by unanimity rule, the resulting libertarian anarchy, the degeneration of the agrarian problem into a racial and religious conflict, and also the rise of an unrealistically imperialistic spirit of expansionism toward the east.

Before proceeding to appraise these various internal weaknesses, which eventually led to Poland's disappearance from the map, some basic understanding of the Polish situation in the sixteenth century may be reached by having a look at the Polish Reformation.[5] It lasted just about fifty years, from 1522, when it appeared in the city of Danzig, to 1573, when the new confessions were granted toleration. By 1563 all anti-Protestant edicts had been practically annulled and the execution of all measures decreed to combat reform had become impossible. During these fifty years Protestantism showed the same characteristics in Poland as elsewhere: rapid spread, territorial differentiation (Lutherans in Great Poland in the northwest and among German elements; Calvinists in Little Poland southeast of the Vistula River), sympathy in the royal court, severe prohibitory legislation followed by only sporadic enforcement (the burning at the stake of an eighty-year-old woman in Cracow in 1539 was and remained a rarity), the appearance and spread of vernacular literature spurred by religious polemics and the use of printing presses, the customary radicalization, and a Calvinist-Unitarian split in 1562.[6]

The Protestant movement was further strengthened in Poland by the conversion of the Teutonic Knights to Lutheranism in 1525; the arrival in 1548 of the Hussite-descended religious community of the Bohemian Brethren, who had been driven from their homeland; and by the political support provided not only by some of the great nobles but also by some of the more numerous lesser nobility, the *szlachta*. Between 1552 and 1565 Protestants, under a Protestant presidency, dominated all the sessions of the *Seym* (Diet). In the Diet of 1569, of

133 senatorial seats 58 were occupied by Protestants; the Protestant temporal peers outnumbered their Catholic counterparts by three. One-sixth of the total number of Roman Catholic parishes had gone Protestant; and 2,000 Roman Catholic churches had been converted to Protestant places of worship.[7] A growing movement toward co-operation and union among the various Protestant denominations—Lutheran, Calvinist, and Bohemian Brethren—was enhanced by the Union of Sandomierz in 1570. An edict of religious toleration was issued in Warsaw in 1573, one year after the St. Bartholomew's Day massacre of the Calvinists in Paris. Yet, in spite of impressive strength and apparent triumph during the closing decades of the sixteenth century, Polish Protestantism was no longer a religious or political factor to reckon with. From the seventeenth century on Poland presented to the outer world a uniformly Roman Catholic image.

Standard histories of Poland in English list several reasons to account for the decline and decay of Polish Protestantism. They enumerate class restrictions, lack of deep roots in the population, political and economic opportunism, absence of internal unity, discrimination against Protestants in the civil service and the army beginning at the end of the sixteenth century, the vigorous Jesuit counteroffensive, the renaissance of the Polish Roman Catholic Church immediately following the Council of Trent (1545-1563), the hostile attitude of seventeenth-century rulers, and immoderate Anabaptist and anti-Trinitarian excesses.[8] To these factors, some weighty but equally applicable to countries other than Poland where Protestantism has to this day remained either a dominant or a strong minority religion, should be added the possibly decisive reason: lack of continuing patronage or protection by the politically supreme power. The re-Catholicization of Poland began more than a century earlier than the Counter Reformation in Hungarian and Transylvanian territories liberated from the Turks. It was spearheaded by the energetic and usually irresistible Jesuits, who appeared in Poland in the 1540s but could enter formerly Catholic areas farther south in large numbers only after the rollback of the Turks at the very end of the seventeenth century. By 1565 there were so many Jesuits in Poland-Lithuania that for administrative reasons it became necessary to divide them into separate Polish and Lithuanian chapters.[9] Thus, by his absence the infidel Turk and by his presence the indefatigable Jesuit were both responsible for the return of Poland to the Roman Catholic fold.

While Poland was moving back to religious unity, which (according to contemporary political theory) should have served to strengthen her politically, she was in fact drifting toward an internal power vacuum. The intransigence of the great nobles and their resistance to the growth of a strong centralized monarchy sapped the strength of the state. The last two of the Polish Jagiellos, Sigismund I (1506-1548) and Sigismund August II (1548-1572), had to rule in the face of the recalcitrance and occasional rebellion of the great nobles. Glinski's rebellion in 1508 had to be put down with great difficulty and almost resulted in the loss of eastern territories to Moscow. King Sigismund I, as he grew older, seemed to acquiesce in the limitation of his royal prerogatives by the great nobles, though his Italian Queen Bona Sforza continued to struggle against them in a double effort to strengthen the monarchy and to enrich the family.[10] Nonetheless a state of aristocratic anarchy was slowly coming into existence. A glaring example of the lawless trend was the defiance of the gentry, called to arms in a military emergency during 1537, to obey the command of the king unless he accepted their political demands.[11] Arrests and trials during 1537-1538 of revolting great nobles had only a temporary effect.

The extinction of the Jagiello line in 1572 was followed by a further weakening of the prestige of the crown in the eyes of the powerful great nobles. The domains of the Polish Potocki and Lubomirski families and those of the Lithuanian Radziwills and Sapiehas exceeded the size of the royal estates. The kings, in an effort to check the countervailing power of the high nobility, attempted to make common cause against it by an alliance with the more numerous lesser nobility. In the Poland of the time this group was a social force substituting for the yet undeveloped middle class. The immediate result was the insistence of the lesser nobles on equality of status with the great oligarchs. Royal concessions in the economic sphere to the lesser nobility led to an extension of serfdom; in the political arena, to an immobilization of both legislative and executive power. The extension of serfdom and the atrophy of central power let loose a whole series of insoluble problems. The kingdom was bled white by runaway serfs and by the rise and spread of the freebooting Cossack population. The exacerbation of Polish-Ukrainian and Catholic-Orthodox antagonisms were an ill augury of the coming clash with a reviving Muscovy during and after its time of troubles. The withering of state power made it impossible in the final emergency to resist Russian encroachment in the east and to prevent the cession of western and southern territories.

Interaction among historical processes originating in seemingly independent events shaped the course of developments in sixteenth-century Poland and set the stage for action during the seventeenth and eighteenth centuries. The enactment of the *nihil novi* constitution in

1505 had provided that nothing new could be undertaken in the Polish state without the joint consent of the Senate and the Chamber of Deputies.[12] *Nihil novi* had signalled the ascent to supreme political power of the nobility, which was the Senate and the Chamber, and heralded a disastrous curtailment of royal power. Implicit in the unfolding of legislative sovereignty was the principle of parliamentary decision by unanimity. This, however, was still being practiced with moderation during the sixteenth century.

The introduction of serfdom into Poland in 1511 and its first appearance in the eastern, Ukrainian provinces during the second half of the sixteenth century coincided with the beginnings and development of the *kozatstvo*, the lawless, free, pioneer life of Cossack frontiersmen moving into the southeastern wilderness.[13] These virgin territories were reportedly flowing with milk and honey. There were no masters and landowners, and brave men could lead an untrammeled and abundant existence in disregard of the Turkish-Tartar threat from the southeast. In 1552 the records showed only 500 "registered" or government-controlled Cossacks.[14] By the 1590s the combined Cossack military forces, registered and unregistered, were said to be 20,000 men.[15] The number of the Cossacks increased partly because of the spread of serfdom and the consequent worsening of the peasants' lot. Hordes of serfs fled the great estates to join in the Cossack way of life in the borderland steppes. The Cossacks incited the peasants to rebel against their landlords, if only by the example of freedom they were setting. Mass flights of peasants into the Cossack no-man's land usually followed unsuccessful revolts of serfs.

In 1569 the federation of Poland and Lithuania assumed a closer form of association under the Union of Lublin. As one of the provisions of the new Union, the Ruthenian, Orthodox populations of Lithuania were detached from the Grand Duchy, and the lands they inhabited were opened to the Roman Catholic Polish nobility.[16] With the new landlords came the Polish institution of serfdom and the imposition of feudal obligations on once-free farmers. The economic antagonism between landlord and serf was already, before the coming of the Polish gentry, sufficiently inflamed to burst forth in uprisings of Ruthenian Orthodox peasants against Ruthenian Orthodox landlords (1590-1593).[17] With the large influx of the Polish, Catholic landowning nobility, the economic antagonism was exacerbated into a latent conflict between two nationalities, two religions, and two populations: one rich and Polish-speaking; the other poor and clinging to the Ruthenian (Little Russian) language.

The first great rising of the Orthodox Ruthenian serfs against their Catholic Polish masters took place in the year 1596. This tragic year also saw a politically fostered merger of two-thirds of Poland-Lithuania's Orthodox populations of four million with the Roman Catholic Church. The merger was the famed Union of Brest, the establishment of the "Uniate" or Greek Catholic Church. This hybrid organization retained the Slavonic-language Byzantine ritual, married clergy, and the ancient metropolitan see of Kiev, while accepting the supreme authority of the pope.[18] In bringing about the union the hope was to create the religious homogeneity then deemed necessary to serve as a foundation for state power. The results were different. Internal squabbles began taking place among the Ruthenian bishops. Religious rivalry rent the Ukrainian faithful. Forced conversions from Orthodox to Catholic allegiance increased the resentment of the Orthodox peasants, who had nothing to gain from following their Polonizing and Catholicizing landowners into the Roman fold. The Vatican is said to have originally opposed the union and to have considered it imprudent. Pope Clement VIII nevertheless confirmed it by the issuance of a papal bull in 1596.[19]

Hardly was the ink dry on the Vatican document when the Cossacks, deeply resentful of the new Uniate bishops and of anyone friendly to the Church of Rome, incited the equally embittered Orthodox serfs to join them in raiding and plundering the estates of both Catholic and Uniate landowners. The ensuing *Jacquerie* turned into a savage civil war more serious than any of the earlier middle-zone peasant uprisings. It gradually turned into a Cossack war against the Polish government. The Commander-in-Chief of the Royal Polish army, Stanislaus Zolkievski, faced and finally forced the surrender of the Cossack chief Nalivaiko, who was executed in 1596 in a manner similar to the atrocious punishment inflicted on the peasant leader Dozsa in Hungary in 1514.[20] According to the legend which soon began circulating and fanning new hatreds among the Orthodox peasants of eastern Poland, Nalivaiko was tortured to death seated on a hot iron horse, crowned with a glowing iron hoop symbolic of his alleged intention to become "King of the Ukraine." The flights of desperate and outraged Ruthenian serfs to the Cossacks rose to mass proportions. Efforts of the Polish government to force the fugitives to return to the serfdom from which they had fled proved to be of no avail. The Cossack host around the inaccessible rapids of the Dnieper grew more numerous.

At the same time, the danger from the Turks and their Crimean Tartar subjects also began to loom larger and larger. In an attempt to use the Cossacks as a military shield against the Moslem menace from the southeast, the Polish government stepped up its recruitment of "registered" Cossacks into special Polish regiments commanded by a *hetman* or general appointed by the king. A hidden, secondary motivation behind the establishment of Cossack military units was the hope of splitting of the Cossack host.[21] The stratagem was successful only to a small extent. A minority of the Cossacks registered to serve in the king's army, and these could not always be trusted to fight against their unregistered comrades. The majority of the host preferred to remain self-governing and to continue enjoying the considerable advantages of the Cossack way of life. They wanted freedom in the borderlands from oppressive Polish landowners and from Catholicizing Uniate bishops. They were willing to die for liberty to fight either with or against the Tartars for plunder and just for the sheer joy of fighting.

The king under whose long reign these events occurred was Sigismund III (1587-1632), of a junior branch of the Swedish Vasa dynasty; he had been raised by German Jesuits as a zealous militant of the Counter Reformation. Sigismund considered the manipulated return to Rome of nearly a million and a half Orthodox "heretics" only the beginning of the re-establishment of the Universal Church triumphant over its enemies.[22] He saw two terrains on which to launch offensives. One field of action was his native land of Sweden, which was becoming predominantly Protestant under the elder Vasa branch. The other area to start an offensive was Orthodox Muscovy, where the extinction of the ancient line of Rurik in 1598 was leading to a time of troubles. Against Muscovy, Stephen Bathori (1575-1586) Sigismund's predecessor on the Polish throne, a devout Catholic Transylvanian, had already made a victorious foray in 1581. The Swedish-born king of Poland not only started a war of succession against Sweden, which lasted sixty exhausting years, but also began making plans to conquer Moscow and to convert its people to Catholicism, so as to rule over a united Russian, Polish, and Lithuanian empire as tsar and king.[23] Here was, in a new form, the recurrent imperial dream of the middle-zone ruler, the same chimera which had driven the Bulgarian tsars after Byzantium and the Hungarian Matthias Corvinus after the elusive Holy Roman crown, with the same result: an exhaustion of national resources in pursuit of the unattainable.

Polish hopes for Baltic hegemony were dashed in the Treaty of Oliva in 1660, which resulted in the loss of both Livonia and Estonia. Instead of Poland ruling Sweden, Swedish control was established along the northern Baltic littoral down to Danzig. Poland managed to hold onto this seaport, although after 1621 both East Prussia to the north and Brandenburg Prussia to the south had fallen into the hands of one of the seven prince-electors of the Holy Roman Empire.[24] The two Prussias were then under the rising dynasty of the Hohenzollerns. Here was an early form of the twentieth-century Polish Corridor, destined to become a Pandora's box of troubles and a source of disaster to Poland between the two world wars.

The Muscovite adventures went through a promising phase from 1605 to 1618, during which Polish armies managed to ensconce themselves in Moscow twice (1605 and 1610-1612) and to have their future king, Vladislas IV (1632-1648), elected tsar (which remained an empty title) against the rival candidacy of his own father King Sigismund III. The Poles heroically held out in the Kremlin against a Russian siege of nineteen months (1611-1612), set a precedent for another famous retreat through the Russian winter two centuries later, then stubbornly returned and failed in a last foolhardy attempt to take Moscow by storm in 1618. The final chapters, without reward for Poland, were written in 1634 by the Treaty of Polianov, in which Poland had to recognize Michael Romanov, the founder of the new and last Russian ruling dynasty, as tsar of all the Russias. In the Treaty of Andrussovo (1667) Poland was compelled to cede to the Russians almost all of her possession east of and on the Dnieper River, including the great and historic cities of Smolensk and Kiev.[25]

The loss of these East Ukrainian territories was in no small measure due to the most sanguine and ferocious of all middle zone uprisings, the great Cossack rebellion (1648-1654) under Bogdan Khmelnitsky.[26] Cossack armies fought a war of extermination against the Polish landlords and the Polish armies, treated with the sultan and the Tartar khan in the Crimea, and finally placed themselves under the protectorate of the Romanov Tsar Alexis (1645-1676), their Orthodox coreligionist in Moscow. Khmelnitsky's rebellion thus led to a new Polish-Russian war (1654-1667), in which the Poles suffered not only defeat and severe territorial losses, but also reaped the bitter harvest of nationalistic Russian hatred for Poland. The seeds of this hatred had already been sown by Orthodox-Catholic religious antagonism, which had been ripening since Polish military intervention during Russia's time of troubles.

Another dream of King Sigismund's, the expulsion of the infidel Turk from Europe by a Christian league under the leadership of the pope, the emperor, and the Christian kings,[27] used up Polish resources in blood and treasure for a century. The Turkish wars from 1589 to 1685 were not fought by Poland for nationally indifferent dynastic interests or as chimerically imperialistic adventures for aggrandizement. They were waged in a common European cause, to repel the intrusion of another culture from another continent.

The intrusion of the Turks into Europe became a serious threat to Poland in the middle of the sixteenth century, for three reasons. First, after the fall of Hungary in 1526, there was no other military power left in the middle zone to resist constant Ottoman expansion to the north. Second, Poland was open to Turkish inroads via the invasion corridor along the western shore of the Black Sea, through the Danubian Principality of Moldavia (in which some of the great Polish oligarchs had family interests), across the no-man's land of the southern Ukraine. It was also vulnerable from the adjacent Crimea, which was held by the sultan's Tartar vassals, remnants of the once mighty Golden Horde. Third, the unruly Cossacks on the lower course of the Dnieper could not be prevented from conducting private wars and raiding parties against the Moslems. Nor could they be kept from shifting sides as their mood and interests dictated, inciting Turkish or Tartar attacks against Poland. From the Ottoman point of view, the constant Cossack harassment was not only an annoyance but also a repeated strategic reminder that a flanking movement east of the Carpathians might place Turkish armies on the main east-west invasion route across Poland, leading straight into the heart of a Germany religiously and politically divided against itself.

In 1589, when the Cossacks repulsed a Tartar raid from the outskirts of Lvov and Tarnopol and continued in hot pursuit of the invaders into Ottoman territories, the Porte protested, and a Polish-Turkish war seemed imminent. It was averted only because the Diet refused to vote the king war credits. In 1593 the Cossacks, stirred up by the Habsburg emperor, again invaded Turkish territory, so that the Polish army was forced to march against the Crimean Tartars to forestall Turkish retaliation. In 1595 the Diet actually voted conditional subsidies for Polish participation in a Christian league against the Turks. However, it set conditions which could not be met. The emperor and the king of Spain would have had to join; the Habsburgs would have had to renounce their pretensions to the Polish throne and stay out of the Danubian principalities.[28] Consequently, peace continued to reign between Warsaw and Constantinople, except for a three-day battle at Cecora in Moldavia, which ended in a treaty establishing friendly relations between the two countries. With minor Cossack interruptions, the friendly relations lasted until 1613. Then the Cossacks, emboldened by Polish reverses in Moscow, launched a major attack down the Dnieper and across the Black Sea on the Turkish Anatolian coast, where they sacked the rich trading cities of Trebizond and Sinope. Again the Porte protested, and once more peace was temporarily preserved by Polish protestations of inability to control the Cossacks. But Cossack depredations went on for four years and made Polish-Turkish hostilities unavoidable.

At Kamieniec, north of the Dniester, the Poles were victorious in 1618, but in 1620 at Cecora, in the disputed province of Moldavia, they suffered a disastrous defeat. A year later another Polish-Turkish battle at Chocim ended in a draw. For nearly half a century the two potential adversaries were occupied at home with problems other than fighting each other. By 1676, however, the Turks were again on the offensive. They took Kamieniec, wrested Podolia from Poland under the Treaty of Buczacz in 1672, and forced Warsaw to recognize their protectorate over the Western Ukraine.

It was at this point that John III Sobieski (1674-1696), a man of providence, was elected king of Poland. He defeated the invading Turks at Lvov in 1675. In the Treaty of Zuravna in 1676, he regained some of the lost Ukrainian territories. Subsequently he conceived a grand strategy to end the Turkish threat to Poland through a joint diplomatic-military effort with the Habsburgs. An Austro-Polish alliance was initialled in September 1682.[29] It was approved by the Diet (in spite of resistance, intrigues, and foreign bribes to deputies) in April 1683. The bilateral treaty, open to all European sovereigns, provided for an offensive alliance against the Ottomans in the event that either Cracow or Vienna should be attacked by them. Should a *casus belli* arise, Poland would rush to the aid of the emperor with an army of 40,000 men; the emperor, to the rescue of the Poles with 60,000. The *casus belli* arose sooner than expected. The Turks hurled their armies against Vienna. On August 15, 1683, Sobieski marched out of Cracow at the head of an enlarged Polish army of 48,000 men to meet the Ottoman forces advancing across Hungary to besiege Vienna. The great Christian victory over the infidel under the walls of the imperial city [30] was not only a last glorious page in the long history of the Kingdom of Poland but also the signal given for the liberation of states and peoples who had long since lost their liberty. This was the brave, final effort of a state and people which lost their freedom before another century was over.

It may be rhetorical to describe liberty lost in Europe as the price paid for remaining European. In assessing the stark realities responsible for the disappearance of Bohemian, Moravian, Slovak, Polish, and Lithuanian independence, it is, however, logical to come to the conclusion that in the areas inhabited by these peoples dependence set in, as it had it the south, because geography, compounded by political, social, and economic factors, made defense impossible against attack from the nearest imperialism.

12

The Ottoman Rollback—
What Price Liberation?

The defense and relief of Vienna in 1683 were diplomatically and militarily preplanned operations. The pursuit of the defeated Turks from the walls of the imperial city into the Balkans was not. The rollback became a possibility, and then a reality, when the cocksure Turks, unaware of their progressing impotence, imprudently went on the offensive to convince the world and perhaps themselves that they were still the conquering great power they had once been in the fifteenth and sixteenth centuries. The Habsburg emperor, on the other hand, was unsure of the forces he could marshal for the defense of his capital, let alone for a possible pursuit of the besiegers, especially in view of French alarums and inroads in the west from across the Rhine. This western border strife was all but incessant from 1683 until the Peace of Utrecht in 1713. Still, Vienna had to be defended, come what might. Polish support had been pledged. Sobieski kept his word and Ottoman power was broken under the walls of the imperial city.

When the irresistibly furious charge of Sobieski's Poles and Charles of Lorraine's Germans down from the Kahlenberg heights above the city of the Habsburgs fragmented, crushed, and utterly routed the besieging Turks,[1] so that Grand Vizier Kara Mustafa took to flight and did not stop running until he reached Belgrade, it was revealed to the world that the Ottoman Empire had a fatal weakness that could not be left unexploited by its opponents. The pursuit began. In 1686, three years later, the old Hungarian capital Buda, in Turkish hands since 1541, was recaptured after a bloody siege. In four years, the imperial armies stood on the Lower Danube within the walls of Belgrade, where the Ottoman breakthrough had begun in

1526. In five years, they were victorious at Nish and Vidin, in the heart of the Balkans, where no Christian armies had trod since the days of the Hunyadis. In six years they reached and were checked at Kossovo, where exactly three centuries before, in 1389, the Serbs had gone down in defeat before the Ottoman onslaught.

The successes of the Habsburg armies and their allies during 1683-1689 had two side effects. First, the wavering populations north of the Danube, which in 1683 had not yet made up their minds whether they wanted to be liberated by the Germans from the Turks or by the Turks from the Germans, took sides. They began jumping on the imperial bandwagon, which seemed to be rolling with apparent ease after the fleeing Ottoman forces. South of the Danube the Bulgarians and the Serbs jumped too early; their ill-timed revolts occurred on the eve of the Habsburg defeat at Kossovo (1688-1689).[2] Those who could fled north with the retreating imperials; those who could not stayed on for two more centuries of Ottoman domination. North of the Danube, Thököli, the leader of the anti-Habsburg Hungarian resistance, stayed with the Turks till the bitter end. When, under their new and charismatic Grand Vizier Mustafa Köpörülli, the Turks began their counteroffensive in 1690, it was Thököli at the head of a Turkish-Tartar army who invaded Transylvania and inflicted a resounding defeat on the liberating Habsburg forces at Zernyest in 1690.[3]

The next step, after the Ottoman successes at Kossovo and Zernyest, was the Turkish recapture of Belgrade, the gate guarding the Hungarian plain. A Turkish reconquest of this region had to be prevented by the Habsburgs at all costs. The strategic task of containment was successfully carried out by Louis of Baden, the new imperial commander. The Turks were stopped at Szalankemen (1691), a short distance north of Belgrade and just south of the point where the Tisza River flows into the Danube. This was the bloodiest battle of the rollback. The northward-marching Ottoman army of 100,000 men left 20,000 dead on the battlefield, among them the Grand Vizier Mustafa Köpörülli himself. The Ottoman counteroffensive had failed and readvertised Ottoman debility.

The second side effect, which appeared a year after the relief of Vienna, was the formation in 1684 of an anti-Turkish military alliance uniting the papacy, the emperor, Poland, Venice, and eventually Russia, known as the Holy League.[4] This was the old dream of the popes and of Sigismund III of Poland come true: the grand, united Christian host assembled for the expulsion of the Turk from Europe. The imperial forces agreed to operate down through Hungary; the Poles, east of the Carpathians, via Moldavia; the Venetians, across the Adriatic into the Balkans. Later, the Russians moved in the direction of the Black Sea and the Crimea. The French, who had fought so bravely, though not too wisely, during the very early phase of the Turkish wars at Nicopolis in 1396, were now conspicuous by their absence. Indeed, the Habsburg-Polish alliance of 1683 and the Holy League of the following year were difficult diplomatic accomplishments, almost frustrated by the opposition of Louis XIV (1643-1715), an enemy of the emperor and an ally of the sultan.

On the eve of the rollback the interests of the European states, whose unity was necessary to launch any joint military action against the Turks, were in seemingly paralyzing conflict. Poland under Sobieski was French-oriented because French and Polish interests coincided in antagonism to expansionist Brandenburg and Sweden.[5] In the beginning France and Poland did not disagree, each for reasons of its own, on supporting Thököli's anti-Habsburg *kuruc* insurgents in Hungary. Both powers appreciated the fact that Thököli was a thorn in the flesh of the Habsburgs. It was only when a Turkish offensive against Vienna became once more a possibility that Sobieski, apprehensive over this Turkish vassal's control of the Carpathian passes from Slovakia into Poland, stopped his support of the *kuruc* (1682).[6] By dropping Thököli, Sobieski removed one obstacle from reaching a Polish-Habsburg entente, though Polish and Habsburg interests were still clashing for dynastic reasons in the Moldavian principality. But the most serious opposition to an alliance between Sobieski and the Emperor Leopold I (1658-1705) came from the king of France, whose main interest lay in promoting insecurity and in preparing, in case of European hostilities, a useful secondary theater of war in the rear of his Habsburg antagonist. To attain these objectives, Louis was ready to ally or associate himself with any anti-Habsburg force in the middle zone: the sultan, Thököli, or Sobieski, just as long as the king of Poland refrained from bolstering the emperor.at Vienna. Sobieski, however, entered into the Polish-Habsburg alliance of 1683, in disregard of Louis's objections.[7] This was a serious step in light of the close diplomatic and emotional ties between the two countries. Consequently, in 1684, after the relief of Vienna, French diplomacy was directed toward immobilizing or exploding the Holy League.[8] The time seemed opportune. The Habsburgs and the Venetians were disputing, in advance, sovereignty over Dalmatia. Sobieski, who had been treated by Emperor Leopold I with cold formality after his brilliant feat of arms at Vienna, had moved on to Moldavia, where he was doing very poorly. In the meantime the Russian advance toward the Black Sea and the Crimea had bogged down. Only the imperial forces were still being carried by their elan south into the Balkans and toward Constantinople. The interruption of their victorious advance and the end of the first phase of the rollback in 1689 at Kossovo was in no small measure due to the renewal of the war in the west, where the French again crossed the Rhine in 1688 into the Palatinate area surrounding Heidelberg. This was the beginning of a long European war, which required the transfer of imperial regiments from the eastern to the western front. Hostilities in the west did not end till the Treaty of Ryswick in 1697.

At last the results of the first rollback phase could be gathered. The gathering was done by a French military genius, Prince Eugene of Savoy (1663-1736), who had been contemptuously assigned by Louis XIV to a subordinate military command under one of the royal bastards.[9] The insulted and alienated prince managed to get higher military rank in the imperial forces from Louis's great adversary, the Habsburg emperor. By 1697 he was commanding on the Lower Danube, where he won the greatest and final victory of the first rollback phase at Zenta, below the confluence of the Tisza and Maros rivers. Zenta was a crushing defeat for the Ottomans. It forced them, after two years of negotiations, to accept the terms of the Peace of Karlowitz in 1699. Interestingly, the peace conference included not only the belligerents in the east, but also diplomatic teams sent by the maritime powers of England and Holland, enemies of Louis XIV's. The task of the English and Dutch emissaries was to speed the negotiations toward the best possible terms for the emperor, so as to free his forces for a likely resumption of the war in the west.[10] The probability was increasing that the emperor and his coastal allies would have to fight again soon to lay low the Sun King's hegemonial ambitions on the continent. United western diplomatic effort did succeed in getting the best possible terms. In the tents at Karlowitz, on the south bank of the Danube across from the modern Yugoslav provincial capital Novi Sad (Ujvidek), where the Ottoman delegates sat cross-legged on red plush divans, the Porte yielded the Habsburgs all of Hungary except the Banat of Temesvar (Timisoara) plus Transylvania, Slavonia, and Croatia. Venice got most of Dalmatia; Poland, Podolia.

Sixteen years of war, which had begun at Vienna, thus came to an end, to be followed by sixteen years of peace in the east, because of the approach and outbreak of the War of the Spanish Succession (1701-1713). Again, military operations in the west plus an anti-

Habsburg military diversion in Hungary supported by Versailles, made the continuation of the rollback impossible in the east. The diversion in Hungary was the national uprising under Prince Francis Rakoczi II, subsidized, and militarily assisted by Louis XIV. Rakoczi's freedom fight (1703-1711) became the eastern phase of the War of the Spanish Succession, a second front for the emperor, who, having regained Hungary from the Turks, then had to reconquer it from the Hungarians, while fighting the French in the west.[11]

As far as Louis was concerned, the Hungarian insurrection was a continuation by other means of French diplomacy which, since the days of Francis I (1515-1547) and Cardinal Richelieu (1622-1642), had sought to outflank the Habsburg emperor by making common cause with his actual or potential enemies to the east: the sultan, the German Protestants, the Swedes, the Poles, and the Hungarians. From the Hungarian insurgents' point of view, the national aim of re-establishing an independent and sovereign Hungary, as it had existed before 1526, except for an up-to-date centralized government, was contingent on obtaining the aid of an anti-Habsburg great power. Charles XII of Sweden (1697-1718) was approached early during the insurrection in 1704, but left Rakoczi's letter unanswered because he would not deal with rebels against their legitimate sovereign. Peter the Great of Russia (1682-1725) was less finical; he entered into a secret alliance with Rakoczi in Warsaw in 1707 and in 1711 personally met him on the Polish-Hungarian frontier as the freedom fight was approaching its unhappy end. The tsar, however, was unable to extend more than sympathy because of the unsuccessful war he was conducting against the Turks.[12]

This left the sultan and Louis XIV as the only two possible sources of outside support for Rakoczi. The first of these sources was politically undesirable. Weak Ottoman power could not have served as a barrier to Habsburg encroachment. Help from a resurgent and strong Turkish Empire, on the other hand, would have meant not the restoration of independent pre-1526 Hungary but a return to the vassal kingdom before Karlowitz. The only possible provider of foreign support was therefore Louis XIV. During his long reign (1643-1715) the Sun King had been a supporter of Francis Rakoczi's ambitious grandfather George Rakoczi II (1648-1660), who attempted but failed to emulate the precedent set by his predecessor Stephen Bathori (1533-1586) in rising from the princely Transylvanian to the royal Polish throne. These family connections are stressed in the correspondence exchanged between Rakoczi and Louis.[13] Versailles knew the Rakoczis as a princely and immensely wealthy post-

Mohacs landowning family who returned to the Catholic fold during the Counter Reformation, and had become leaders of the anti-Habsburg national resistance in Hungary. Francis Rakoczi II was the stepson of the *"kuruc*-king" Thököli, a descendant of the heroic Turk-resister Nicholas Zrinyi, and married a Princess Hesse-Rhein-fels from the empire. The haughty Louis XIV accepted the Rakoczis as protégés but, since they were rebels against his fellow-monarch, the emperor, never as allies.

The overall strategic concept of the new European war was a victorious advance of the French and allied Bavarian armies from the west to Vienna for a meeting with Rakoczi's Hungarians irrupt-ing into Austria from the east. But hope for this bearding of the emperor in his own den was soon and irretrievably lost after the Battle of Blenheim in 1704, in which Eugene of Savoy and Marl-borough stopped the Franco-Bavarian march down the Danube toward Vienna. Rakoczi's fate was sealed. In his post-Blenheim instruc-tions to the Marquis Pierre Puchot Des Alleurs, the French diplo-matic representative at Rakoczi's headquarters (he had no ambassa-dorial rank and also served as a cavalry general in engagements against the imperials), Louis's Foreign Minister, the Marquis Jean-Baptiste Colbert de Torcy expressed the hope that "the Hungarians might be kept in arms until the end of the Spanish War." [14] Rakoczi had been asking for a French landing on the Adriatic coast of the Balkans and for funds to raise an auxiliary army of Albanian mer-cenaries. When help via the Balkan littoral failed to materialize, *pourparlers* and truce negotiations with Vienna began and contin-ued through 1706. As at Karlowitz in 1699, English and Dutch diplomatic observers were present, because London and The Hague had a vital interest in getting Rakoczi off the emperor's back so that the war against the French king might be prosecuted in the west without a diversionary drain on the allied forces.[15] A truce was ar-ranged but lasted less than a year. The rebel Hungarian Estates convoked by Rakoczi then voted and proclaimed the dethronement of the Habsburg family in Hungary in 1707. The prince sought to place on the vacant Hungarian throne either the Bavarian Elector Maximilian Emanuel or the Prussian Crown Prince Frederick Wil-liam. For himself he was content with his election as reigning Prince of Transylvania and Prince-Commander of Hungary.

The imperial forces then went into a major offensive against the menacing Rakoczi, while keeping a weather eye on the Turks still north of the Danube in the Banat. The *kuruc* armies, reeling under the imperials' blows, retreated step by step, their ranks thinned by defections to the emperor and by the ravages of the plague, whose victims were in the hundreds of thousands. In April 1711 the insurrection ended in a surrender without the consent of its supreme commander, who fled via Poland to Versailles. He ended his days in Turkey, "cultivating his garden" on the shore of the Sea of Marmara, in a glimpse caught and left for posterity by Voltaire in the epilogue to his *Candide*. The Peace of Szatmar in 1711 between the emperor and the *kuruc* made twice-reconquered Hungary safe, it was thought, for Habsburg centralism and absolutism. It also permitted, after the end of the Spanish war and the death of Louis XIV in 1715, the resumption of the Habsburg military effort to roll back Ottoman power farther south in the Balkans.[16]

In the year of the Sun King's death the Turks were readvertising their enfeebled state to the world by a dismal showing in the war against Venice. In the meantime French expansionism had been checked (at least until the Revolution and the Napoleonic Wars) by the treaties of Utrecht in 1713 and Rastatt in 1714. The second phase of the rollback thus became a strategic possibility. Prince Eugene, again in command on the Danube after his great triumphs with Marlborough in the west, resumed the offensive and led his armies to victory in 1716 over the Turks at Petrovaraden (Petervarad). A year later he recaptured the key fortress of Belgrade. These imperial victories ended the second liberating phase under the terms of the Treaty of Passarowitz in 1718. Peace was made in a small village south of the Danube and east of the Vardar. The Porte had to cede, on top of the territorial losses it had sustained at Karlowitz, the Banat of Temesvar, Cis-Oltenian Wallachia, and northern Serbia. With these cessions, the rollback reached the line below the Danube, where the northernmost limits of Ottoman advance had lain at the end of the fifteenth century, in the days of Matthias Corvinus.

But for the Spanish war and the Rakoczi uprising, the interrupted rollback might have been resumed perhaps sixteen years sooner. Among the grievances which had triggered the Hungarian insurrection was the unbearable price the country being liberated had to pay for its new Turk-free status. In the beginning, during the early 1680s, the war effort and military operations were financed out of the papal treasury and from the income of the large Church estates in Habsburg Hungary. In the mid-eighties, however, the liberating armies were kept in the field by taxes levied to a large extent on the liberated populations. The Hungarian share in the military taxes collected fluctuated between 51 and 75 per cent of the total war appropriations.[17] In the meantime the country was devastated and depopulated by two armies, the advancing imperials and the retreating Turks. To both sides the land fought over was a conquered province in the process of being evacuated by the Turks and invaded by the Germans. The attacking Christian armies numbered fifty to sixty thousand men, who had to be supplied, fed, billeted, and transported. After 1685 the liberated populations were made responsible for these logistical functions. Reconquered areas were placed under military rule, marked by anarchy, brutality, and corruption. Fortunes were made not only by suppliers to the imperial armies but also by local commanders from the highest to the lowest ranks. Even common soldiers got their share of the booty by engaging in rarely controlled pillage, extortion, arson, rape, and robbery. The soldiery acted like a state within the state. It arrogated to itself the right to erect customs barriers and checkpoints on roads, bridges, or even at ordinary sentry posts to collect payments of arbitrarily assessed duty. Commanders of forts had self-issued licenses for the sale of liquor and meat. High-ranking officers were also in the duty-free cattle-export business. Pfeffershoven, the military commandant of Buda in 1690, levied a special tithe on the inhabitants of the town, payable in wine. His officers extorted *robota* or forced labor from the townspeople.[18] Sociologically and economically military rule in reconquered areas at the end of the seventeenth century resembled unbridled feudal exactions from the peasantry during the introduction of serfdom at the beginning of the sixteenth.

The imperial treasury itself was being drained by the mounting cost of the rollback. A financial genius by the name of Hans Samuel Oppenheimer, (†1703),[19] resembling in the wizardry of his transactions his Scotch contemporary John Law (1671-1729) of "Mississippi Bubble" fame, managed to cover the rising deficit of the state for the first two decades of the campaign. He did so through the issuance of copper coins, devaluation, introduction of indirect and hidden taxation, as well as by the granting and renting of monopolies for the sale of salt, tobacco, cattle, wheat, wine, textiles, coffee, hops, mineral water, scythes, playing cards, chocolate, and vegetable oil.[20] These were only temporary remedies. By 1698 the state deficit rose to catastrophic proportions. Taxes had to be doubled in and behind the areas of military operations. One-sixteenth of the new taxes were assessed on the towns, two-thirds on the serfs, and one-third on the indignant nobility. In 1702 a large area in the central plains was sold to the Teutonic Knights for half a million florins. When Oppenheimer died, there was no one to fill his shoes. The imperial treasury in 1703 was unable to make good a five-million-florin line of credit and went into a state of undeclared bankruptcy.[21] The deficit had to be shifted to the population in the form of new military exactions.

At the approach of the imperial armies the villagers took to flight. Depopulation of habitable areas, in process since the Ottoman breakthrough in 1526, spread. Once fertile regions deteriorated into scraggy, scrubby, fallow wastes covered by impenetrable brushwood or into impassable sodden swampland. The population of the territories being liberated, which had been somewhere between four and five million at the end of the fifteenth century, was estimated, in spite of the large influx of refugees from the south, at about three or four million at the end of the seventeenth century.[22] The largest and most populous city in the lowlands was the "Calvinist Rome," Debrecen, with a population of 12,000. The ruins left in Buda by the siege were razed and the rubble used to fill in and terrace the area around the medieval palace to serve as a firm foundation for the new Habsburg royal castle.[23] Across the river, in Buda's twin city Pest, only 228 houses were left standing in 1696.[24] Having observed the process of depopulation and environmental decay, the loyalist Prince Paul Esterhazy dared to warn the emperor himself: "What will it profit Your Majesty to rule over nought but forests and desolate mountains?"[25] In his petitions Esterhazy estimated that during the first two years of liberation the populations freed from the Turks had to pay to the invading Christian soldiery more than the Ottomans had extorted from them during the entire preceding century. Military depredations, forced levies, and spoliations had, according to the prince, produced endemic famine and driven the population to suicide, the murder of family members, flight by the thousands, or to selling their children, wives, and young daughters to foreign soldiers. Incidentally, having obtained the salt monopoly in the closing years of the seventeenth century, the Esterhazys were not doing badly for themselves financially. But at least they showed social conscience at this early stage, as they showed a flair for artistic patronage at the end of the eighteenth century.

The dominant economic philosophy in the Habsburg empire at the turn of the seventeenth into the eighteenth century was mercantilism, the program to produce national wealth by attaining trade and payment surpluses measurable in gold specie. In this scheme the role assigned to the reconquered territories was similar to that given to the Indian and American colonies of the contemporary maritime powers: to supply raw materials for the industrializing metropolis at a minimum cost and to serve as marketing outlets at a maximum price. The task of devising and putting into effect a general economic policy for the regained territories of the Crown of St. Stephen was entrusted in 1688 by the emperor to Bishop Leopold Kollonich (1631-1707), a loyal Germanized Croatian. The bishop is reputed to have declared, with reference to both the collapsing economic situation and the heavy Protestant coloration of the Hungarian populations re-emerging from Turkish rule, that the reconstruction agenda should consist in "making the Hungarians first paupers and then Catholics." [26] As for the "heretical" Rumanians and Ruthenians in the eastern provinces, they were to be weaned from Orthodox allegiance and brought into "Uniate" Greek Catholic churches organized on the model of the Polish Union of Brest of 1596.

Yet Bishop Kollonich was not without some enlightened ideas. His economic planning included ending the tax exemption of the nobility, the gradual reduction of internal duties levied on domestic commerce, the development of towns through municipal self-government independent of the surrounding county authority, the modernization of the courts of justice, the resettlement of depopulated areas by the encouragement of immigration, the introduction of standard weights and measures, and higher pay for schoolmasters. He had a hard time trying to carry out his ideas.[27]

The bishop's plan was not accepted by the emperor because of strong opposition by both the foreign military and the native nobility. Yet, individual features of the plan were independently adopted and carried out. Thus, in November 1696 Kollonich was ordered by Leopold I to inform the Hungarian aristocracy and high clergy that thenceforth they also would have to shoulder part of the tax burden. When the spokesman of the nobles indignantly protested that a change in existing tax laws could be made only by the Estates (which had last met in 1687 to vote the Hungarian crown hereditary in the male line of the Habsburg family, in gratitude for the recapture of Buda during the preceding year), the emperor refused to convoke the Estates and used the imperial army to collect taxes if not from the top aristocrats, at least from segments of the lesser nobility. The plans for urbanization were also pushed. The towns received German and South Slav artisans; the villages, especially in the southern (now Yugoslav and Rumanian) areas, immigrants recruited from all parts of Central and Western Europe. The colonists were enticed by exemptions from taxation and by other allurements both economic and administrative. Decrees issued in 1722-1723 had granted immigrant farmers tax exemptions for six years, immigrant artisans for fifteen.[28] The result was the greatest immigration movement of European populations prior to the trans-Atlantic wave of resettlers in the New World during the late nineteenth century. A side effect was a radical alteration in the original ethnic composition of the reconquered and depopulated territories. Because of immigration, the population doubled to about nine and a half million by the end of the eighteenth century. The Magyar ethnic element was swamped by the influx, thus losing its absolute majority.

An interesting feature of the way in which the titles of landownership in the reacquired areas were dealt with was the preference shown the clergy over the nobles. This was so presumably because the former had financed the early rollback and were greatly in demand by the devout Habsburgs to further the work of the Counter Reformation. The *Commissio neoacquisitica,*[29] organized to preside over the reacquisition of landed property once held in formerly Ottoman-occupied areas, returned estates free of charge only to ecclesiastical owners. Nobles claiming their former property had to submit documentary evidence to a title search. If the title was certified by the *Commissio,* the noble titleholder could re-enter his property only after paying a fee amounting to 10 per cent of the assessed land value. This established his exemption from military service, which was an indirect way of extending taxation to the nobility. Municipalities also were assessed taxes before they could repossess landed property they had held before the coming of the Turks. If titles could not be established to the satisfaction of the *Commissio* or taxes and fees paid by the claimant as assessed, landed property reverted to the imperial treasury. There it was used to pay debts outstanding to army suppliers or to reward deserving military officers and civilian bureaucrats in the form of land grants.

The political price for liberation was paid by the liberated partly at once and partly on an installment plan over the next two centuries. As in the more fortunate countries of the west, though retarded by about half a century, the emerging centralized monarchy's modernizing tendencies provoked the resistance of the nobles, who were jealously guarding their archaic constitutional liberties. Even under Rakoczi, during the most critical periods of the freedom fight, the landowning nobility was able to enforce its constitutional right —since the *Tripartitum* of 1514—to obtain the return under military guard of serfs serving in the *kuruc* armies without the permission of their masters.[30] Against the foreign Habsburg dynasty, ruling from Vienna, the nobility put up an even more assiduous resistance in defense of its constitutional prerogatives. As noted before, these privileges included freedom from military service, exemption from taxation, and the right to prevent or cancel the free movement of serfs away from the estates. Because these were native liberties threatened by a foreign dynasty, the resistance of the nobles was seen in a xenophobic and nationalistic light by the rest of the population. The burghers in the towns, even when they bore German names, were resentful of the depredations of the imperial troops and looked to ancient charters to maintain their autonomy against military rule. The process of alienating the townspeople was begun as early as 1685 by the imperial General Antonio Caraffa (1646-1693). This military martinet started by laying a special military levy of 1.8 million florins on the lowland town of Debrecen, which at that time had a population of only about ten thousand. Then he continued by setting up bloody assizes in the northern town of Preshov (Eperjes) to stamp out an allegedly "widespread and dangerous" conspiracy. Between March and May 1687, death sentences were passed and executed on twenty-four burghers and nobles, whose names (Keczer, Feldmayer, Zimmermann, Rakovszky, Medveczky, Palasthy, etc.) [31] indicated the forging of an incipient national unity among ethnically and socially heterogeneous elements by the depredations of a foreign invading army.

The impoverished peasantry ranged itself on the side of the nobles and the burghers against the Habsburgs. They were driven to despair by the heavy tax burden, the excesses of the imperial army, and abductions by military press gangs. Like the Cossack host of Bogdan Khmelnitsky a century earlier, the *kuruc* armies of both Thököli and Rakoczi were swollen by desperate serfs who had been promised emancipation and relief from feudal obligations if they continued to serve until victory. But victory was to perch on the imperial banners and not on the *kuruc* standards. The landowning nobility continued its resistance to the modernizing but foreign Habsburgs. In the meantime the peasants' lot was not improving. The last notable rising of the serfs between the second and third phases of the rollback took place in 1735, when the Magyar rustics of Bekes on the middle Tisza joined forces with the Serb military under Pero Segedinatz on the Lower Danube in a typical *Jacquerie,* which was suppressed by the authorities with the customary severity.[32]

The third rollback phase was opened in 1737 by a joint Habsburg-Romanov offensive against the Turks. The latter retreated down to Nish but then counterattacked and advanced to Belgrade. There in 1739 the Porte succeeded in depriving the Habsburgs of all their gains made twenty-one years earlier at Passarowitz. Once again north Serbia, Cis-Oltenia, and Belgrade came under Ottoman rule. For the next one hundred years the Habsburgs had to be satisfied with the Danube and the Sava rivers as the frontier between the two neighboring empires ruled from Vienna and Constantinople.

The portentous feature of the third rollback phase was the joint move by the Austrians and the Russians against the Turks. This military co-operation foreshadowed a developing political rivalry between these two powers in the Balkans. The prize of the contest was the territorial legacy of the receding Ottoman Empire. Both the first and second rollback phases had been stopped by the French wars the Habsburgs fought in the west. The third and fruitless phase could not be continued because of Prussian attacks from the northwest against the integrity of the Habsburg possessions. Vienna was too exhausted by the War of the Austrian Succession (1740-1748) and by the Seven Years' War (1756-1763) to start a fourth liberating phase. But while the Austrians were licking their wounds, the Russians under Catherine the Great (1762-1796) began making headway against the Turks in their private war of 1768-1774. It was at the end of this conflict, with the Treaty of Kuchuk Kainarji in 1774, that the ruler of the Russians was recognized by the vanquished Turks as protector of the sultan's Christian subjects in the Balkans and in the Holy Land. It was also in the course of this war that the seemingly imminent Russian annexation of Moldavia prompted Frederick the Great of Prussia to propose the fateful diplomatic step which led to the disappearance of Poland from the map between 1772 and 1795.

The closing years of the eighteenth century in the middle zone thus brought great changes. The Carpathian basin shifted in dependence from Turkish to Austrian overlords who were already in control of Turk-free Bohemia. The Balkans remained under a decaying Ottoman domination, which provoked Russian-Austrian rivalry. In the meantime the Polish-Lithuanian federation was moving toward dismemberment by its imperial Russian, Prussian, and Austrian neighbors.

Liberation had come at a high price to the inhabitants of the plains and mountains north of the Danube. It was disappointing and exacerbating to masses of the liberated. New patterns of resistance and collaboration emerged. If liberation did come about, it was not only because of strategic compulsion on the part of one great power to exploit an unexpected revelation of weakness by an imperial rival, who was fast becoming known as the "Sick Man" of Europe:

there were other deep pyschological reasons as well. The prestigious leader of the west at the end of the seventeenth century was not a distant, idealistically theorizing figure, but the Habsburg emperor, who sat in the eastern marches of the west, in Vienna. He had vested interests—royal crowns, realms, estates, and other income-producing enticements in the middle zone. The emperor also had an unwavering religious commitment to a still powerful crusading creed. His family tradition inspired him not only to further dynastic interests by happily marrying while others were making war, but also to send forth conquering armies when the constellation of European powers appeared propitious for the success of his arms. All these psychological motivations must be taken into account if we want to understand the conduct of the rollback between the relief of Vienna in 1683 and the territorial gains made at Passarowitz in 1718. The reward to the Habsburgs for the exertions and sacrifices of the thirty-five years between these two military-political milestones was exactly two more centuries of grandeur, until 1918.

13

The Other Sick Man—
Poland Partitioned

For reasons inexplicable to the student of history, the closing years of the seventeenth century constituted one of those periods of recurrent, sweeping historical change during which the old order yields to the new. In coastal Europe old dynasties were being replaced by antithetical successors: Catholicizing Stuarts by Protestant Hanoverians (after an interlude under the House of Orange) in England; German-Burgundian Habsburgs by French Bourbons in Spain. In landlocked Europe the fateful year of 1697 saw both the epoch-making victory of Prince Eugene over the Turks at Zenta and the bodeful ascension of the Saxon Wettins to the Polish throne. The victory of Zenta in the south signalled the replacement of Ottoman by Habsburg overlordship in the central tier of the middle zone. In the north two generations of Wettins (1697-1763) presided over the course of the fateful political debility which rendered Poland unfit to survive the adverse changes occurring around it.

Until its shipwreck at the end of the century, the unseaworthy Polish ship of state sailed perilous seas, manned by a crew drunk with self-interest. The ebbing of Ottoman power in the south went on apace with a rising tide of Prussian, Russian, and Austrian imperialism in the north. Dependence was thus not disappearing with the receding Turkish flood. It was in fact expanding from the south, where the sultan was yielding to the Habsburg emperor, to the north, where Berlin and St. Petersburg as well as Vienna were at the beginning of a historical process which before the century was out provided them with common frontiers in the heart of the Polish state. The only improvement in the situation was a decrease in cultural divisiveness: while the area of Asiatic dependence was shrinking, that of European imperial rule was spreading.

The shifting power balance during the opening years of the eighteenth century induced a dismembering and partitioning fever in the European powers. They were ravenously watching not only the infidel Turk but each other as well for signs of weakness. The Ottoman doom was sealed when the Turkish armies went into a headlong flight after their failure to take Vienna in 1683. Then the Habsburg control over their vast domains was placed in jeopardy by the imminent extinction of their male line. The Emperor Charles VI (1685-1740) concluded that he was unlikely to leave a son to wear his crown. To prevent the extinction of his dynasty, he therefore gave orders for the drafting and promulgation of the Habsburg family law known as the Pragmatic Sanction.[1] This law provided for dynastic succession in the Habsburg female line and declared Habsburg-ruled states "indivisibly and inseparably" united. In 1713 the Pragmatic Sanction was accepted in the Austrian hereditary provinces as a binding family law. It assumed the force of public law upon enactment by an affirmative vote in the Estates of Transylvania during 1722 and also in the Estates of Hungary during 1723. The Austrian enactment of 1713 and the Hungarian version voted in 1723 agreed on the point of succession in the female line but contained divergencies [2] on the handling of "joint affairs"—state debt, shared budget, interstate commerce, customs management, etc. —of the Habsburg empire. During the following century these differences led to near disruption and a radical reorganization of the Habsburg monarchy.

There was trouble brewing in Versailles also. French hegemonial ambitions were checked by the fiasco of Louis XIV's costly wars, which left France too exhausted to prevent the dismemberment of Spain's European empire. Spanish Belgium, Naples, and Sardinia went to the Habsburgs at Utrecht in 1713. The following year at Rastatt, France's middle-zone clients, Rakoczi's Hungary and Transylvania, were also recognized as Habsburg possessions. This left Poland, a shadow of its former self under Sobieski, as the next logical victim for territorial cannibalism by its neighbors. In secret *pourparlers*, Poland's first Saxon king, Augustus II (1697-1733), was already offering his newly won kingdom for partition to further his personal, half-cocked schemes.[3]

The history of Poland during the eighteenth century provides a unique, egregious, and terrifying example of a state heedlessly preparing and blithely rushing to its own destruction. During the seventeenth century Poland had fast become a political paradox.[4] The whole political structure was kept in a state of precarious equilibrium by a system of checks and balances among the legislature, the senate, and the king. Both within and beyond the legislative body, the system was controlled by an asocial and factitious dictatorship of the nobility. On reaching a deadlock in the legislature, or in a struggle against the king, opposing factions proceeded against each other by forming constitutionally recognized armed confederations. Unlike the Diet these Solemn Leagues and Covenants required, not unanimity, but only a majority vote in their action against rival formations.[5] The end result was the perpetuation of embattled extraparliamentary factionalism among the ruling elite. The factions developed the habit of making appeals for arbitration to outside powers, even though these had designs on Poland's territorial integrity.

By the beginning of the great and shattering European wars of dynastic succession and territorial spoliation in 1701, Poland was a house divided against itself, threatened with foreclosure by its neighbors, but prevented by irrationally quaint domestic customs from acting in unison to forestall seizure. The throttling parliamentary device which could and did prevent united action was known as the *liberum veto*. This was a sole dissenting vote cast in the Diet, which could not only block passage of a particular piece of legislation but also had the procedural force of "breaking up" or terminating whole sessions of the Diet, thus rendering invalid all other laws already enacted by it. Given the poverty and the venality of the lower nobility, any parliamentary action which was needed to steer a course beneficial to the state but was opposed by vested interests, domestic or foreign, could be easily stopped by bribery. Patriotic, enlightened, and deeply apprehensive Poles sought to arrest this headlong rush toward self-destruction in the increasingly menacing international climate. Uppermost in the minds of such people as the century progressed was the burning question: would the Polish political system be reformed before the Polish state was overtaken by irrevocable calamity?

By the time reform came, in 1791, it was too late. During the preceding century, beginning as early as 1645, in interaction with social, economic, religious, and other political symptoms of decadence, the *liberum veto* was a spade in the hands of Poland's gravediggers. On the eve of the Khmelnitsky uprising in 1645, a single dissenting vote cast in the Diet prevented an appropriation of funds necessary to equip an army against the threatening Tartars.[6] When King

Vladislas proceeded nevertheless to recruit effectives, the Diet compelled him to abandon all military preparations. When the Cossacks in due course learned of the parliamentary opposition to strengthening the military forces, they entered into alliance with the Tartars and attacked and defeated a royal army sent against them. The terrible uprising of the Cossacks and serfs, aided by the Tartars, began. It led to the loss of the Ukraine.

Another notorious exercise of the *liberum veto* occurred in the Diet of 1652, when in the controversy between King Jan Casimir and the Radziwill family, the session was "broken" by a *szlachta* hanger-on of the latter.[7] All he had to do was cast the fateful veto and then walk out of the Diet chamber. By 1658 the increasingly frequent use of this nefarious parliamentary device had produced parliamentary paralysis (five Diets were "broken up" between 1658 and 1668),[8] extending all the way down to the dietines or district assemblies. The Swedes were invading. The defending Polish armies were in a state of recurrent mutiny for not receiving their pay, which could not be voted by the Diets. The king in 1658 proposed the replacement of unanimity rule by majority vote, but his proposal was defeated. John Sobieski's preparations against the Turks were greatly handicapped by the continuing use of the *liberum veto*. In 1681 the Diet debating military appropriations was broken up by another petty noble in the pay of Sobieski's inveterate enemy, the Hohenzollern Prince Frederick William.[9] Prussian, French, and Russian agents were hovering around the Diet, lobbyists for foreign powers, tempting and seducing venal deputies with bribes.[10] During the year of Vienna's liberation in 1683, the price of the *liberum veto* was quoted at 100,000 gold pieces in the parliamentary corridors, but patriotic fervor ran so high during that year that the standing offer found no taker even among the most corrupt of the deputies.[11] Still patriots and scoundrels continued to coexist. Under the Polish parliamentary system one scoundrel out of 182 deputies [12] was enough to bring deliberations to a dead halt and to cancel all legislature already voted.

The situation continued to deteriorate under the Wettin dynasty. Available statistics indicate that half of the Polish Diets biennially assembled during the first twenty years of the eighteenth century were broken up.[13] The ratio rose to between 50 and 60 per cent between 1720 and 1740; during 1740-1760 every single Diet was dissolved and dispersed without being able to enact any legislation or to solve any national problem.[14] This spectacle gave rise to the axiom freely bandied about by German and Russian diplomatists of the period that "despite their eight centuries of history, the Poles were incapable of independence." [15] Indeed, the Poles seemed to be motivated by a political death wish for dependence.

During the year of interregnum that elapsed between the extinction of the Saxon dynasty in 1763 and the election of Stanislas Poniatowski as the last king of Poland in 1764, the movement for parliamentary reform and abolition of the *liberum veto* gathered momentum. The new king and his kinsmen, the Czartoryski family, were for abolition. Their intellectual alimentation, which reinforced their political conviction to bring about reform, came from a work by the great Catholic-Piarist educator, the Abbé Stanislas Konarski. entitled *On the Effective Conduct of Debates,* in four volumes, written between 1744-1748 but not published until 1761-1763.[16] Konarski proposed far-reaching reforms of the Polish political system on the English model, including the replacement of unanimity rule by majority vote as a requirement of parliamentary approval. But this noble resolve came to nought against the insidious and Machiavellian resistance of a succession of astute Russian diplomatists—Kayserling, Saldern, Repnin, and Stackelberg, ably assisted by such highly sophisticated Prussian colleagues as Benoit and Solms—whose instructions specified and whose secret funds provided the means for preventing reform and keeping the *liberum veto* in force.

The ostensible reason for Russo-Prussian intervention in Polish internal affairs was the issue of the Dissidents—non-Roman Catholic Christians in Poland—whom Orthodox Russia and Protestant Prussia agreed to take under their protection in the secret articles of their Treaty of Mutual Defense, signed for twenty years in 1762. The religious pretext for diplomatic and military intervention worked so well in the case of Poland that twelve years later the Russians used it again in the Treaty of Kutchuk Kainardji to establish treaty rights for the protection of the sultan's Christian subjects.

The Dissidents consisted of about two hundred thousand Protestants in western Poland and of perhaps from three to four million Russian Orthodox in the eastern provinces and Lithuania. The early onset of the Counter Reformation had changed the tolerant visage of Polish Catholicism by the early eighteenth century. Until the rise of Prussia as a great power around 1700, Polish Protestants had been without political utility to any nearby, potential intruder planning to carry out a disruptive design. As, however, the fortunes of Prussia rose, those of the Protestants in Poland declined, creating the possibility of a diplomatically reasoned Prussian intervention on their behalf. While the Habsburg armies were driving the Turks below the Lower Danube from Protestant-inhabited territories in the south, in Poland official energies were being used to exclude Calvinists and Lutherans (the Unitarians had been driven out in 1658) from the national and provincial legislatures, from the Senate, and from the bench. The right to build churches was taken away from Protestants in 1717. In 1724, during a riot in the town of Torun (Thorn), the Host and the image of the Virgin were desecrated by an iconoclastic Protestant mob. The incident [17] might have passed without being noticed beyond Poland had it not been for the severity of the penalties meted out. Not only were the Protestants deprived of one of their churches, which was turned into a Catholic place of worship, but ten death sentences were imposed and carried out: one on the burgomaster for being derelict in his duties in not preventing the desecration and nine on actual participants in the riot. This was grist to the Prussian mill. A formal diplomatic protest from Frederick William I of Prussia was joined not only by Peter the Great but also by the new Hanoverian King George I of England. By 1733, the opening year of a war which saw foreign armies on Polish soil, Polish Protestants had become a disfranchised minority barred from holding any office except, within established quotas, in the heavily German-populated towns of Danzig and Torun.

As for the Russian-speaking Orthodox millions in the east, the establishment of the Uniate Church at Brest in 1595 was considered by devout Catholic Poles only a first step in bringing Greek schismatics back into the Roman fold. The Uniate hierarchy—metropolitan, archbishop, and bishops—were excluded from the Senate, where their Roman Catholic confreres held seats ex officio.[18] The equal civil status of their Ruthenian flock remained a promise on paper. The vast majority of Orthodox peasants, serfs, and Cossacks, had only obligations and no privileges, except, if "registered," to serve in the army of the Polish king. This was considered an honor.

By 1766 the stage had therefore been set for Russia and Prussia to come to the rescue of their oppressed coreligionists in Poland. So convincing was their case, that the Protestant powers of Great Britain and Denmark innocently joined in their protest. The four demanded the restoration to the oppressed Polish antipapists of their ancient rights and privileges. These included rights taken for granted for Protestants (though not for Catholics) in England, Denmark, Holland, Scandinavia, and other Protestant countries, but having a propensity for political dynamite in retrograde Poland. Prussia and Russia asked for freedom of Protestant and Orthodox beliefs, worship, instruction, removal of official disabilities, and equality before the law. These extorted Dissident rights were subsequently listed in a treaty imposed on Poland in 1768. So was the immutability, except for some minor alleviations, of the unreformed Polish constitution: an elective king and *liberum veto* in all essential matters as well as continued feudal privileges. Russian and Prussian interests demanded a perpetuation of Polish internal weaknesses. Ironically the sole Polish deputy ready to cast a *liberum veto* against the retention of the *liberum veto* had to flee the Diet building for his life.[19] Two confederations were then formed, one with Protestants among the leaders, the other under Catholic resisters. An appeal for Russian support by the opponents of reform (who presented themselves as proponents of religious toleration) placed Russian forces stationed in Poland at the disposal of this antireform and avowedly pro-Dissident confederation.

The presence of foreign armies, including Russians, on Polish territory was hardly a novelty at this late date. It had occurred as early as the Great Northern War of 1700-1721. During this conflict Swedish troops invaded Poland, took Warsaw and Cracow; Prussian forces occupied Szczecin (Stettin); and the armies of Peter the Great (who was an ally of Poland's Saxon King Augustus the Strong) freely maneuvered and countermaneuvered on Polish territory. Russian forces next invaded Poland as enemies during the War of the Polish Succession (1733-1735), which was fought over the rivalry for the Polish throne of the Russian-supported Saxon Augustus II and the native Polish pretender Stanislas Leszczynski,[20] Louis XV's father-in-law. The war ended with the enthronement of the Russian candidate, Augustus III, and the final exile of Leszczynski. At Vienna, where peace was made in 1735, Austria tacitly acknowledged a Russian protectorate over Poland. At the Treaty of Belgrade in 1739, which ended a Russo-Turkish war (during which Polish territory was repeatedly violated), the usual clause guaranteeing Polish territorial integrity was omitted without explanation.

The next two great wars of territorial spoliation, the War of the Austrian Succession (1740-1748) and the Seven Years' War (1756-1763), withdrew the preoccupation of the European powers from Poland to the Habsburg domains and also to France's North American empire. But the Poles could not safeguard their territorial inviolability by remaining outside the conflict. Russian armies marched unimpeded through Poland and Lithuania twice in 1748, and again in 1756, 1758, 1759, and 1761. The Prussian army did likewise on several occasions between 1759-1761. From 1758 on there were Russian garrisons more or less permanently stationed in Great Poland, the area which included Warsaw, Poznan, and reached the Baltic coast at Danzig.

A year after the treaties of Paris and Hubertusburg in 1763, in which France lost Canada to the British and Prussia was confirmed in its possession of the Habsburg province of Silesia, Berlin and St. Petersburg once again turned their attention to the inert and chaotic Polish state. Undefended and indefensible Polish territories provided an irresistible temptation to both. A Russo-Prussian treaty in 1764 placed on the Polish throne, in effect, one of the Empress Catherine's discarded lovers, Stanislas Poniatowski—suave, sophisticated, patriotic, but not a leader of men. The treaty also provided for co-operation between the two powers in Poland and contained a clause placing the oppressed Dissidents (Protestant as well as Orthodox) under the protection of the Prussian and Russian monarchs. Consequently, when civil war broke out in Poland in 1768-1770 between the anti-reform and pro-Dissident Confederation of Radom, financed and supported by Russia and Prussia, and the proreform, anti-Russian Confederation of Bar, sympathetically treated by distant France and decadent Turkey, the three essential elements of a two-power intervention—a *casus belli* (protection of the Dissidents), a Russo-Prussian entente (the treaty of 1764), and the military instrument (Russian and Prussian armies of occupation in still sovereign Poland)—were present. It was then possible to reduce Poland to a state of dependence.

The Polish Civil War of 1768-1770 was, however, not a completely foreign-engineered domestic disturbance to justify intervention. It was also a culmination of long-brewing social and economic discontent. The decline and fall of Poland during the eighteenth century exhibited symptoms familiar to students of the dissolution of the Roman Empire fourteen centuries earlier. There was the same concentration of purchasing power in the hands of the minority group of patricians and latifundia owners, who spent it on imports of luxury goods. Since the value of these imports exceeded the income to the state provided by exports (in spite of a modest economic revival and upswing in the production of textiles, pottery, and mining toward the middle of the century),[21] a chronically unfavorable balance of trade had developed. The growing atrophy of trade led to the decline of the cities. The wars of succession and territorial spoliation, for which Poland had become a theater of military operations, turned decline into urban devastation and ruination. The picture the great Polish noble Anton Potocki left of his country in the middle of the eighteenth century is not much different from the Hungarian Prince Esterhazy's melancholy description of his war-ravaged homeland during the early part of the same century. "The ruin of the cities is so universal and so evident," wrote Potocki in 1744, "that with the single exception of Warsaw the best ones in the country can well be compared to caves of robbers." [22] Other contemporary observers speak of the disappearance of the Polish burghers, the complete vanishing of once prosperous towns, people living in the cellars of ruined mansions, foreign armies quartered in the streets, a few wretched householders trying to eke out a miserable living in the rubble of collapsed buildings. [23] The Reconstruction Commission appointed by King Stanislas Poniatowski in 1765 reported a composite urban picture in the words: "Every street an open field, every square a desert." [24] Security of person and possession was threatened, even in Warsaw, which managed to triple its population from the mid-seventeenth century to the mid-eighteenth to about 100,000, but the nobles lived in fortified enclosures during the increasingly turbulent sessions of the Diet.

Nor were social conditions in the Polish countryside in the eighteenth century much different from the plight of the small farmers in the Apennine peninsula during the declining years of Rome. The series of wars had depopulated the agricultural areas and left them fallow. Serfdom brought about greater degradation. In western Poland serfs could be seen wearing boots, but in Lithuania they walked barefoot. [25] There were estates where the *corvée* had risen to six days a week. Elsewhere serfs could be bought and sold. In the southeastern part of the country, where socioeconomic antagonism between serf and master was heightened by ethnic and religious differences between Poles and Ukrainians, Catholics and Orthodox, peasant riots with increasing frequency accompanied the decline of Polish authority. The subsequent proclamation of Catherine the Great to Europe in July 1772 that she had been compelled to resort to armed intervention in Poland in order to "quell the Polish disorder," may have been hypocrisy but not without an element of truth.

The Polish Civil War lasted only two years because, in an attempt to relieve pressure on the anti-Russian Confederation of Bar, the French government of Louis XV prevailed on the Turks to declare war on Russia in 1768. [26] Ottoman territory had indeed been violated by Russian troops in hot pursuit of defeated Polish freedom fighters. The Porte was worried about Russian policy in Poland. But the sultan flung down the gauntlet to the Muscovites without realizing how far the decay of his empire and armies had progressed. The Russians cut through the Turkish defenses as a knife through butter, overran Moldavia and Wallachia, penetrated the Crimea, and inflicted a crushing defeat on the Turkish fleet at Chesme in the Aegean, between the Anatolian mainland and the island of Chios. Austria, Russia's rival for the Ottoman Sick Man's mantle, grew alarmed at excessive Russian gains in the Danubian Principalities. Moldavia in Russian hands would be a threat to newly reconquered (1690) Transylvania and an opening wedge into the Balkans, where Austrian advance had been stopped by the Treaty of Belgrade in 1739. Vienna consequently began considering a preventive war against the Russians in order not to be done out of its expected Balkan legacy.

Sitting in Berlin, Frederick the Great had nothing but contempt, from recent personal experience, for Austrian military capabilities. He was certain that a war between Austria and Russia could end only in victory for the latter. As a result Moldavia would fall to Catherine the Great. This would cause a serious disequilibrium in the relations of the three expanding empires. In Moldavia a victorious Russia would get all, Austria and Prussia nothing. Such an increase in Russian power and prestige would probably make Poland the next target of Russian expansionism. With defeated Austria out of the picture, Russia would then probably be able to seize all of Poland, without having to worry about compensating Prussia. If, therefore, the tsarina could be prevailed upon to turn to Poland from Moldavia, she could satisfy her territorial appetite without upsetting the balance of power, by matching her gains through concessions to Prussia and Austria at Poland's expense. This was the basic plan of tripartite partitioning Frederick proposed to Catherine. She reflected and accepted.

Twenty-seven years elapsed between the outbreak of the Polish Civil War in 1768 and the disappearance of Poland from the map in 1795. The first partition among Russia, Prussia, and Austria, deprived the country of between one-third and one-fourth of its territory, inhabited by about five million people. Russia got the lion's share: Livonia and White Russia, to a line drawn west of Vitebsk from the Dnieper to the Dvina rivers, with an estimated Russian Orthodox population of 1.8 million. Austria took an area north of the Carpathians, known as Galicia, Podolia, and Halicz, including the great city of Lvov and part of Cracow, inhabited by approximately 2.7 million people of mixed Catholic, Orthodox, and Jewish religions. Prussia in the west got less than half a million new subjects in the strategic Baltic areas of Pomeralia and Ermeland, excluding the cities of Danzig and Torun.[27]

The second partition in 1793 was triggered by the long-overdue enactment (while Russia was busy fighting the Turks) of the Polish reform constitution of May 3, 1791. The reform abolished the *liberum veto* and made the royal succession hereditary instead of elective. Disapproving Russia used reforms as an excuse to take a large slice of Lithuania and almost all of the western Ukraine, with a total population of approximately three million. Prussia seized Great Poland plus Danzig and Torun with more than one million inhabitants. This time Austria abstained. Poland was thus reduced to 80,000 square miles of territory around Warsaw and to a population of four million.[28]

The third partition in 1795 was in retaliation for the patriotic uprising in 1794 under Thaddeus Kosciuszko. This leader was a veteran of the American Revolutionary War. He set himself at the head of a national army of middle-class freedom fighters, intellectuals dubbed "Jacobins," students, and a few peasant contingents armed with scythes. He led this army first to victory and then to defeat, when the three partitioning powers tore asunder the last vestiges of the Polish state and even abolished, for perpetuity, the name "Kingdom of Poland." Russia took all of Lithuania, Courland, and the Ukraine, with the cities of Vilno, Grodno, and Brest, inhabited by 1.2 million people. Austria moved up north along the Vistula, nearly to Warsaw, by adding the Lublin and all of the Cracow regions to its Galician possessions, with about a million people. Prussia took Warsaw itself and along with it Mazovia.[29]

Prussia and Russia had a common frontier for the first time. The borders remained largely unchanged until the end of the First World War (except for about six years at the end of the Napoleonic Wars, when a rump Poland known as the Duchy of Warsaw was re-established by the French emperor). The multinational Romanov, Habsburg, and Hohenzollern empires devoured their middle-zone neighbor Poland just as effectively as the expansionist Ottomans in the south had gobbled up countries they found in their path: Serbia, Croatia, Albania, Bulgaria, Wallachia, Moldavia, and Hungary. The rape of Poland, however, occurred during an eighteenth-century crisis of European conscience and concurrently with the rise of the idea of the nation as a sovereign power during the French Revolution. Early in the sixteenth century Sir Thomas More, beset with personal tragedy, had shown concern for the Hungarian disaster. Rousseau, that tenderest of French *philosophes,* found the inevitability of Polish dependence so tragic that he advised the Polish nation to prove itself indigestible in the entrails of its predatory neighbors.[30] The Poles followed Rousseau's advice. In 1795 they lost their state but kept their cultural entity and their nationhood.

14

The Revolutions that Failed

Inside a hollow square formed on May 20, 1795, by squadrons of Habsburg soldiery under the landside walls of Buda Castle, five heads fell in halting succession under a bungling executioner's axe. The men beheaded had been convicted of the double crime of lese majesty and treason for being the leaders of a conspiratorial movement of French Jacobin inspiration. The last head to fall, after those of the Freemason Count Jacob Sigray, the cashiered army captain John Laczkovics, the former student leader Francis Szentmarjay, and the retired county official Joseph Hajnoczy, belonged to the Abbot Ignatius Martinovics,[1] a sometime professor of physical sciences at the Polish (Austrian since 1772) University of Lvov (Lemberg) and at the time a defrocked Franciscan. The sentence passed on Martinovics, the confessed instigator of the conspiracy, required him to witness his companions' executions. On June 3 two more heads rolled in the dust: those of the law student Alexander Szolartsik and the Protestant erudite Paul Öz, unsuccessful candidate for a professorial chair in philosophy. Twenty-seven lesser conspirators were sentenced to long prison terms.[2] The terrified populations understood the official message: there would be no revolution east of Vienna!

In Paris, where Robespierre had been carted off to the guillotine just ten months before and where padlocks had recently been placed on the Jacobin Club (November 11, 1794), the conspirators of Buda would probably have stood somewhere to the right of the moderate Girondists in the political spectrum. But in the middle zone, where the French and Polish revolutions had stirred up a metapolitical great fear and a witchhunt unprecedented since the Inquisition (Jacobin Clubs did indeed come into existence in Warsaw during the fateful summer of 1794), the Martinovics movement was considered dangerously subversive, dubbed Jacobin, and politically utilized for the purposes of a preventive and precautionary white counterterror.

Martinovics and his fellow conspirators had to atone with their lives not only for the excesses and success of the French Revolution but also for the failure of the royal revolution vainly attempted in the Habsburg lands by the enlightened despots Joseph II (1765-1790) and Leopold II (1790-1792).[3] Martinovics had been an informer, probably a double agent, for the secret police of these two brothers of Marie Antionette. He made a living by submitting reports on the activities of members of the ultraconservative Hungarian nobility, who clung to their ancient feudal constitutional privileges and resisted, amidst the plaudits of an anti-German nation, the centralizing, modernizing, reformist edicts of a foreign ruling house resident in Vienna. The French Revolution healed the political feud between the dynasty and the traditionalist nobility because it posed a threat to the interests of both. By the end of Leopold's reign, and especially during the opening years of the rule of his son Francis II (1792-1835), revolutionary events in France created a community of interests between the Habsburgs and their oligarchic opponents. Vienna and the landowning nobility of the east joined hands to nip in the bud any revolutionary burgeoning among intellectuals, commoners, and that part of the nobility which, filled with the ideas of the Enlightenment, could be suspected of reformist and conspiratorial tendencies. People like Martinovics, who had been useful tools for the enlightened despots Joseph and Leopold before the conservative reaction to the French Revolution set in, lost their utility. The police no longer needed reports on the activities of the conservative nobles. Its new mission was to keep under surveillance and, if need be, to stamp out, radical underground "Jacobin" movements. Dropped from the imperial payroll but still filled with the ideas of the Enlightenment and the French Revolution, bitter and resentful because of the loss of an easy livelihood, former police informers, Martinovics among them, turned to conspiratorial republican agitation and thus became a prime target for the reinvigorated regime so badly frightened by the French bogeyman.

Both the revolution in France and the precautionary counterrevolution in the Habsburg lands were explosions in a chain reaction. In both coastal and inland Europe violent change was provoked

by the success of entrenched aristocratic interests in preventing the
enlightened despots' regeneration of the spent and decomposing old
regimes. In the middle zone the decadent socioeconomic structure
was even more in need of reform than it was in the coastal areas.
After repopulating and rendering once again productive the areas
reconquered from the retreating Turks, the Habsburgs failed to
integrate their enlarged domains into world commerce. Charles VI
(1711-1740) got British and Dutch recognition for his *Pragmatic
Sanction* (Habsburg dynastic succession in the female line) only by
dissolving the newly formed Austrian East India Company.[4] When,
some years later, this venture-capital organization was re-established
exclusively for trade in the markets of the Ottoman Empire, it
quickly failed because of the inability of Austrian goods to compete
successfully with British, Dutch, and French products. The loss of
Silesia to Frederick the Great in the 1740s and the first partition
of Poland in 1772 entailed the loss of northern markets for Danubian
cattle and wine exports. At the same time, industry was practically
nonexistent; factories, manufacturers, river shipping, all rare. The
French wars from 1792 on produced an economic boom by creating
a rising demand for supplies for the armies. But this demand also
increased the need to maintain, within the existing economic system,
a large captive labor force at minimum cost and maximum exactions.
In other words, the pressures to debase the economic status of the
serfs increased.

Steadily, during the second half of the eighteenth century, feudal
obligations exacted from the serfs by the landowners rose in the
middle-zone areas of the Habsburg domains. The reaction to this
retrograde economic process came in a series of peasant uprisings:
in the Trans-Tisza region in 1753; in Croatia in 1755; in the Csik
region of eastern Transylvania in 1764; and in the Transdanubian
counties south of Lake Balaton in 1765-1766. In order to preserve the
social equilibrium of the realm in a *modus vivendi,* the Empress
Maria Theresa promulgated in 1767 her *urbarium*—a series of edicts
regulating the feudal obligations that could be exacted from the serfs
according to the size of the parcels they were cultivating.[5] In 1780
the *urbarium* was extended to Croatia and the Banat, providing for
the cash redemption of the *robota.* A year later, against the vehe-
ment opposition of the landowning nobility, the enlightened Joseph
II abolished serfdom in the western areas of his domains. Two years
later, in 1783, again in the face of opposition from the nobility, a
modified form of emancipation was introduced in the realms of the
Crown of St. Stephen. It was forbidden to exact feudal obligations

above the limits set by the *urbarium,* to evict the serf from his parcel of land, to limit him in his choice of a vocation, or to prevent him from marrying in accordance with his wishes. Even more far-reaching alleviations were decreed by Joseph II for the Hungarian and Transylvanian serfs in 1785. The very term "serf" was abolished and the right of free displacement was assured. No change, however, was made in the exaction of feudal obligations as set by the *urbarium.* This came as a bitter surprise to the peasants, who had looked on Joseph as their messiah and who had mistakenly interpreted his gradualist road to emancipation as the total abolition of serfdom.

Most bitter was the disappointment among the Orthodox Rumanian peasants of Transylvania. These rustics were being victimized not only as serfs but also as minority nationals and religious dissidents. In their ignorance they interpreted the emperor's introduction of military conscription in the eastern frontier regions during 1784 as a legal way opened by imperial grace to terminate the quality of being a serf by becoming a soldier. Thousands of Rumanian peasants flocked to the imperial military posts under the leadership of Orthodox priests to enlist as frontier guards. The swarm eventually absorbed the total population of about four hundred villages, numbering about thirty thousand men, commanded by the serfs Crişan, Horia, and Closca. Horia had been to Vienna and was alleged to have had an audience with the emperor. He quoted Joseph to his followers as being sympathetic to the abolition of serfdom. In a manifesto he demanded not only the suppression of all feudal privileges and obligations, but also a division of the noble landed estates among the peasants.[6]

As in the eastern areas of Poland, the Transylvanian situation was exacerbated by the division between landowners and serfs along ethnic and religious lines. A Hungarian Catholic-Protestant gentry faced a Rumanian Orthodox peasantry. Also, as in the Ukraine during the earlier uprisings, the fury of the insurgents was directed against the dwellings of the landowners and, in general, against all non-Orthodox inhabitants of the province. After a series of unspeakable atrocities, the imperial regiments of the Transylvanian garrison were ordered into action. By the end of December 1784 the peasant bands had been dispersed and their three leaders captured. Crişan was fortunate in being able to commit suicide during an unguarded moment. Horia and Cloşca were broken on the wheel and then quartered. But the lesson of the uprising was apparently not totally lost on the rulers, because Joseph's partial emancipation proclamation of 1785 followed by six months the execution of Horia and

Cloşca. In spite of this cruel, though at the time not unusual, punishment in the middle zone, Joseph II still continued to be revered
as "the good emperor" by the peasants of Hungary, Transylvania,
and Croatia. His death in February 1790 was a signal for country-
wide peasant unrest from the Zipser region in the northern Carpathians down to the Croatian border on the Drava River. But all
these stirrings failed and were of no avail. Serfdom remained a legal
institution in the lands of the Crown of St. Stephen until 1848.

Joseph's enlightened despotism failed in Hungary because of the
opposition of the nobility and the high clergy. At the end of the
eighteenth century these two estates together numbered only about
three hundred thousand souls out of a total population of approximately nine million (excluding Croatia). On his deathbed the disil-
lusioned emperor is said to have revoked with a stroke of the pen
most of his reformist decrees, with the notable exception of the Edict
of Toleration (1781) and the Serfdom Ordinance (1785). The toleration decree removed the disabilities placed on Protestants during the
darkest days of the Counter Reformation in 1731, when office holding was made conditional on the swearing of an oath in the name
of the Virgin and the saints. From 1781 on, government employment
was, at least by the letter of the law, open not only to Protestants
but also to the Orthodox, and full freedom of worship was guaranteed to all non-Catholics. The Hungarian Diet of 1791 confirmed the
Edict of Toleration. Yet, in the conservative reaction following
Joseph's death, more and more stringently exclusive restructions were
placed on office holding. Thus Hajnoczy, one of the "Jacobins" executed in 1795, who was a Lutheran and a nonnoble, had to resign
his county office as vice sheriff within two months of the enlightened
emperor's demise. We have his farewell address to his associates, delivered on April 29, 1790. In this sad document he points out that,
as he leaves office, in all Europe only two countries are left, Poland
and Hungary, where noble birth is still a prerequisite to government
employment.[7]

Did Martinovics and through him the Hungarian Jacobins have
contact with or receive support from revolutionary Paris? The abbot
was not a stranger to the French capital. He had visited it in the
early 1780s, in company with Count Ignace Potocki, a Polish friend
from Lvov. While in Paris he probably joined a Masonic lodge or
some other secret society of the *illuminati*. Later, during his stay in
the Austrian capital in the early 1790s, he is known to have been in
contact with the Vienna Jacobins. This underground organization
secretly sent two emissaries to Paris in April 1794 to report to the

Convention on conditions in Austria.[8] We also know that Martinovics had communications with George Forster, a scholarly protégé of Catherine the Great and subsequently a liaison agent between the Convention and its Rhineland German sympathizers.[9] Was the First French Republic following the foreign policy of the Valois and Bourbon kings of France in attempting to incite and subsidize malcontents in the middle zone in order to create a diversion in the rear of the Habsburg emperor? The police protocol of Martinovics's interrogation, dated September 9, 1794, quotes the abbot as admitting that, under the cover name "Démocrite la Montagne," he maintained contact with and received at least one visit from a clandestine agent of the Committee of Public Safety, the twelve-man ruling body of France during the Terror (June 1793—July 1794).[10] At the trial, testimony was given by witnesses that the voluble Martinovics had been able to convince some of his codefendants that he had moral and financial support from the Convention and even Robespierre's personal approval for his plans!

What were these plans and what were Martinovics's ideas? The abbot's early writings, such as, for example, his anonymous open letter of October 7, 1792, to the emperor, contain a rehashing of Rousseau's social contract, a condemnation of archaic noble privileges, and a demand for careers open to talent.[11] The principal sources for his conspiratorial aims are the two pamphlets he drafted for his underground organizations: the *Catechism* of the Society of Reformers (in Latin) and the *Handbook* of the Society of Liberty and Equality (in French). The two societies were organized on a Masonic hierarchical model. Only the higher-level Libertarians were aware of the existence of the subordinate Reformers but not vice versa. The first organization was intended primarily for anti-Habsburg political malcontents of the gentry; the second, for radical intellectuals bent on reorganizing both state and society. The *Catechism* accordingly excoriated the king-emperor, the upper aristocracy, and the high clergy. It recommended independence from Austria. It proposed the transformation of Hungary into a federal republic, in which each nationality would live in a state-province of its own language. The supreme federal legislature would be bicameral, with an upper house for noble and a lower for nonnoble deputies. The language of parliamentary debates and publications would be Hungarian. The executive branch of the government was to be composed of ministries specializing in finance, defense, foreign relations, administration, agriculture, and other state functions. Nobles would remain exempt from taxation and exclusively qualified to hold landed property. Serfs would become freemen, though paying rent to the landlord whose parcels they cultivated in produce and by *robota* labor. To accomplish these objectives, an armed uprising would be necessary. The revolt was to succeed with French, Polish, and some rebel Austrian backing.[12]

The *Handbook* of the Society of Liberty and Equality went much farther. It proposed a democratic republic based on Rousseau's social contract and contradicted the *Catechism* of the Reformers. It attacked all noble privileges instead of promising to safeguard them. The three great scourges of mankind, said the *Handbook,* are kings, nobles, and clergy. A "holy rising" will be necessary, based on an alliance of the bourgeoisie with the peasantry, to overthrow the existing unjust social order. Only after the overthrow of the throne and the substitution of the shrine of reason for the altar, will there be a free, egalitarian society, in which the nobles will cease their bestial exploitation of their serfs.[13] These deviations of the *Handbook* from the *Catechism* clearly show Martinovics's awareness of the impossibility of conducting a successful revolution in the middle zone without the nobility, the local substitute for a nonexistent bourgeoisie. But they also point to his conspiratorial naivete in supposing that the nobles could be kept in the revolutionary ranks in ignorance of their role as ultimate victims after the overthrow of kings and priests. Perhaps the abbot was proceeding on the assumption that the revolution must, in any event, devour her own children. Or perhaps, having been a double agent during his early career, he had acquired the characteristics of double dealing and dissembling.

In any event, he and his Jacobins failed, as had the Polish Jacobins and Kosciuszko a year before, as had all the peasant uprisings from the fifteenth century to Horia and Cloşca in 1785, as had the heretics and the Hussites, as had the enlightened despots by the late 1780s, Rakoczi in 1711 and all his insurrectionist predecessors, the hasty Bulgarian and Serbian rebels in the late 1680s, and the Polish reformists who had vainly striven for a century and a half to save their country from ultimate destruction. Indeed, a search of middle-zone annals from the beginning to the end of the eighteenth century fails to reveal a single revolution or uprising that did not fail, with the possible exception of Bogdan Khmelnitsky's revolt in 1648, which was a failure in achieving the independence of the Ukraine but a success in bringing about its detachment from Poland.

During the early nineteenth century a curious geographical factor entered into deciding the fate of middle-zone revolutions. The Lower Danube, the previous dividing line between history and prehistory, became the boundary between revolutions that failed and revolutions that succeeded. South of the great river, down to the Mediterranean, successful revolutions, starting among the South Slavs in 1804, gradually brought into existence a system of minor states divested of their centuries-old state of dependence. North of the Danube, up to the Baltic, the tenaciously and desperately fought revolutions of 1830-1831, 1848-1849, 1863-1864, all failed and only a compromise solution in 1867 produced semi-independence for the Hungarians. An explanation of this geo-revolutionary riddle of the nineteenth-century middle zone must be sought first of all in the persistence in one area and the waning in another of the external power potential. In the Balkans the decline of Ottoman power and the intervention of other rising imperial powers made it possible for revolutions to succeed and to terminate dependence. The sultan, it should be remembered, did not belong to the Holy Alliance of European rulers, who condemned all revolutionary, nationalistic stirrings in the name of a vague Christian mysticism. In fact, the Ottoman ruler encouraged such stirrings in order to keep his unruly army under control. In the lands of the Danube and the Vistula, on the other hand, the persistence of the external power potential in Austria, Prussian Germany, and Russia, all members of the Holy Alliance, doomed every revolution until the final exhaustion of this triple imperial potential in the First World War. The middle zone thus passed through a period of political bifurcation during the nineteenth and the early twentieth centuries: independence in the south; dependence in the north; semi-independence, after 1867, in the middle, Danubian tier.

But the failure of the nineteenth-century middle zone revolutions was not exlusively a corollary of external power factors. It was also influenced by the countervailing forces of centrifugal nationalism negating and cancelling out clashing national aspirations and efforts in the multinational Ottoman, Habsburg, and Romanov empires. Additionally, the revolutions that failed in these vast realms during the nineteenth century were also adversely affected by social and economic contradictions within the same national group seeking to terminate dependence. The conflict existed mainly between the interests of the large landowners and those of the poverty-stricken peasantry. To understand the abortive revolutions of the nineteenth century, we must therefore next turn to centrifugal nationalism and its historical environment between the Napoleonic wars and the great conflict which was to make the world safe for democracy.

15

Centrifugal Nationalism

The revolutions that failed in the north and succeeded in the south of the middle zone during the nineteenth century were violent efforts of dependent peoples bound together by ethnicity, language, and common traditions. Autonomy was an early, moderate goal. Resistance to reasonably modest reform proposals gradually led to emotionally charged mass movements to establish or re-establish sovereign states. In post-Napoleonic Europe, from the Atlantic to the Urals, Christian rulers (with the exception of the pope) joined to treat nationalism as a subversive, anti-status-quo doctrine, much as the succeeding popular sovereignties considered Communism after World War I. Unlike twentieth-century Communism, however, early nineteenth-century nationalism had no central directing and co-ordinating apparatus to guide toward a common goal mutually antagonistic ethnic groups of the multinational empires which bestrode the middle zone.[1] Additionally, in landlocked Europe sovereignty had not yet been transferred by the rulers of their subjects; the ethnically heterogeneous state had not yet been inherited by the people. State and nation consequently became antithetical entities.

The result of ·retarded development was a drastic alteration in the political dynamism of nationalism. In coastal Europe nationalism acted as a centripetal force emanating from a unitary ethnic group to keep or to bring together territories as states. In the middle zone nationalism functioned centrifugally to explode and to fragment imperially bound, ethnically heterogeneous units into self-proclaimed nation states, which were still and could not help being multinational. North of the Danube in the middle zone during the nineteenth century, history did not favor nationalism. The large units remained powerful enough to resist disruption. Consequently, what we have in this vast continental area, from Napoleon to Lenin, is a dissatisfied and frustrated form of nationalism without an outlet, similar to the pent-up sexual urge which finds gratification in rape.

There may be some justification for considering the nationalism of coastal and north-central Europe as a reaction to Napoleonic conquest. Not so in the middle zone. If nationalism is correctly defined as a doctrine that upholds as an objective the political unity of a people speaking the same language, then Matthias Corvinus was a nationalist in 1458 when he styled himself *"rex Hungariae et magnae Hungariae,"* king not only of Hungary but also of those distant tribes of the Hungarians who had remained in the Eurasian steppe after the Patzinak disaster of the ninth century.[2] The Hussite freedom fighters who, in the name of religious distinctiveness, vainly struggled during the fifteenth century for a self-governing Bohemia free of German domination, were also protonationalists.[3] Veneration of the national traditions in their external aspects was present in Hungary after Mohacs in the sixteenth century as Scythianism, an organized nativist political movement, which was used to promote John Zapolya's aspirations to the throne. The devotees of Scythianism went to the extreme fad of riding bareback, on the historical assumption that the ancient Scythians had disdained saddles.[4] In declining eighteenth-century Poland, fashions were dictated by Sarmatism, another political fad, which took its inspiration from the supposedly superior virtues and sartorial styles of the early Slavs who had once lived on the northern fringes of the Roman Empire.[5] Scythianism and Sarmatism were mock-heroic movements among ethnic groups with experience of statehood. Illyrianism, the early eighteenth-century protonationalist movement of the South Slavs emerging from Ottoman domination, was, on the other hand, the intellectualized aspiration of a stateless people for political autonomy.[6] Its opponents charged that its aim was the establishment of a state within a state. Modest as such an objective may have been, its attainment north of the Danube proved impossible during the persistence of Habsburg power. Yet south of the Danube, due to the debility of the Ottoman Empire, the same Serbs were able to forge an autonomous Serbia under the sultan during the first two decades of the eighteenth century.

The record of centrifugal Serb nationalism, frustrated in the north but gratified in the south during its pre-World War I phase, begins with the three national congresses. These assemblies were held in 1744, 1769, and 1774 by Serbs who had fled north of the Danube from the pursuing Turks and settled in the Hungarian Voyvodina. The three congresses behaved much in the manner of constituent national assemblies. They addressed the imperial crown for the recognition of already existing ecclesiastical self-government as a political organ separate from the administrative and judicial authorities of the Hungarian and "associated" Croat Kingdoms. The response of the imperial authorities to these demands was conciliatory but consistently negative. An "Illyrian Commission" was established in 1745 under a Royal Commissioner to oversee Serbian affairs in Hungary and Croatia. The commissioner at first acted on instructions sent from Vienna. Later he had to comply with the provisions of three Illyrian *regulamenta* [7]—administrative guidelines—issued in 1771, 1777, and 1779. Political autonomy remained out of the question. To ecclesiastical self-government under a Serbian Orthodox metropolitan there was no objection. The metropolitan was acknowledged as the ecclesiastic but not as the temporal head of the Serb people on imperial territory. His investiture was made dependent on imperial approval. An imperial permit was required for the holding of Serb national congresses.

In the military sphere the Habsburg emperor-king continued to recognize, until 1871, the administrative separateness of the Serb Military Border Guard Territories. This lateral strip of land was first organized as a defense zone against the Turks and as settlement reservations for Serbian refugees crossing the Danube under their Metropolitan Arsene in 1702.[8] The strip ran along the north bank of the Sava River from the Adriatic Sea to the Transylvanian frontier. It had a width of about 25-30 kilometers, except in the west, where it covered a distance of approximately 75 kilometers from the Adriatic coast to the Una River; and east of Zagreb, where it linked the Sava and Drava rivers across a south-north distance of roughly 80-85 kilometers. These military territories were considered *in comitatu non de comitatu;* [9] in other words, only territorially in the administrative county subdivision, for purposes of administration directly tied to the central government under military rule and law. The transfer to regional civilian administration was delayed by almost two centuries and was a ten-year political process (1871-1881), fraught with explosive nationalism.[10] In sharp distinction, the diocesan areas under the ecclesiastical jurisdiction of the Serb Orthodox metropolitan remained, from the eighteenth century on, integral parts of the Hungarian and Croatian administrative and judicial systems.

It was this situation, crystallized by 1779, that Napoleon found when he first appeared in the Slovene city of Ljubljana (Laibach) in 1797. He did not create but rather capitalized on already existing Serb nationalism by acquiring from Austria in the Treaty of Vienna in 1809 the so-called Illyrian Provinces. These territories were organized as eight French territorial Departments extending from Kotor (Cattaro) and Dubrovnik (Ragusa) into the Border Guard Territories and into Croatia proper. The Illyrian Provinces of the French Empire, like the Duchy of Warsaw (a miniature, independent Poland resurrected by Napoleon) were functions of and coterminous with French imperial power.[11] They disappeared from the map with the shadow of the emperor. Illyrian nationalism north of the Danube then continued unsatisfied and frustrated until 1918. In Croatia the great apostle of Illyrianism was Ljudevit Gaj (1809-1872), editor of the literary journal *Novine Hrvatske* (New Croatia), which patriotically disseminated the idea of cultural and political unity among all South Slavs, who then numbered about seven million.

South of the river, Slav nationalism began a victorious march which led to political autonomy in 1817 and to full independence, recognized by the great powers, in 1878. The revolt of the Serbs [12] under Ottoman rule began in 1804, not so much against the central authority of the sultan but rather as a protest provoked by the depredations of his lawless janissaries. During this period the Ottoman Empire was still in a state of gradual decomposition. Not only was it becoming incapable of defending itself against Russian and Austrian encroachments, but it had to use its waning strength to control the internal disobedience of the ulemas (religious leaders) and the unruly janissaries. When, in December 1801, these mutinous occupation troops murdered the Turkish vizier commanding in Belgrade and savagely sacked the city, the Serb population resorted to guerrilla warfare. Resistance began with the tacit agreement of the sultan. A partisan leader was found in Kara George Petrovich (Black George [1752-1817]), an illiterate but militarily trained and strategically gifted peasant, a dealer in pork. Kara George annihilated the janissaries in Serbia during 1804-1805, thus setting a precedent for the sultan to follow in Constantinople itself in 1826.

The Serb war against the janissaries gradually turned into an armed clash with the central Ottoman authority. Victorious over the sultan's army at Nish in 1806, Kara George entered liberated Belgrade but saw the fortunes of war turn against him after the Treaty of Tilsit in 1807, in which Napoleon agreed to act as a mediator to help restore good relations between Turkey and Russia.[13] A temporary Russo-Turk cease-fire enabled the Ottoman army to turn against the rebel Serbs and to crush their resistance at Chegra. When, however, the Russians once again resumed their offensive against the Turks, the relieved Serbs completed the liberation of their country. After Serb victory, the Serb military command in 1808 was made hereditary in the Karageorgevich family (against the opposition of the rival Obrenovich clan). The sultan, eager for peace, granted an amnesty to the Serb military rebels and autonomy to a small area designated as Serbia.

In the Treaty of Bucharest in 1812 between Russia and Turkey, the name Serbia first appeared in a modern diplomatic document. This was not due to the Russians, who had abandoned the Serbs to their fate when the Ottoman army, once more relieved of defending the frontiers of the empire, could concentrate anew on disciplining the sultan's recalcitrant subjects. The Turks, victorious at Negotin in 1813, re-entered Belgrade. Kara George fled north across the Danube to Habsburg territory, where he was perversely imprisoned, in the spirit of the Holy Alliance, as a nationalist rebel against his sovereign monarch. After a period of Ottoman retaliatory atrocities and terror lasting two years, a new Serb insurrection broke out in 1815. This time the rival leader Milosh Obrenovich (1780-1860) was in command, with better luck than his Karageorgevich rival. Waterloo in 1815 permitted the Russians to renew their pressure on the enfeebled Turks, who in their turn were unable to resist the Serb insurgents. At the smell of gunpowder Kara George returned to Serbia from Austria, but was assassinated by the Obrenovich faction, whose head, Milosh, gained recognition from the sultan as hereditary prince of autonomous Serbia in 1817.[14]

In two *hatti-sherifs* (imperial decrees) issued during 1829-1830, the sultan laid the constitutional foundations, for the time being, of the new Serbian state. Prince Milosh was to reign as a personal representative of the sultan, his imperial master, but to share power with a pasha resident in Belgrade. He had to pay an annual tribute to the Sublime Porte, but did not have to accept Ottoman military units except in the towns of his principality. Under a new *hatti-sherif* in 1833, six more Ottoman territorial divisions were added to renascent Serbia.[15] The newly autonomous unit then began to play its historical role as a Balkan Piedmont, foreordained, it seemed, eventually to unite under its dynasty the other ethnically related provinces of the peninsula. As for the Serbs north of the Danube, they remained Habsburg subjects during this historical process until the fall of the multinational empires in 1918.

The role Russia played in the unfolding nationalist developments was ambivalent. Its imperial power, while it lasted, was used north of the Danube to crush Rumanian, Hungarian, and Polish nationalism. South of the river, it was employed to give gradual satisfaction to Serbian and Bulgarian nationalist appetites. Obviously, during the nineteenth century, as in the twentieth, national or imperial interests were considered by sophisticated states as superior to ideologies. The interests of the Russian empire during the nineteenth century called for supporting centrifugal nationalism when it was working toward the disruption of a rival empire. But the same interests demanded that Russia suppress nationalism without mercy when it threatened its own security and territorial integrity.

If the history of Serbian nationalism during the early nineteenth century is geographically divided into unsuccessful northern and successful southern sectors of development, the progress of Rumanian nationalism north of the Danube is chronologically marked by the fluctuating power relationship between advancing Russian and receding Ottoman imperialism.[16] The ideology of Rumanian nationalism (based on the eighteenth-century recognition of the Rumanian language as a descendant of Latin and on the assertion of Rumanian ethnic continuity north of the Carpathians) sought the disruption of the Ottoman Empire by a union of Moldavia and Wallachia as well as the dismemberment of the Habsburg domains through annexation of the third Rumanian-inhabited province of Transylvania. The fourth province claimed by Rumanian nationalism was Bessarabia, a strip of territory between the Pruth and Dniester rivers, and more significantly, a border area between Rumanian Moldavia and Russia. Beginning with the Napoleonic wars, Russian policy operated on the horns of a diplomatic dilemma: to continue expansion south toward the warm sea by the acquisition of Rumanian-inhabited Ottoman territory and yet at the same time to support centrifugal Rumanian nationalism. Bessarabia became a barometer of Russian state power: whenever strong, Russia incorporated this border province, as was the case in 1812 (and today); whenever weak, Russia disgorged it, as will be seen in the following pages.

Tsarist annexation of Bessarabia was an affront to Rumanian nationalism. It was compensated for by Russian support for the establishment of a unitary, autonomous, and eventually independent Rumanian state to be carved out of Ottoman and Habsburg territories. After the Treaty of Kuchuk Kainarji in 1774, Russia had been a protector of the sultan's Moldavian and Wallachian subjects. Petersburg was in a better strategic position than the Serbs to help these Rumanians in the satisfaction of nationalist appetites. The recognition in 1817 of an autonomous Serb state within the Ottoman Empire served the Rumanians as a tantalizing example. Accordingly, in the Treaty of Adrianople in 1829, the tsar extracted from the sultan complete autonomy for the two Danubian Rumanian provinces under his protection, on the Serbian model. When, however, in June 1848 a nationalist-liberal revolution broke out in Wallachia, Russia and Turkey got together in the face of the common threat. Russian troops moved into the rebellious province and remained in occupation until 1853. Then, with Turkish consent, they were replaced by Austrian forces, which stayed on until 1857. By then evacuation had become possible. During the previous year the great powers at Paris forced a weak Russia staggering from her defeat in the Crimean War (1853-1856), to cede coastal Bessarabia down to the Danube delta, to give up her protectorate over the sultan's Christian subjects, and to recognize the union of Moldavia and Wallachia, renamed the United Principalities and placed under the collective guarantee of the Great Powers.[17] Six years later, in 1862, the name Rumania first appeared in diplomatic and cartographic usage. Rumanian nationalism was thus gradually though incompletely satisfied during the first half of the nineteenth century, first, by taking advantage of progressively decaying Ottoman power; second, through exploitation of temporary Russian weakness; and third, by fighting shy of as yet undiminished Austrian imperial might.

In fact, both Russian and Austrian imperial power remained sufficiently strong during the first half of the nineteenth century, either alone or in combination, to hold in check the forces of centrifugal nationalism pressing against the status quo north of the Danube. Russian and Austrian armies dealt with the Poles in 1830-1831 and 1863-1864, and with the Hungarians in 1848-1849. The first test of strength came in November 1830 with the outburst of pent-up Polish nationalism against the rule of Tsar Nicholas I (1825-1855), autocratic successor of the mystic Alexander I. While an antinationalist at home, Tsar Nicholas I was a firm protagonist of Greek independence at the expense of the Ottoman Empire.

The revolution staged by Polish nationalists in 1830 drew its inspiration from the abortive Russian Decembrist uprising against autocracy in St. Petersburg (December 26, 1825). Its immediate stimulus came from the success of the French July Revolution in replacing the old regime reign of Charles X with the bourgeois monarchy of Louis Philippe. The cadets of the military academy in Warsaw touched off the revolt in Poland at the news that the tsar intended to make use of

Polish army units for an invasion of revolutionary France and Belgium to "restore order," in the spirit of the Holy Alliance. The cadets of Warsaw served as the catalytic factor in speeding up the coalescence of nationalist elements. They were soon joined by army units, by Lithuanian and Volhynian patriots; by workers, students, professors, and intellectuals. The Romanov dynasty was declared dethroned; the ancient union with Lithuania was proclaimed restored. The Diet was on the point of offering the Polish crown to Napoleon's only legitimate son, the Duke of Reichstadt, a resident of the Habsburg capital since his father's first abdication in 1814. At this moment, the Russian forces, which had been expelled or had withdrawn from Polish territory during the early phase of the revolt, counterattacked. In the bloody Polish defeat at Ostrolenka (May 26, 1831), the Russian commander Ivan Paskievich and the Polish general Joseph Bem, a veteran of Napoleon's 1812 Russian campaign, faced each other for the first time.[18] They did so again nineteen years later, with the same result, farther to the south in Transylvania. It was the consistently vanquished and not the permanent victor whose name served as a nationalist shibboleth in the middle zone until 1956.[19]

Paskievich besieged and took Warsaw in September 1831. The Polish army laid down its arms. Once more it looked like *finis Poloniae,* with deportations to Siberia, flights to the west, oppression and Russification at home. While in far-away Greece the tsar, in alliance with Britain and France, had just helped the Hellenic nationalists wrest the independence of the sovereign Kingdom of Greece from the sultan (1829), closer to home he acted in accordance with enlightened Russian self-interest and crushed nationalism in his own empire.

The next contest of strength between imperialism and nationalism in the middle zone was a challenge to the Austrian army by the Hungarians. The Austrians could cope with the rebel Magyars only by joint military action with the autocratic Russians and with other, anti-Hungarian Slav and Rumanian nationalist forces. The immediate occasion for this major conflict was the chain reaction of revolutions released in February 1848 in Paris by the overthrow of Louis Philippe and the subsequent proclamation of the Second French Republic. By March and April the revolutionary ferment spread beyond Vienna to Hungary, Bohemia, Moravia, Galicia, Transylvania, Croatia, and Dalmatia. In Hungary and Bohemia the antecedents of the nationalist flare-up could be traced to opposition to the Habsburgs' becoming the ruling dynasty in 1526. In Hungary, more specifically, Magyar nationalism, rooted in the tradition of a once strong and independent state, had been intensifying since the centralizing efforts of the enlightened despots Joseph II and Leopold II at the end of the eighteenth century. In the course of a great debate between the reformist but functional gradualist magnate Stephen Szechenyi (1791-1860) [20] and the charismatic people's tribune Louis Kossuth (1802-1894),[21] the nationalism of the Magyars became associated with the popular, liberal cause. The March Laws, extracted from the Habsburg emperor in the irresistible sweep of mass enthusiasm agitated by Kossuth's charisma and fired by the oratory of the romantic poet Alexander Petöfi (1823-1849), were in no sense radical or revolutionary. They merely provided for a liberal, monarchic constitution, leaving the Habsburg dynasty in hereditary possession of the throne, to rule with the aid of an appointed cabinet responsible to an elected bicameral legislature. This liberal constitution was repudiated through the contrived replacement of the feeble-minded Ferdinand V (1835-1848), who had sworn to uphold it, by his young nephew Francis Joseph (1848-1916), who had not. Vienna then pitted Croatian nationalist forces employing regiments from the Border Guard Territory against the Hungarian nationalists. The invasion of Hungarian territory provoked a revolutionary war of independence. The Croatian forces were quickly defeated, but an Austrian army under Prince Alfred Windischgrätz took the Hungarian capital in January 1849, only to be driven out by the counterattacking Hungarian nationalist army in May.

In the meantime the impact of war was showing itself in a process of political radicalization. The government and the parliament, which had fled to Debrecen at the approach of Windischgrätz, proclaimed the dethronement of the Habsburgs in the Great Calvinist Church and elected Kossuth chief of state. Emperor Francis Joseph appealed to Tsar Nicholas I for military aid in the interest of the European antinationalist status quo. A Russian army under the supreme command of Paskievich crossed the Carpathians into Hungary. Polish General Bem, who didn't care where he fought Russians, showed up unexpectedly from his Viennese exile in command of the Hungarian army corps defending Transylvania and was again defeated by a subordinate of Paskievich's in the battle of Segesvar (Sighisoara). Here the great poet Petöfi, the incarnation of romantic nationalism, disappeared during the rout. The Hungarian general Arthur Görgey (1818-1916), commanding on the western front with dictatorial powers, surrendered to the Russians and pointedly not to the Austrians, at Vilagos (now Siria, Rumania) in August. Kossuth fled to Ottoman territory across the Danube, never to return to his native land. Paskievich could now report to the tsar: "Hungary lies prostrate at the feet of Your Majesty." [22] He might have added, though without historical foresight: a country purged of subversive nationalism!

The last nineteenth-century attempt of middle-zone nationalism to break out of the bonds constraining it was the desperate Polish uprising of 1863-1864. It was an essentially urban revolt of soldiers, workers, and students fighting in guerrilla bands against occupying tsarist army units. Unrest had been brewing for about three years, in spite of the conciliatory attempts of the moderate Alexander II (1855-1881). The immediate cause was the drafting of rioting nationalist Polish students into the Russian army in January 1863.[23] Before long resisting nationalists sprang to arms not only in Poland proper but in Lithuania and White Russia as well. Public opinion in the west was outraged, but the Polish freedom fighters received no foreign help. Sympathetic England and France, joined by Austria, tried to ameliorate the situation by diplomatic protests. The Russians, on the other hand, got not only diplomatic support but also military co-operation from the politically congenial Prussians. By the spring of 1864 the unequal struggle had degenerated into sporadic maquis fighting. The Russians resorted to increasingly severe punitive measures. Executions were still going on in August 1864.[24] The last vestiges of Polish autonomy were wiped out. Obviously, nationalism on the Vistula did not have a chance as long as it faced unimpaired Russian power.

The persistence of the imperial power potential in northern Europe was the principal but not the only reason for the frustration of nationalism in Poland and Hungary and for its partial satisfaction in Rumania. A very important role was played also by the conflicts among rival nationalisms of differing ethnicity. Thus, in 1821, during the early stirrings of Rumanian nationalism in Wallachia, nationalistic resentment was directed not so much against the Turkish overlords as against their ruling agents, the Greek Phanariots. This was at the moment when the Greek war for independence (1821-1830) flared up under Alexander Ypsilanti (1792-1828) in Moldavia, the other Rumanian principality. Bucharest was entered by both nationalist groups: Ypsilanti's Greeks and Rumanian insurgents under the popular leader Tudor Vladimirescu. Before long the rival Greek and Rumanian nationalists were fighting each other rather than the common overlord. When the tsar, alarmed by this precocious outbreak of nationalism (Napoleon was still alive at the time on St. Helena), repudiated the Greek nationalists at the Congress of Ljubljana in 1821, Ypsilanti's followers were driven to extremes. They seized and brutally executed Vladimirescu,[25] whose Rumanian nationalist movement then collapsed, at least for the time being. The Greeks were also overcome and scattered. Like Kara George in 1813, Ypsilanti fled to Austrian territory. There he was kept in prison while the Greek national movement marched toward its triumph in the Morea far to the south.

Nowhere, however, were the countervailing forces of rival nationalisms more destructive of nationalist aims than in the lands of the Crown of St. Stephen during the 1848-1849 revolution. Here the Magyars, fighting for the attainment of their nationalistic aims, which entailed the dismemberment of the Habsburg empire, carried on a simultaneous defensive struggle against the onslaught of Croatian, Serb, Slovak, and Rumanian nationalist counterinsurgents. The first battles of the Hungarian war for independence from Austria were fought against Serb and Croat nationalists (July–September 1848), who were demanding independence from Hungary. In October there was a three-cornered fight in Transylvania among Austrian, Hungarian, and Rumanian armies and insurgents, with occasional Saxon inroads against the Hungarians. The Rumanians of Transylvania protested the union of that multinational province with Hungary. A Rumanian national council under the patriot Avram Jancu (1824-1872) cast in its lot with Vienna against the Magyar nationalists. The Habsburg strategy was to divide and conquer. The subject nationalities of Hungary were encouraged to fight the Magyars until the latter surrendered to the Russians. After the surrender, Hungary was pacified and all nationalist movements, Croat, Serb, Slovak, Rumanian as well as Hungarian, were equally suppressed. The oppressed had failed to learn the lesson of unity from the oppressors, Austria and Russia, who knew how to act in concert when it came to partitioning a country or to putting down a rebellion which threatened the European status quo.

The survival of serfdom and the wretched condition of the peasantry were also powerful factors in frustrating nationalist aspirations in the north. One advantage of prolonged Ottoman occupation of the Balkans had been a resultant social leveling. The South Slavs emerging from Ottoman rule were peasant members of egalitarian societies, at the beginning of social differentiation through the rise of a merchant class. Kara George in Serbia was a simple peasant who rose to a position of command because he had served as a sergeant in the Austrian army and later became a rich man with many armed employees in the wholesale pig business. In the north, in contrast, there was a persistent conflict between the interests of the landlords and their serfs. Already during the seventeenth century serfs in Poland preferred to fight with the Tartars against Polish landlords rather than for the Polish king. In Hungary and Transylvania during the eighteenth century the Estates upheld the landowners' right to force serfs to leave military service in the armies fighting for national liberation and to return to forced labor. A Polish nationalist revolution in Galicia, the part of Poland annexed by Austria in 1772, was brought under control in 1846 by the Habsburgs, who again used their divide-and-conquer strategy. They fomented revolts of Ruthenian peasants against their Polish nationalist masters and broke the back of the revolt. In Hungary the nationalists of 1848 were able initially to get peasant support, because the March Laws included the emancipation of the serfs upon payment of indemnity to the landowners. The emancipation article, however, did not abolish all the feudal obligations of the peasantry nor did it carve parcels for all liberated serfs out of the large estates.[26] As a result, the revolutionary government's call to the nation for a general armed rising in June 1849, at the moment of the Russian invasion, found a weak response among the peasantry.[27] The same attitude was manifest in Poland during the rise and expansion of nationalism. The personal magnetism of Kosciuszko in 1795 had brought peasant bands armed with scythes into the ranks of the patriot armies, but the nationalist uprisings of 1830, 1846, and 1863 met with peasant indifference, if not hostility, because of social and economic grievances.[28] Indeed, the Polish nationalist movement during the second half of the nineteenth century was divided and therefore weakened on the question of what kind of independence was to be fought for: with or without agrarian reform. Rumanian nationalism also suffered from the aloofness and suspicion of the peasant masses, who were more interested in economic and social emancipation than in the political union of Rumanians living under foreign rule.

A final factor which must be taken into consideration while appraising nineteen-century nationalism in the middle zone is the relationship between the new nationalist ideology and the various churches. In looking at this problem, we must keep in mind the political differences which by the eighteenth century had fully developed between coastal and inland Europe. Let one example suffice. In the west, absolute monarchies had risen under native dynasties. In France, French Huguenots were persecuted and driven out of their native land by French kings. In the middle zone, Czech and Hungarian Protestants felt victimized by German Habsburgs. Rumanian, Serbian, and Ruthenian Orthodox peasants were kept in bondage by the Hungarian and Polish gentry. Even within the same general ethnic group, the South Slavs, the Catholic Croats and the Orthodox Serbs were at each other's throats, divided by implacable religious animosity. Thus, in the middle zone, in contradistinction to France, religion was a major factor in the rise of nationalism. The historical process here resembled remotely the development of English nationalism under an anti-Catholic impulse and the growth of Catholicizing Irish nationalism influenced by resented political dependence on a Protestant state and a Protestant dynasty.

At the same time, while religion in the middle zone served to intensify centrifugal nationalism working against political cohesion, it also tended to frustrate nationalist aims. Members of the lower clergy, both Catholic and Orthodox, had in earlier centuries fought with and even led peasants revolting against oppression. Priests therefore found it relatively easy to join popular nationalist movements. It was a different story with the high clergy, who were often of aristocratic origin, possessors of great landed wealth, and with a special affinity for the Catholic monarchs under whose sponsorship the Counter Reformation had restored the Church to its dominant position and gradually excluded all but Catholics from government employment. In Poland, nationalism was closely associated with Catholicism. Religious dissidents, both Orthodox and Protestant, were regarded by the end of the eighteenth century as pawns in the hands of anti-Polish foreign powers. In Habsburg-ruled areas, on the other hand, the nationalist movement had a strong Protestant coloring inherited from the sixteenth and seventeenth-century anti-Habsburg resistance. Consequently, when nationalism reached a revolutionary pitch in mid-century, the attitude of the high clergy was ambivalent. A pastoral letter of the Hungarian Bench of Bishops issued in October 1848 called for support of the nationalist government then in control.[29] In January 1849, however, the entry of Austrian troops into the capital occasioned a second pastoral letter from the bishops, calling for submission to the emperor.[30] Catholic Bishop Mihaly Horvath, who was serving as Minister of Culture and Education in the anti-Habsburg revolutionary government then sitting in Debrecen, refused to accept the pastoral letter as authentic. In a special appeal to the faithful, he warned them not to believe that it had originated with the Hungarian high hierarchy.[31]

Recent Hungarian research, published during the anticlerical phase of the post-World War II regime, has produced some documentation of antinationalist attitudes among the high clergy in 1848-1849. The romantic, nationalist literature of the period contains sporadic instances of strong and occasionally vulgar anticlericalism. It is probably not without foundation that in a conflict separating conservative from liberal, aristocrat from democrat, loyalist from revolutionary, the highest local dignitaries of the Catholic Church found themselves more in sympathy with the guardians of the status quo than with the insurgents bent on destroying it. In other middle-zone areas, however, such as Poland, where the bond between Catholicism and nationalism had become strong and where the enemies of the nationalists were Orthodox Russians and Protestant Prussians, both high and low clergy took its stand with the patriots.[32]

During the second half of the nineteenth century nationalism became a seemingly lost cause north of the Danube. The exception was Rumania, where it had received partial satisfaction and was awaiting full gratification. In the Habsburg domains, after the first shock of defeat in 1849, nationalist leadership gradually passed from romantic into moderate hands. In Poland, on the contrary, it was the romantic extremists, the "Reds," who gained the upper hand and swept the moderate "Whites" into renewed rebellion in 1863.[33] The Polish Catholic Church rallied to the nationalist cause. Priests fought in the guerrilla bands along with students, workers, and soldiers. When Russia triumphed over the nationalists, the Catholic Church also became an object of persecution and oppression. This was due not only to the participation of the clergy in the uprising but also to the longstanding antagonism between Russian Orthodoxy and Polish Catholicism. With the resultant rupture between the Vatican and Russia the papacy itself seemed to side with Polish nationalism.[34]

Centrifugal nationalism failed, even during its most dynamic phases, to explode the multinational empires of the middle zone during the nineteenth century. The disintegrating Ottoman Empire was an exception. All its European subject nationalities became independent by the early twentieth century. While the Balkan nations were moving toward independence and while the Poles were vainly struggling to end dependence, an unusual *modus vivendi* between nationalism and centralism, not thought of since the days of the attempted Greco-Hungarian dual monarchy in the twelfth century, was worked out and put to test in the Habsburg realms.

16

Liberation through Compromise: Austro-Hungarian Interdependence

When, during the late summer of 1848, the Habsburg *camarilla* (court cabal) contrived a revocation of the liberal Hungarian March Laws, it did so because seemingly the dynasty was in a position of strength firm enough to maintain the status quo, by the force of arms if need be. The Austrian Marshal Joseph Radetzky had just won a resounding victory over the Italian nationalists at Custozza on July 24. The Croatians and the other nationalities of the Crown Lands of St. Stephen were ready to march against their Hungarian overlords at Vienna's bidding. Should things still go wrong, in a final emergency the monarchs of the Holy Alliance would not permit a nationalist revolution to succeed anywhere in Europe. The soldiers of the tsar, who would carry out the will of the alliance, stood just across the eastern frontiers.

When, on July 11, 1848, Kossuth, amidst the thunderous ovations of the Hungarian Parliament, asked for and was voted 200,000 recruits for national defense, he acted out of the romantic nationalist conviction that there was no tyrant powerful enough to destroy a nation fighting for a just cause. Or, as he rhetorically put it in his speech, not even the gates of hell could prevail against a Hungary armed for freedom. There was, in addition, a misunderstanding between Vienna and the Hungarian nationalists, which went back as far as the *Pragmatic Sanction* of 1723. Under this Habsburg family law, which had been enacted by the Diets of both Hungary and Transylvania, Hungary and other Habsburg-ruled areas became "indivisible and inseparable." States indivisibly and inseparably tied together have joint affairs. These joint affairs were ignored by the March Laws and left a legalistic vacuum which soon turned into chaos. The end result of monarchist and nationalist miscalculation was a bloody revolutionary war dragged out to a final tragedy, in which the clash between Austrian and Hungarian overconfidence was settled only through Russian intervention. In any event, it was the Habsburgs and not the nationalists, Hungarian or anti-Hungarian, who in 1849 demonstrated their ability to draw from a power reservoir to make their cause prevail.

Eighteen years later the political ground no longer seemed resilient with success for either of the contestants. For the Habsburgs' defeat by the Prussians at Königgrätz in July 1866 meant reduction to a position of weakness between German nationalisms in the west and middle-zone nationalisms in the east. At the same time, the growth of the Pan-Slav movement after the 1848 Congress of the Slavs in Prague turned the majority of the empire's non-Magyar nationalists from supporters into potential destroyers of the monarchy. As for Russia, the leader of the new Pan-Slav idea of collective nationalism, it had become alienated by Habsburg ingratitude when Vienna chose to forget the help it got from the tsar in 1849 and remained menacingly neutral to Russia at the outbreak of the Crimean War in 1853. In conquered Hungary the nationalist movement still looked for leadership to the exiled magnetic Louis Kossuth but was gradually shifting to the sobering views of the moderate Francis Deak (1803-1876), who had chosen to remain in his homeland. Deak's views were based on the pessimistic lesson learned from the nationalist defeat of 1849 that "without secure and strong support, alone and by its own strength, the Hungarian nation is unable to defend its country and its national existence against the overwhelming power of its enemies." [1] Hungary, Deak kept explaining to his countrymen during 1866-1867, had been placed by fate among great powers, any one of which could wipe it off the face of the earth. If these great powers, he once wrote, "should fall to fighting among one another, in this struggle not we ourselves but the interests and caprices of others would decide our fate, swallowing or dismembering our country." [2] The political equation in which Deak summed up the problem was simple: "For us [Hungarians] Austria's existence is just as necessary as our existence is for Austria." [3] It was the painstakingly negotiated acceptance of this basic equation, prompted this time by a sense of political realism in both Vienna and Budapest, that made possible the Austro-Hungarian Compromise of 1867.

Under the new compromise arrangement Hungarian dependence on Austria did not end but was mitigated by Austrian dependence on Hungary. After Königgrätz the Habsburg center of gravity shifted from west to east. The Compromise mirrored this eastward shift in a legalized reconciliation between the Hungarian Parliament, heir to the 1848 national legislature, and the Habsburg dynasty. On the one hand, the reconciliation involved the restoration, with minor modifications, of the liberal, monarchic Hungarian Constitution of 1848. On the other hand, in return for a restoration of this constitution, the Hungarian Parliament accepted the unity of the Habsburg empire and invested Francis Joseph and his successors as kings in Hungary while reigning as emperors in Austria. The Austrian and Hungarian halves of the monarchy thus became coequal partners in the empire, each governing its own territories. Three state functions—foreign affairs, war, and finance—became "joint" affairs under common Austro-Hungarian ministries. Other "affairs of joint interest" were the state debt, the shared budget, interstate commerce and customs.[4]

A year later, in 1868, another compromise compact between Hungary and its "associated" kingdom of Croatia tried to establish a form of Croat-Hungarian interdependence. In this subsidiary relationship, however, the element of the Austro-Hungarian *quid pro quo* was missing. Not only did the Croatians have no political leverage to move the Hungarians from their dominant position, but the very fact of the Compromise between Vienna and Budapest had a reinforcing effect on the Hungarian position of strength vis-à-vis Croatia. Bishop Josip Juraj Strossmayer (1815-1905), leader of the Croatian People's Party from 1860 to 1873, led the struggle for a larger measure of political autonomy but had to be content with cultural achievements, which included the establishment of a university, an academy, museums, and a theater giving performances in the vernacular.

A new Hungarian nationalities law guaranteed equal linguistic rights to all the nationalities of the Crownlands of St. Stephen. It seemed like the dawn of a new era. The Hungarian nationalists, in a position of relative strength as regards Austria, which had been weakened by the rise of Prussia to hegemony in Germany, were able to obtain far-reaching concessions from the dynasty. The Habsburgs gave up their traditional policy of governing their Hungarian kingdom as a territory as dependent on Vienna as the Austrian hereditary provinces. The Hungarians desisted from their perennial demand to restore the status quo before the Ottoman breakthrough of 1526, when Hungary was still a fully independent kingdom. The other nationalist groups of the empire, renamed the Dual Monarchy in 1867, willy-nilly acquiesced in the new *modus vivendi* and settled down grudgingly to live for the next half century under joint Austro-Hungarian rule. On February 18, 1867, Julius Andrassy (1823-1890), a nationalist sentenced to death in 1849, was entrusted by the king with the formation of the first responsible Hungarian cabinet since 1848-1849.[5] On June 8 of the same year Francis Joseph and his beautiful Bavarian Queen Elizabeth were crowned in Matthias Corvinus's cathedral in Buda as King and Queen of Hungary.

Deak was not the sole architect of the new structure of interdependence. His fellow craftsman on the Austrian side was Friedrich Beust (1809-1886), Habsburg Foreign Minister and a recently imported anti-Prussian Saxon, who needed Hungary to show Bismarck that Habsburg Austria, even after the defeat at Königgrätz, was still in the same power category with Hohenzollern Prussia. Beust flitted like a blithe spirit to and fro between Vienna and Buda during 1866. He was at the coronation of Buda in 1867 and recalled with pleasure in his memoirs the words of recognition the king-emperor addressed to him. "No Austrian minister has ever been received in Hungary as you have!" [6] He told with relish how, during the festivities held in the Hungarian capital, he (being fifty-eight years old at the time) had his hand kissed by a hoary-maned and white-bearded Magyar octogenarian who knelt before him in the flower-bestrewn street and with grateful patriotic exuberance hailed him as "Our Father!" [7] Indeed, the Saxon Beust considered the Austro-Hungarian Compromise as the greatest achievement of his career. His pride of accomplishment ran through his Vienna Reichsrat speech of December 12, 1867, in defense of his and Deak's joint accomplishment. A deputy of the opposition had addressed to him the ironic question: "What will happen to the statesman counseling the king of Hungary not to recognize debts incurred by the emperor of Austria?" Beust handled the question with triumphantly aphoristic evasiveness: "The emperor is [now] not merely king of Hungary but also king in Hungary!" [8] The amused Reichsrat ratified the Compromise.

Placed in its world-historical context, the Austro-Hungarian Compromise was part of the late nineteenth-century modernizing process on the peripheries of the west, analogous to the attainment of dominion status for Canada, the Meiji restoration in Japan, and the reconstruction of the American Union after the Civil War. In all these reorganizational arrangements the retreat from political romanticism and from anachronistic survivals of the past coincided with the advance of the industrial revolution and of the age of the new, oceanic imperialism. Why did the change in the middle zone occur only in the Habsburg middle tier and neither to the north nor to the south? Possibly because the Habsburg form of absolutism in ruling dependent nations had always been more enlightened, more progressive, and more European than either Ottoman or Russian overlordship. Reconciliation between Russia and dependent Poland was made impossible by the bloody events of 1864. There was Hungarian blood spilled in 1849 by the Austrians too, but by 1867 most Hungarians were able to convince themselves that the martyrs had not died in vain.

In the narrower, middle-zone framework, the Compromise was historically a continuation of earlier attempts, last tried by the enlightened despots during the eighteenth century, to organize the ethnically heterogeneous but existentially interdependent population groups of the Danubian basin into one political entity for internal viability and the external exercise of power. The novelty in the Compromise structure was the hedged acceptance of nationalism as the predominant political force of the nineteenth century. It took diplomatic astuteness to convert this centrifugal political force into a centripetal, cohesive power to safeguard state survival for half a century.

The advantages of the dualistic, interdependent state were manifest. Dualism made possible until 1914 the maintenance of peace based on the European balance of power by preventing the opening of a vacuum north of the Danube. Dualism also stimulated half a century of material and cultural progress in the middle zone, permitted an incipient integration with the economy of the world through a development of the free enterprise system as well as of the trade-union movement. It enabled people to live with their problems in security and peace, surrounded by a simulacrum of permanence, in contrast to the situation on the Vistula Plain or in the Balkans.

The most serious shortcoming of the dualistic system was the insistence of the Hungarian ruling elite on keeping the non-Magyar nationalities of the realm of St. Stephen in a state of dependence, denying their aspirations for the sake of Hungarian nationalistic aims. Interdependence. therefore, was limited to the relationship between the Austrian and Hungarian ethnic elements and excluded the minorities who together constituted the majority of the monarchy's inhabitants. As it was said in a moment of exuberance during the early days of dualism by an Austrian to a Hungarian politician: "Henceforth you rule your barbarians; we will rule ours." The "barbarians" were the Serbs, Croats, Slovenes, Czechs, Slovaks, Poles, and Rumanians. The first three of these had an Illyrian nationalist tradition antedating the French Revolution. Czech nationalism had roots as early as the fourteenth century and was emotionally influenced by the tragedy of John Hus and the fifteenth-century revolt of the Hussites. From the early nineteenth century it was provided high-caliber intellectual and political leadership by the great historian Frantisek Palacky (1798-1876) whose *History of Bohemia to 1526* was first published (in German) during 1830. A strong Slovak nationalist movement had been launched by Ludovit Stur (1815-1856), a professor in the Lutheran Lyceum of Bratislava, who fled Hungary and found refuge in Prague. The main targets of Polish nationalism were Russia and Prussia but its goal remained the reconstruction from its three partitioned components of an independent Poland, glorified by the exiled Romantic poet Adam Mickiewicz (1798-1855). Rumanian nationalism in Transylvania was nourished by pride in Latinity and in the antique Daco-Roman past. It found a gifted leader in Avram Jancu (1824-1872), a liberal lawyer whom the clash between Rumanian and Hungarian nationalisms forced to compromise with Habsburg absolutism.

The nationalism of these dependent peoples remained centrifugal after 1867 and continued to press against the seams of the dualistic structure with increasing force. It was especially short-sighted to reject Czech demands in 1871 for an expanded system of political accommodation under which Bohemia would have received under the monarchy the same rights and privileges as Hungary. As late as 1898 Woodrow Wilson, under the impact of whose Fourteen Points the dualistic structure fell to pieces twenty years later in the moment of defeat, could only express admiration for Hungarian skill in winning a "highly favored place in the Dual Monarchy." [9] But the French historian Auerbach writing in the same year as Wilson, expressed a contrary opinion. He was the first to accuse the Hungarians of "committing an anachronism in attempting to found a nation . . . on the corpses of diverse nationalities." [10]

Auerbach's views prevailed over Wilson's. Liberal western opinion makers, who had been admirers of the Hungarians in their 1848-1849 freedom fight against Habsburg absolutism, became protagonists of Hungary's non-Magyar nationalities. A typical example was the Norwegian Nobel-Prize winner Bjornstjerne Bjornson, who as a young man in the 1850s had extolled the freedom-fighting Hungarians of Louis Kossuth, but as an old man at the turn of the century condemned them for denying freedom to others.[11]

There was no question that the Compromise, while terminating the state of complete dependence for Hungarians, prolonged it for their subject nationalities, the Croats, Serbs, Rumanians, Slovaks, and others. However, western observers had trouble seeing into the Hungarian microcosm and observed only the ruling class, which enjoyed quasi-independence from above while maintaining dependence below. The outside world did not see the Hungarian opponents of the "uncompromising compromise," who championed the non-Magyar minorities' right to liberation and equality.

The ruling elite in Hungary during the second half of the nineteenth century was the product of a social process which Ortega might have cited to illustrate his theory of the rise of the historical level,[12] the appearance as actors on the stage of history of previously submerged population strata. The Compromise of 1867 had not been the work of the high aristocracy of Hungary. Many of the greatest landowners of the kingdom were "old conservatives," who would have been satisfied with much less than a return to the liberal constitution of 1848. This faction had a key role in breaking the political impasse, but the Compromise was the achievement of the middle nobility, the landowning class of moderate means. This group numbered probably not more than four thousand families in a population of around fifteen million at mid-century, increasing to nineteen million by 1900. During the early part of the nineteenth century the sons of these gentry were cultivated men in the western sense. They had sparked the nationalist revolution because they were steeped in the ideas of the Enlightenment and were fired by reading about barricades periodically rising in the streets of Paris from 1789 to 1848. After the failure of the Hungarian revolution, the families of the middle nobility rusticated on their country estates, shielded from the intellectual currents of the west.

Historically this segment of Hungarian society was heir to centuries of political resistance by the autonomous counties to the central governing authority. But the country squires, the political bosses of Compromise Hungary, were numerically insignificant. Consequently, after rising to the "historical level," they were compelled, step by step, to accept into their well-defined caste members of the petty nobility, the next lower social class, some of them landless and hardly distinguishable from the peasantry. The assimilable part of this submerged stratum was gradually admitted into the middle nobility to share top political leadership. The lesser fry supplied the rank and file of the state and county bureaucracy. The petty nobles had to resort to a proletarian existence, to which they were being driven by their inability to adjust to the partially free-labor type of agriculture created by the emancipation of the serfs in 1848. Thus, increasingly during the last three decades of the nineteenth century, Hungarian political leadership and the bureaucracy it commanded were recruited from provincials of limited horizons, under whose stewardship Deak's liberal concept of the "political nation," in which acceptance of the idea of a quasi-independent Hungarian state would be rewarded by equal nationality rights, slowly withered to a form of "quietistic conservatism." [13]

The ideas of the new ruling elite on the question of nationality had been conditioned by personal origins and roots in the Hungarian kingdom's sixty-three counties, the majority of which were multinational. To squires from multinational counties ethnic differences appeared largely as social distinctions between master and servant. Non-Magyar nationalist strivings struck them, especially if they were among the growing number of ethnic assimilants, as menacing their newly won class status. In addition, some of these men had retained ancestral memories of horrors perpetrated on the rulers and their families during the non-Magyar peasant uprisings of earlier centuries in the peripheral areas of the realm. In many a squire's mind the armed struggle of 1848-1849 lived on as an interracial, intercultural war, a sort of Sepoy rebellion against a Magyar *raj*. The liberal traditions of early nineteenth-century Hungarian nationalism thus atrophied within the span of two generations into a chauvinistic legend, to a form of stereotyped literary romanticism.[14]

Western observers saw the Hungarian upholders of the system of Austro-Hungarian interdependence but not its antagonists. Already in his "Cassandra Letter" of 1867 [15] the exiled Kossuth warned his former colleague Deak that the Compromise would prove to be a point "beyond which Hungary could no longer be master of its future." [16] In his mellowing years the idolized leader of the Hungarian nationalists counseled political coexistence with other Danubian nationalities. By 1862 he had worked out the broad outlines of a Danubian confederation to unite independent Hungarians, South Slavs, and Rumanians as equal partners in a Habsburg-free federal state.[17] Lajos Mocsary (1826-1916), president of the anti-Compromise Hungarian Independence Party formed in 1875 and "the purest repository of the traditions of 1848," [18] broke with his own followers on the nationality question and became the champion of a new deal for the minorities. As early as 1861 he had warned against the approaching Compromise. In 1881 he raised his voice to declare that, without making peace with the other nationalities inhabiting Hungary, the Magyars could not attain true independence. "It would be an absurd policy," he wrote, "to oppose the nationalities on the one hand, and to form a front against Austria on the other." [19] At the turn of the century Mocsary called on the ruling group to choose between two policies: either Magyarization or independence, because the two, he said, could not be pursued together in good faith. Peace with the non-Magyar nationalities, he counselled, was within reach, provided that they were given equal constitutional status with the Magyars.[20]

Agitation to terminate the dependent status of the non-Magyar minorities was carried on by Magyar intellectuals at mid-century and continued right up to the outbreak of World War I. Foremost among these men was the brilliant political scientist Oscar Jaszi (1875-1957), who was to finish his days as an exile on the distant shores of Lake Erie. Jaszi saw the Compromise of 1867 as a compact of the "Austrian Emperor with the Hungarian feudal classes, which the liberal German high bourgeoisie accepted, though not without serious hesitation, in order to secure its own hegemony against the will of the Slav majority." [21] According to him the basic arithmetical fault of the Dual Monarchy was the attempt to balance on its apex a pyramid formed of six million Austro-Germans and five million Magyars, exposing skyward its base containing eighteen million Slavs and Rumanians.[22] Amazingly enough, this gravity-defying balancing act lasted half a century.

It lasted fifty years because no external shock upset the precarious equilibrium until 1914 and because the combined eleven million Austro-Hungarians had a common interest in the prevention of an external force of attraction operating on the eighteen million Slavs and Rumanians over whom they were jointly ruling. This force of attraction could be exerted by a united South Slav state, a "Yugoslavia," which might rise south of the Danube on the ruins of the Ottoman Empire. Austro-Hungarian foreign policy, therefore, attempted to forestall the rise of such a state, which would probably seek to incorporate Austrian Slovenia as well as Hungarian Croatia, Voyvodina, and the Banat. Serbia, which seemed to be readying itself to play the role of a Balkan Piedmont, had to be contained and kept within an Austrian sphere of influence. Both Austro-Hungarian diplomacy and military intervention in the Balkans were motivated by a domestic concern to preserve the unity of the Compromise-based Dual Monarchy.

As the collapse of the Ottoman Empire became apparently imminent in 1875, a sense of urgency seized the Austro-Hungarian Ministry of Foreign Affairs in Vienna's Ballhausplatz. The monarchy was in danger: if parts of the Sick Man's legacy were allowed to fall into Serbian hands, the Yugoslav threat would arise on the Lower Danube. As fate would have it, it was exactly the preventive military diplomacy of the Monarchy in the Balkans that not only failed to forestall the rise of the South Slav state but also touched off a world conflict whose destructive fury overwhelmed states far less heterogeneous than the Compromise-based Austro-Hungarian Empire. The immediate chain of events which led to the demise of dualism may be traced to the crisis stage reached in the dissolution process of the Ottoman Empire during July 1875.

17

The Eastern Question
and Balkanization

The partitions of Poland at the end of the eighteenth century and the Polish uprising at the end of the nineteenth evoked a few diplomatic notes of protest from the maritime powers of Europe but did not produce a "Polish Question" of vital importance to them. The attempted dismemberment of the Habsburg empire by nationalists in the mid-nineteenth century aroused public interest in coastal Europe, even French armed intervention in its Italian phase, and applause for the Magyar freedom fighters during the prolonged struggle in Hungary, but no other western diplomatic or military involvement. The United States, which in 1849 sent a diplomatic agent to the revolutionary Kossuth government (he never got beyond Vienna),[1] came the closest to intervention. The Great Powers never had to grapple with a "Hungarian Question" to maintain their own relations on an even keel. The only middle-zone political issue which became a major problem of modern world politics was the Eastern Question: what to do about the void Turkey would leave in the Balkans by disappearing from the rank of great powers.

The term "Eastern Question" was first used in a French diplomatic note of 1839 to denote the Gordian knot which had to be disentangled before the approaching collapse of the Ottoman Empire could seriously disturb the European balance of power. The gradual disintegration of this huge and sprawling agglomeration of territories which, *de jure*, at least, during the last quarter of the nineteenth century, still covered the entire non-European coast of the Mediterranean from the Black Sea to the Atlantic, was of vital concern to the maritime powers. Primarily it was a source of deep anxiety to England's diplomacy because the future of Turkey involved the guardianship of the strategic straits—the Dardanelles and the Bosporus—which could be kept closed by an Anglophile Turkey but through which an aggressive Russia could freely irrupt into the Mediterranean if Turkey were no longer the guardian. Such a Russian irruption would constitute a threat to the new British lifeline to India, in existence since the opening of the Suez Canal in 1869. How important this shortened sea route appeared to be to the British Empire was advertised to the world by Prime Minister Disraeli's acquisition, during November 1875, of the controlling share of the stock in the International Suez Canal Company. The Eastern Question thus took on a new dimension during the 1870s. It ceased to be a regional problem involving only the dependence or independence of the sultan's Christian subjects in the Balkans. It became a major diplomatic concern in the chancelleries of the major powers affecting global relationships.

The world-wide interests of the great powers [2] paved the way from dependence to independence in the Balkans. Russia wanted to hasten the collapse of Turkey by inciting the Balkan Slavs to rebellion and by supporting them in their struggle. England was anxious to maintain a strong Turkey, in firm control of the straits, and strongly suspected that Russia, in fomenting trouble among the Balkan Christians, had designs on its imperial holdings. Like England, Austria-Hungary had an interest in the maintenance of the status quo, because of those problems in the Balkan peninsula which it considered dangerous to its own interests. In the 1860s and 1870s the Dual Monarchy had become the prime target for the Pan-Slav agitation of such supernationalist Russian writers as Fadeiev and Danilevsky, who were preaching the destruction of the Habsburg empire as a prerequ·ite for the union of all Slavs under the tsar's scepter.[3] To counter such a dangerous eventuality, Austria-Hungary followed a policy designed to prolong the life of the Sick Man without recurrent crises, if possible. Vienna also tried to prevent the aggrandizement of a catalytic Serbia, which might pull into its orbit sloughed-off Ottoman territories.[4] At the same time, however, Austrian militarists, who had the ear of the emperor, looked with covetous eyes on the mountainous hinterland of the Dalmatian coast, on the Turkish-held provinces of Bosnia and Herzegovina. These wild highlands were marked for eventual annexation to the monarchy for purely strategic reasons.[5]

It was at the urging of his generals that the Emperor Francis Joseph went in the spring of 1875 to visit his faithful subjects in Dalmatia. There he ostentatiously received malcontent delegations from neighboring Bosnia and Herzegovina. The outbreak of the insurrection in these two provinces during July may have been triggered by this imperial demonstration of sympathy. The situation became further complicated in September, when the Bulgarian subjects of the sultan also rebelled, because of grievances of their own. The Turkish irregulars sent to quell the rebellion used the same savagely atrocious methods which had outraged the European conscience in incidents such as the massacre on Chios during the Greek war for independence early in the century.[6] When news of these "Bulgarian horrors" reached England, the public feeling of humanitarian revulsion against the "unspeakable Turk" was turned into a domestic political issue by the anti-imperialist opposition.[7] The pro-Ottoman stance of the British government was shaken to its very foundations at a time when the Eastern Question had just reached a crisis stage.

The dependent Slav peoples of the Balkans, whom the crisis of 1875 willy-nilly set on the road of independence and unity, showed different degrees of political development. In Bosnia and Herzegovina the insurgents were for the most part wild mountaineers who rose against the corrupt local administration the central Ottoman government was absentmindedly maintaining in their provinces. Bosnia, it will be remembered, was the area where the Bogomil heretics of the thirteenth century had embraced Islam and in the course of five centuries had become assimilated to Turkish ethnicity. While there was dissatisfaction among the Christian population due to the slowness of the Porte in decreeing and applying reforms to improve their social and economic status, there was also a great deal of resentment among the Turkicized landowning classes, whose privileged feudal position was to be undermined by the promised reforms.[8] Independence at this stage was definitely not yet the goal of the insurgents, Moslem or Christian. The only objectives appear to have been relief from the depredations of local Ottoman officialdom and a general improvement of the human condition.

The Bulgarian rebels were far more advanced politically. Their ill-timed uprising had been preceded by years of revolutionary plotting and conspiratorial organizing, stimulated by nationalist dreams of the two medieval Bulgarian empires. Russian rubles and Pan-Slav ideas from the north kept the secret societies going and reaching into population strata slowly awakening to national consciousness. The Serbs, who had already obtained quasi-independence under their own prince and among whom nationalism, Pan-Slavism, and the Russian influence were at least as strong as among the Bulgarians, had a strong sense of serving the holy cause of Slav unity in the Balkans. But neither the Bosnians, nor the Bulgarians, nor even the Serbs, had any thought or desire in 1875 to destroy the Ottoman Empire. In his casual declaration of war against Turkey in June 1876, Prince Milan Obrenovich of Serbia professed an intention to preserve Ottoman territorial integrity.[9] But nationalism was already motivating the political action of all concerned parties in the St. Petersburg-Constantinople-London triangle. Serbia and Serb Montenegro went to war against Turkey under the impelling pressure of Russian-aggravated Slav nationalism, whose Balkan votaries saw in the Bosnian uprising an opportunity to move closer to the idea of a territorial Yugoslavia under the sultan's suzerainty.

By 1876, however, nationalism had also developed its Turkish variant, which set as its objective the defense of the Ottoman Empire. In the ensuing clash between two nationalistically inspired armies— Serbian-Montenegrin on one side, Turkish on the other—the latter proved superior under inspired military leadership. At this point the Great Powers intervened, because the defeat of Serbia (the Montenegrins as usual held their own in their mountain strongholds) posed the immediate threat of a territorial squabble between Austria and Russia. Such a controversy would have had far-reaching consequences for the other Great Powers. England, Germany, and France were certain to be affected in the pursuit of their interests elsewhere, even though they did not seek to profit from an imminent dismemberment of Turkey in the Balkans. The Constantinople Conference of 1876, hurriedly called by the Powers to maintain the European equilibrium, was, however, torpedoed by the newly established Turkish regime. Istanbul unexpectedly proclaimed reforms, turning the Ottoman Empire into a constitutional, parliamentary, liberal federation of equal nationalities—on paper at least. In any event, the conference thus lost its *raison d'être,* which was to settle the crisis through reforms rather than through war, which might end no one knew where. The meeting therefore adjourned sine die.

If there were no open convenants openly arrived at, a secret Austrian-Russian convention was negotiated behind the scenes. Its purpose was to delineate Balkan spheres of influence, looking forward to an ultimate Ottoman collapse. Under the terms of the secret convention,[10] Austria-Hungary was to have a free hand in Bosnia-Herzegovina to satisfy its strategic interests and to keep in existence a territorial gap—the Sanjak of Novi Bazar—between Serbia and Montenegro. Russia would not be challenged in Rumania and Bulgaria, the two client states which lay athwart the narrow invasion route between the eastern Carpathians and the Black Sea littoral connecting Russia with the Balkans. Nobody was to tamper with the fulcrum of

South Slav nationalism: Serbia and its kindred principality of Montenegro.[11] If carried out, the secret convention would have prevented a clash of Austrian and Russian imperialisms in the Balkans and might have contained the pent-up forces of Serb nationalism. But it proved to be an unequal struggle of diplomacy against onrushing change replete with the contingent and the unforeseen.

Nationalism could be checked by armies if no Great Power intervened on its behalf. Nationalism, however, proved too difficult to keep within bounds by diplomatic means. Essentially it was nationalism running amok in Russia and Turkey, as well as in the small Balkan nations emerging into independence, that brought on the Russo-Turkish War of 1877-1878. The heroic and mock-heroic episodes of the major conflict, which Russia declared in April 1877 after the defeat of the Serbs, have been told in great detail in historical narratives: [12] the victorious advance of the tsar's armies through Rumania and Bulgaria to within ten miles of Constantinople, after a bloody contretemps in the Shipka Pass across the Balkan Mountains, where Osman Pasha, the "Lion of Plevna," immobilized them from July to December; the ludicrous maneuverings of the British fleet in the straights toward and away from the threatened Turkish capital; the rise of the war spirit in England, christened "jingoism" from the popular ditty chanted by the superpatriotic mobs surging through the streets of London—

> "We don't want to fight, but by jingo, if we do,
> We've got the men, we've got the ships, and
> we've got the money, too!"

The war ended in the Treaty of San Stefano, dictated by the victorious but diarrheic Russians to the bloody but unbowed Turks. The treaty was then promptly undictated at Berlin under the presidency of the "honest broker," Bismarck, in the midst of the most glittering assembly of European powers since the Congress of Vienna in 1815 and of Paris in 1856.

The Treaty of San Stefano, a purely bilateral arrangement in March 1878 between Russia and Turkey, was a triumph of Pan-Slavism. The sultan was forced to recognize the independence of Serbia, Montenegro, and Rumania and to grant autonomy to a huge Russian-sponsored Bulgaria extending from the Danube down to the Aegean and from the Black Sea west to Albania, including Macedonia and Rumelia. Montenegro was to receive a new seaport on the Adriatic. Bessarabia would revert to victorious Russia, and compensation would be made to Rumania from the Dobrudja, south of the Danube delta. Bosnia and Herzegovina were to remain Turkish but under a reform constitution providing equal rights and human dignity for their motley population.[13]

San Stefano violated the interests of both England and Austria by its establishment of a large Bulgaria. London objected to the northern Aegean coastline falling under the control of a Russian satrapy which would dominate the sea-lanes to and from the Dardanelles and Gallipoli. Austria saw its interests threatened by the rise of any large South Slav state, whether Serbia or Bulgaria. Bismarck, looking out for the future of the Hohenzollern Reich, then not quite eight years old, could not permit a rift between Austria and Russia, both friendly to Germany. Even a slight rift between these two powers might frustrate his policy of securing the eastern frontiers of Germany, so as to be able to deal, in case of need, with a revenge-seeking France in the west. Nor could he allow a rapprochement between France and an England seeking to buttress its position against Russia. The result was the unmaking of the Treaty of San Stefano and the regulation of the Balkan shift from dependence to independence, not simply to satisfy Russian and Pan-Slav appetites, but also to safeguard the interests of other directly or indirectly concerned Great Powers.

The Berlin Congress,[14] which sat from June to July 1878, was a milestone in the establishment of independent Balkan states. Rumania, Serbia, and Montenegro were recognized as fully sovereign states. Montenegro got its port (Antivari) on the Adriatic. Rumania ceded Bessarabia to Russia but was compensated in the Dobrudja. Bosnia and Herzegovina and also the narrow strip of the Sanjak of Novi Bazar separating Serbia from Montenegro were to be occupied militarily, though not annexed politically, by Austria-Hungary. Serbia and Montenegro were limited in their territorial gains, moderately as compared to Bulgaria, which was cut down to one-third of its San Stefano size. Macedonia was returned to Turkey with a promise of reforms. Rumelia, south of the Balkan Mountains, remained under Ottoman military and political control, though under the supervision of consuls reporting to the Great Powers. North of the chain of the Balkan Mountains there was permitted an autonomous Bulgaria paying tribute to the Sublime Porte. England, incidentally, made sure to strengthen its control of the imperial lifeline by acquiring the island of Cyprus from Turkey.

But the greatest loser at Berlin was the Ottoman Empire, at its lowest ebb of power in Europe since the fourteenth century. After nearly half a millennium of dependence, the Albanians, the Macedonians, and some Bulgarians were still *de jure* subjects of the sultan. The inhabitants of Bosnia-Herzegovina and the Sanjak of Novi Bazar remained technically under Ottoman sovereignty. On the other hand, Rumania, Bessarabia, Serbia, and Montenegro were excised from the empire. A precedent was thereby set for the dismemberment, forty years later, of other multinational empires which were considered obstacles to the exercise of the right of self-determination by dependent nations which wanted to become independent.

Independence had thus either become or was about to become a reality in the middle zone south of the Danube. The Great Powers, which had made independence possible, played an ambivalent role. The vicinal land powers, Russia above all, which farther to the north had stamped out independence and continued to maintain full or semidependence, helped establish independence in the south. Insular Englishmen naively asked the question: Why is the tsar oppressing Slavs in Poland and liberating them in the Balkans? For that matter, the rest of Europe, especially the émigré Poles in England and France, were also posing embarrassing questions: Why, for example, were the maritime powers, which had maintained a policy of nonintervention in 1863-1864 when Polish freedom was trampled in the dust, seeing to it, through multilateral diplomatic intervention, that Rumanians, Serbs, and Montenegrins would live free and Bulgarians partially free in their homelands? [15] Nobody asked, on the other hand, where the establishment of a minor league of bickering states, with political habits rooted in dependence, would lead. Nor could the general public foresee that a systemic imbalance in a regional microcosm of minor states, outraged in their nationalism would, in a matter of decades, totally destroy the general European balance of power so assiduously maintained for a century.

For none of the newly independent Balkan countries was satisfied. Rumania bewailed the loss of Bessarabia and continued looking wistfully across the mountains into Transylvania. Bulgaria mourned her unredeemed provinces of Macedonia and Rumelia. Serbian nationalism was raised to a white heat over Austrian military presence in Bosnia, Herzegovina, and the Sanjak. The Montenegrins came to the verge of war with the Albanians over the Adriatic coast. The Balkans became a hornets' nest, full of resentful, spiteful, feuding, plotting, vengeance-seeking, assassination-bent nationalists, determined to pay off scores and to remake reality to fit their political concepts. The ancient medieval animosity between self-liberated Serbia and Russian-freed Bulgaria reappeared. Serbia, under a native dynasty (with the title of king from 1882), was deeply resentful of Russia for lavishing its hegemonial affections on Bulgaria under its German princes. The Obrenovich King Milan swore that he would never demean himself to the role of a Russian "prefect" or his country to the rank of a Russian "satrapy," but in so doing he imprudently accepted a form of Austrian protectorate over his country, much to the chagrin of his ministers.[16] The sentiment of Serbian intransigence and rejection of Russian dictation began to take root. The diplomatic necessity of using Russia even as just a counterweight to the Dual Monarchy could last only as long as the Habsburgs remained an imperial power in Vienna.

A nationalist insurrection in Rumelia, the southern Bulgarian province that the Congress of Berlin had returned to Turkey, brought Balkan turbulence to a new stage of crisis in September 1885. In disregard of the 1878 decision of the Great Powers assembled in the German capital, the Rumelian rebels proclaimed the union of their homeland with autonomous Bulgaria north of the Balkan Mountains. The uprising came on the heels of a diplomatic revolution. For about five years (1879-1883) Bulgaria had indeed become what Serbia refused to turn into: a Russian "satrapy" under a Russian "prefect," the German Prince Alexander Battenberg. (The family name was changed to Mountbatten later.) In the course of romantic adventures, which read like the story of the *Prisoner of Zenda,* Prince Alexander lost the favor of his uncle the tsar. By the time of the Rumelian uprising in 1885, Russia was dead-set against a greater Bulgaria. She received diplomatic support from Austria-Hungary, which was still opposed to the creation of the large South Slav state whether in the western or in the eastern Balkans. On the other hand, Great Britain, which had been instrumental in reducing the Greater Bulgaria established by the Russians at San Stefano in March 1878 to its truncated size of July 1878, saw Battenberg's principality as a buffer state useful in blocking Russian expansion toward the Aegean and the Dardanelles.

Accordingly, London offered a compromise solution of the new Balkan crisis by prevailing on the sultan, who was the sovereign of Rumelia, to appoint Prince Alexander Battenberg as governor of the rebellious province. This was tantamount to a union of the two Bulgarias. At this point, however, jealous Serbia, fearful that an enlarged Bulgaria would incorporate not only Rumelia but also the disputed province of Macedonia, declared war on Bulgaria. But Macedonia was only one concrete symbol of the deep-seated Bulgaro-Serb rivalry dating from the Middle Ages. What made the Serbs particularly apprehensive in November 1885 was the fact that Bulgarian nationalism had been creating a pro-Bulgarian climate of political preference in Macedonia through cultural and religious means. As a matter of fact, since the creation of a Bulgarian exarchate in 1870 most of the Macedonian populations had been living under Bulgarian ecclesiastical jurisdiction.[17] The Serbs knew from their own tactics in the Voyvodina that the recognition of church autonomy was an intermediate step toward attainment of political self-government.

The Serbo-Bulgarian war of 1885 opened and ended with Bulgarian victories. The Bulgarians invaded Serbia and soundly trounced their fellow Slavs in the battles of Slivnitsa and Pirot in November 1885. Serbia was saved by the diplomatic intervention of the Dual Monarchy, but Russia continued in its anti-Bulgarian stance and managed to engineer the fall and exile of Prince Alexander Battenberg in 1886. Flouting Russian opposition, the defiant Bulgarians replaced him with Prince Ferdinand of Saxe-Coburg, a jovial colonel in the Austro-Hungarian army. The ensuing tension between Vienna and St. Petersburg once again raised the perennial specter of an armed clash of unforeseeable ramifications between the two rival claimants for the Sick Man's mantle. Fortunately, German mediation proved effective. Austrians and Russians both stopped rattling their sabers. A few years later, in 1886, the conversion to the Orthodox faith of Prince Boris, Ferdinand's son and heir to the Bulgarian throne, again made Russia smile benignly on its closest Balkan protégé.

While these diplomatic and dynastic changes were taking place, a new Balkan crisis was brewing in Macedonia. Two rival Macedonian organizations, IMRO (founded in 1893) and EMRO (established in 1895), fought each other and their opponents from Greece to Rumania in a wave of ambushes, kidnappings, political assassinations, and brutal murders. IMRO (Macedonian Revolutionary Organization, Internal) wanted an autonomous Macedonia. EMRO (Macedonian Revolutionary Organization, External) which operated out of Sofia and was Bulgarian-financed, proclaimed the identity of the Bulgarian and Macedonian ethnic elements as one nation, and worked for the annexation of Macedonia to Bulgaria.

EMRO raids into Macedonia across the Bulgaro-Macedonian border finally touched off a major Macedonian uprising in 1902-1903. Turkey, of course, was still sovereign in Macedonia. War was narrowly avoided not only between Bulgaria and Turkey, but also between Bulgaria and Rumania, where Macedonian assassins succeeded in pushing nerves as well as statesmanship to the brink.

By the time the twentieth century opened, political violence and particularly assassination had seemingly become a conventional way of effecting governmental change in the newly independent Balkan states. Plotted assassination was being used as a substitute for the abdication of kings and the resignation of prime ministers. Crisis followed upon crisis at the turn of the century. To quell a nationwide uprising of wretched and discontented Rumanian peasants in 1907, an army of 120,000 regulars was put in the field, and several villages in the immediate vicinity of Bucharest were razed by artillery fire.[18] The next year, nationalism on the defensive produced an internal crisis in the Ottoman empire. The Young Turks, nationistically minded officers in the sultan's army, seized power and were supported by the revolting First Albanian Army Corps in Constantinople (1908-1909).[19] Again Turkey seemed on the verge of collapse. Again both Balkan nationalism and external imperialism hastened to take advantage. Prince Ferdinand of Bulgaria proclaimed the full independence of his country and assumed the glorious Bulgarian medieval title of tsar in 1908. Far more provocative were the consequences of Austria's move. On October 6, 1908, the monarchy proclaimed the political annexation of Bosnia-Herzegovina,[20] which had been under Austro-Hungarian military occupation since 1878. This outrage to their cherished nationalist objective, the hoped-for creation of a catalytic South Slav Piedmont, drove Serbian, Bosnian, and Montenegrin conspirators to a state of political madness and extremism. It was no longer Russia but Austria which was betraying and frustrating Serb nationalism. The Bosnian annexation crisis in 1908 lit the fuse that burned until the great world-shattering explosion six years later.

Those last six years of general peace saw unceasing turmoil and two murderous wars in the Balkans. While the other great powers watched apprehensively, Russia used diplomatic means to bring about a league of Balkan states to serve as a barrier to further Austrian encroachments at the expense of the sultan's moribund empire.[21] Vienna, for its part, became a sponsor of Albanian independence. This was a decision taken to deny Serbia an outlet on the Adriatic Sea as part of the greater Austrian strategic design to prevent the rise of a Yugoslav state. The Albanian tribes rose in rebellion during 1910. With Austrian support, an independent Albania was proclaimed in November 1912. This new non-Slav state was aloof from and hostile to its neighbors from its very inception. Italian imperialism threatened its existence from across the Adriatic. Surrounded by enemies on all sides, semi-Asiatic and divided internally, its hope of survival lay in autocratic rule at home and in the support of some remote imperial power as distant as or even farther away than the Dual Monarchy.

During the year of Albanian independence, the efforts of Russian diplomacy to create a Balkan bloc bore fruit. In March 1912 feuding Bulgaria and Serbia were brought together in the expectation of territorial gains either at Austria's or at Turkey's expense. Tough little Montenegro, always in the forefront for Serb independence, led off by declaring war on Turkey in October. Bulgaria, Serbia, and Greece followed suit. The First Balkan War (October 1912-May 1913) was on. Before long the Turkish armies were reeling back in defeat before the concentric attacks of the four hostile armies. The Serbs and Montenegrins established themselves on the Adriatic coast in areas reserved for Albania. The Bulgarian army, as in 1885, swept ahead to spectacular victories at Kirk-Kilissa and Lule Burgas. By November it was storming the Chatalja line, the last remaining fortification before Constantinople.

No Bulgarian army had come so close to the imperial city since the days of Tsar Ivan Asen in the thirteenth century. At Chatalja, however, a halt was called by the Russians. The tsar did not want to see the Second Rome fall into Bulgarian hands. Both Russia and Austria-Hungary began to mobilize. But British and German diplomacy came to the rescue. London and Berlin had a triple aim: the conflict should not spread beyond the Balkans; the nationalism of the small states should be satisfied at Ottoman expense; and the straits and Constantinople should remain under Turkish sovereignty. This, in essence, was the arrangement made by the Treaty of London in May 1913, under which Turkey surrendered all its Balkan territories west of a line drawn from Midia on the Black Sea coast, just south of the 42nd parallel, to Enos at the Aegean estuary of the Maritsa river, at the northern entrance of the Gulf of Saros. Strategic Turkish control was thus not weakened on the Gallipoli Peninsula to the south. England soon bewailed this fact. But while the Bulgarians were coming into possession of the territories surrendered by the Turks, the Serbs once again were abandoned by the Russians. They were not allowed to hold their conquests on the Adriatic. Finally, in the moment of victory, disappointment over the division of the spoils drove a new wedge between the old-time rivals, Bulgaria and Serbia.

The other Balkan nations from Rumania down to Greece, as well as defeated Turkey, shared Serbia's resentment of Bulgaria. The Bulgarians themselves precipitated the Second Balkan War (June-July 1913) by imprudently taking the offensive. This was exactly what the anti-Bulgarian Balkanites had been waiting for. In the course of co-ordinated military operations lasting less than a month, Bulgaria was brought to her knees by Serbia, Rumania, Greece, and Turkey. In the Treaty of Bucharest in August 1913 she was deprived of her port of Salonika on the Aegean coast, Ochrid on the Albanian border and Monastir on the road to it, northern Dobrudja below the Danube delta, and most of Macedonia. There was still an independent Bulgaria, with an outlet to the Aegean at the minor port Dedeh-Agatch, but it was a dissatisfied and bitter Bulgaria, repeatedly humiliated since the Congress of Berlin in 1878 and separated from its Balkan neighbors by a clash of nationalistic aspirations.

The Great Powers had not tried their hands at making small states since the Belgian experiment of 1830. In that diplomatic exercise, as well as in the repeated Balkan interventions since the 1856 Paris Conference, the double objective had been to satisfy dangerous local nationalism so as to safeguard the security of the Great Powers. Both the diplomatic fiction of Belgian neutrality and the assiduous localization of crises rising from the Eastern Question proved simultaneously ineffective within less than twelve months after the signing of the Treaty of Bucharest—ineffective in the final analysis but not effort totally wasted, because diplomacy was successful in its silent, unseen, antlike work which held back adverse historical change and prolonged the peace of the world by over half a century. Whether this would have been possible if a state system of several rival Belgiums had been created in 1830, as was the case in the Balkans in 1878, is a question difficult to answer. In any event, the creation of Belgium in 1830 did not start a process of Belgianization, a proliferation of small states at the mercy of their predatory neighbors. The triumph of centrifugal nationalism with Great Power assistance south of the Danube during the second half of the nineteenth century, on the other hand, did lead to a process of Balkanization. Small and mutually hostile states were created by the powers, first in Europe after the First World War and later in Asia and Africa, after the Second. The ultimate consequence was the rise in the second half of the twentieth century of 140-odd sovereign nation states, a Balkanized globe, with all the dire implications the pursuit of the interests of such a multitude of sovereignties has for the peace of the world.

18

The Jewish Presence and the Rise of Zionism

The doctrine of Jewish political repatriation from the Diaspora to Palestine was not a product of the middle zone, but Theodor Herzl (1860-1904), the founder of Zionism, was born in what soon became Budapest, spent the first eighteen formative years of his life in Hungary, and got strong early support for his work from the Jewish community in Bulgaria.[1] The Jewish presence in this part of the world, from which Herzl sprang and which later provided a morbid common denominator of political anti-Semitism with Nazi Germany, is therefore of some interest not only within but beyond the middle zone as well.

Cemeteries with Hebraic tombstones and other archeological evidence attest the presence of Jewish communities in landlocked Europe under Roman rule.[2] St. Paul's first European hosts were the Jews of Philippi and Salonika during the middle of the first century. Beginning in the medieval period, the middle zone served as a receptacle for waves of Jewish immigration from coastal Europe, due to persecutions and expulsions from France (1182-1394), England (1290), Germany (1336-1338), and Spain (1492-1496). At approximately the same time the new Christian monarchies to the east, Poland and Hungary, needed skilled manpower from the more developed coastal countries. Jews came during the peaceful phases of the *Drang nach Osten* and were treated as welcome guests. Poland had issued an invitation to Jewish settlers as early as 1133. New invitations and hospitable reception followed after the Mongolian invasions of the mid-thirteenth century, because the shattered economies of Poland and Hungary needed rebuilding. In Poland, King Boleslav in 1264 recruited Jewish

colonists and Casimir the Great issued a special charter in 1345 to safeguard their welfare and liberties,[3] some say because he loved and
cherished a Jewish mistress.

It is probably an exaggeration to say that from the fourteenth
century to the eighteenth Poland was a "paradise of the Jews." [4]
Nevertheless it is true that while religious tolerance lasted in Poland
—the expulsion of the Unitarians in 1658 may be a convenient ter-
minal date—the Jews benefited from it. They lived in autonomous
communities, were considered a guest "nation," developed their own
Yiddish language from the Low German dialect they had brought
with them, and had their own schools, police, and courts. They enjoyed relative prosperity by engaging in commerce, acting as middle-
men, and as contractors for tax collecting. Their close connections
with the landowning gentry may be conjectured from the survival to
this day of the picturesque caftans and fur-brimmed hats of the
Orthodox Jews, which were originally the garb of the medieval Polish
nobility. But all was not sweetness and light: Polish Jews were caught
between noble landowners and rebellious serfs in the perennial struggle between these two antithetical interest groups. Access to certain
cities, Warsaw among them was forbidden to Jews, although they
were permitted representation in the Diet.[5]

After the first partition of Poland, the Russians established the
so-called Hebrew Pale (1773-1776) in their newly won western provinces. Jews from all other parts of Russia were herded into these
territories, which served in the beginning as a catch-basin for Eastern
Jewry and later as a spillway into other middle-zone areas and the
world.

Jews who went into the middle zone from coastal Europe via
Germany were called Ashkenazim (Germans).[6] Those who migrated
from Spain were known as Sephardim (exiles).[7] The Sephardim
spread eastward along the Mediterranean coastline into the Ottoman
Empire and knew no persecution at the hands of the Turks. By
mid-seventeenth century Salonika on the Aegean had a large Jewish
population of more than 60,000.[8] From the Balkans the Sephardim
followed the path of Ottoman conquest north to the Austrian and
Slovak borders. When Buda fell in 1686 to the besieging imperial
armies, the Sephardic Jewish population of the town fought on the
ramparts of the fortress with the defending Turks.[9]

By concentrating their Jewish populations in the Pale at the end
of the eighteenth century, the Russians added a characteristic mark
to middle-zone Jewry. They brought Jews from the Caspian shores
whose ancestors had never seen the Mediterranean and were converts

to Judaism. These Jews were the descendants of the Turco-Tartar Khazars [10] and the related Bashkirs, whose rulers and aristocracy embraced the Mosaic faith at the middle of the eighth century, probably as a compromise solution to avoid politically weighted conversion either to Byzantine Christianity or to Arabic Islam. Contemporary travelers have left fascinating descriptions of the two great Khazar cities, Itil and Sarkel, respectively in the Volga and Don estuaries on the Caspian and the Sea of Azov. At the beginning of the tenth century, according to the Arab voyager Ibn Fadhlan, there were in the capital city of Itil about 4,000 Jews, 10,000 Moslems, and a smaller number of Christians. The *khagan,* or prince, had his fortified castle on the west side of the city, which served as the Jewish quarter. The castle was built of brick and, at the time of Ibn Fadhlan's visit, contained a harem of sixty women. The prince was devout in his Judaic faith. When news reached him of the destruction of a synagogue by the Arabs in their territory, he retaliated immediately, though cautiously, by closing down the minaret adjacent to the capital's largest mosque. Seven judges held court in the town. Of these, two passed judgment according to the Torah; two in obedience to Koranic law; two following the ancient Khazar customs; and one adjudicated on the basis of heathen Russian and Slav traditions.[11]

Among the Russian Jews moved into the territories seized from Poland in 1772, there were descendants of these Turco-Tartar populations of the Azov-Caspian regions, who had during the intervening centuries fused with Ashkenazim arriving from the west. When the periodic pogroms of the late eighteenth and early nineteenth centuries made life unbearable for the Jews in the Pale, they began spilling over into Galicia. This province, Austrian since 1772, then became the great reservoir of Jewry both for the Habsburg empire and for the two Danubian principalities later renamed Rumania.

Ashkenazic Jews fleeing the discrimination, humiliation, and pogroms inflicted on them in the Orthodox-inhabited parts of what used to be Poland (anti-Semitism was one of the few points on which the tsarist government and the Ukrainian serfs found themselves in agreement) chose Austrian rather than Prussian territory as a haven. Both Frederick the Great, who died in 1786, and Joseph II, who survived until 1790, were enlightened despots, but the Prussian king's enlightenment did not extend to Jews. In Prussia under Frederick and his successors Jews were denied government employment, could not serve in the army, were excluded from the professions, and were burdened with special taxes. According to Frederick they were "useless to the state." [12] The Habsburg emperor, on the other hand, saw in the

Jews of his realms victims of infamous treatment originating in the Dark Ages and wanted them to benefit from the reformist spirit of the Age of Reason. Under Joseph's rule the modernizing provisions of his Edict of Toleration in 1781 were extended to the Jews also. Ancient regulations compelling Jews to wear a distinctive garb and to reside in ghettos were repealed. The vocations, some professions, and even military service were opened to them. They were allowed to settle in towns from which they had been excluded; they could make loans on real estate as well as rent it. Some disabilities, however, remained. Jews did not become subjects of the emperor with full and equal rights. They were still prohibited from acquiring landed property. The special taxes levied on them remained in effect. Their exclusion from government employment and the legal profession continued. The use of Hebrew was relegated to the synagogue; German was declared for Jews, as for others, the official language of communication with the authorities. It was during Joseph's reign that Jews, who for the most part still lacked surnames, were ordered to assume or were assigned German family names.[13] The road to Jewish emancipation was thus opened in the Habsburg possessions. The situation of the Jews in Galicia (fully incorporated in the Habsburg empire during 1815) became immeasurably better than in any of the other areas of partitioned Poland. But even Galicia proved only a transiting area to other Jewish destinies.

Across the Carpathian Mountains from Habsburg Galicia lay Habsburg Hungary. Farther to the south were the plains of Rumanian Moldavia. During the first half of the nineteenth century, while Galicia was filling up with Jewish refugees from the Pale, Hungary and Rumania were transforming themselves into nation states. When the process of transformation provided these two countries with temporary working models of independence—the Compromise of 1867 in the case of Hungary and the recognition of sovereignty by the Berlin Congress in 1878 in the case of Rumania—the ensuing burst of economic activity and expansion provided a powerful attraction to the Galician Jews. Large-scale immigration began southward into both Hungary and Rumania.

Immigration into Hungary was preferable because it was easier, inasmuch as both Galicia and Hungary were Habsburg domains.[14] Also, Hungary was ahead of Moldavia in economic development. In addition, Jews were more welcome in Hungary during the second half of the nineteenth century than in Rumania. The reasons in Hungary were political, economic, and demographic. Hungary had always been a multinational state ruled by the dominant Magyar element (or rather by the Magyar nobility, which before 1848 excluded peasants and other nonnobles from the concept of the "nation"). After the reconquest from the Turks, however, the Magyars, nobles and non-nobles, all told, found themselves a numerical minority in their own country. The spirit of the age was liberalism. It had as one of its corollaries the emancipation and assimilation of the Jews. The Jewish immigrants from the north were therefore thrice welcome in moderniz-ing Hungary: as oppressed masses seeking to assert their human potential in a new, rationalist society; as an experienced and business-minded group to assist in the takeoff from a traditional to a free-enterprise economy; and—last but not least—as an assimilable influx of immigrants to help restore the Magyar element to numerical preponder-ance. Post-Compromise Hungarian censuses listed Hungarian-speak-ing Jews as Magyars of the Israelite faith. Classified on the basis of religious denomination, statistics showed 241,000 Jews in the Hungar-ian kingdom at mid-century; 550,000 in 1870; 707,000 in 1890; 831,000 in 1900; and more than one million in 1914.[15] During this same half century the total population rose more slowly, from about 13 million to 19 million.

The rapid increase in the number of Jewish citizens was accom-panied by a process of urbanization. By the turn of the twentieth century Jews constituted 23.4 per cent of Budapest's inhabitants but only about 5 per cent of the country's total population.[16] Most of them were engaged in commerce, rural and urban; in the free pro-fessions of medicine, the law, and journalism; and also in industry, high finance, and banking. The industrialization of the urban areas, especially of the Budapest region, owed a great deal to the imagina-tion, investing skill, and managerial ability of Jewish immigrants from Austria. These began arriving in limited numbers after the Compromise of 1867 in order to participate in the economic oppor-tunities offered by the new spirit of enterprise that was abroad in the land. At the turn of the century a handful of the successful top layer of Jewish entrepreneurs received baronetcies from the king-emperor in recognition of their economic contributions. With or be-fore the titles came conversion to Catholicism and intermarriage with Christians. Since well into the twentieth century social status in Hun-gary depended on landed wealth, the new Jewish aristocracy began acquiring country estates and adapting, amidst the cares of running banks, industrial plants, and credit institutions, to the traditional style of living of the Hungarian country squire. To be sure, Budapest and the other Hungarian cities still had their Jewish quarters built around Moorish-style synagogues, teeming with poor Jews eking out a precarious existence in small shops and ateliers, in devout observance of the Mosaic law. However, the top strata of titled bankers and industrialists, doctors, lawyers, journalists, and literateurs, who had chosen assimilation with or without conversion, sincerely believed that in Hungary a solution had finally been found for the age-old "Jewish question" and reciprocated for their acceptance in the national community by patriotically identifying themselves with Magyar nationalism. Perhaps it was awareness of this experience that had prompted Theodor Herzl (whose three children all became Catholic converts) to propose as one of his pre-Zionist solutions for the Jewish problem a mass conversion of Austria's Jews in Vienna's St. Stephen's Cathedral.[17]

The rapidity of the Jewish influx from Galicia was accompanied by the rise of political anti-Semitism. At first the movement seemed to echo the mouthings of foreign demagogues such as the Prussian Paul de Lagarde. In 1875, when Theodor Herzl was fifteen years old, the Hungarian member of Parliament, Victor Istoczy (1842-1915), demanded immigration and naturalization restrictions on the Jews, whom he vehemently described as an "aggressive caste." [18] In 1883 the accidental drowning of a peasant maid employed in a rural Jewish family was used by professional anti-Semites to whip up latent animosity to the Jews to an affair of nationwide proportions. Moritz Scharff, young son of the kosher butcher in the village of Tiszaeszlar,[19] was bribed and frightened into testifying at the trial of local Jewish religious leaders that he had seen his father cut the girl's throat and collect her blood in a receptacle which was then used in the synagogue for ritual purposes. The body of the missing victim, unexpectedly washed up by the river, showed no wounds. The defendants were all acquitted in response to this act of God and to the prominent liberal lawyers who rushed from the capital to save them from falling victims to unconscionable demagoguery. The damage, however, had already been done. As in the Dreyfus case [20] during the ensuing decade, anti-Semitism became a political force with a considerable following. In the elections of 1884 Istoczy and seventeen of his followers were elected to Parliament on an anti-Semitic ticket. The small group could never muster enough strength to produce more than venomous oratory, which was drowned out by the philo-Semitic pronouncements of leading figures of both government and opposition. Anti-Semitism in Hungary continued as a sociological phenomenon, but failed to turn itself into a political force until the disintegration of the established order at the end of the First World War.

In Rumania it was a different story. The Jews were not welcome. The political leaders in and out of the government pandered to the anti-Semitism of the Orthodox masses, whose behavioral patterns toward the Jews had been set by the pogroms in neighboring Podolia and the Ukraine. Prior to the rise of Naziism on the ruins of the old order, there seems to have been an invisible toleration line drawn across the map of modern Europe between countries that had and others that had not experienced the Renaissance and the Reformation. It was perhaps the spirit of humanism and the importance of the individual instilled in people by these two great intellectual movements west of the toleration frontier which prevented physical brutality against the Jews, while anti-Semitism had free play east of the line. Moldavia, where an incipient economic upturn, intensified by railroad construction in the 1860s and 1870s, began to attract Galician Jewish immigrants, was east of the toleration line. Attacks on synagogues, desecration of Jewish cemeteries, the occasional outbursts of peasant brutality against Jews were part of the traditional sociological climate. The rapidity of the Jewish influx during the second half of the nineteenth century strengthened these sadistic patterns of behavior. By 1859 there were 118,000 Jews in Moldavia and in Wallachia 9,200, because the latter was farther away from Russian territories. Within four years these numbers grew, respectively, to 201,000 and 68,000.[21] On the eve of the Congress of Berlin which granted Rumania full sovereignty, Jews numbered a quarter of a million out of the total Moldavian population of five million. As in Hungary, in fact more disproportionately so, urbanization became a corollary of the increasing Jewish presence. At the turn of the century more than half of the Rumanian city dwellers were of the Jewish faith, between 300,000 and 400,000 out of a total urban population of 700,000.[22]

Rumanian anti-Semitic attitudes were exacerbated by the conflict which developed after the Congress of Berlin regarding guarantees, required by the powers, of equal treatment for Jewish citizens. The same guarantees were demanded of newly independent Serbia also, but no political problem developed there because the Jewish population consisted of a small number of Sephardic Jews who had been there since the early days of the Ottoman Empire. In Rumania, on the other hand, the extent of Jewish immigration and the ingrained pattern of anti-Semitism had produced restrictive legislation by 1866, the kind Hungarian political anti-Semites unsuccessfully sought to put through their parliament in 1875. Article VII of the Rumanian constitution of 1866 provided that "only foreigners belonging to a

Christian confession may obtain naturalization." [23] To protect the Jews of Rumania against such discrimination, Article XLIV of the Treaty of Berlin laid down as a condition of Rumanian independence the following stipulation:

> In Rumania the distinction of religious creed or confession shall not be used against anyone as a motive for exclusion and disability as regards the enjoyment of civil and political rights, admission to public employment and honors, or exercise of different profession or industries. The freedom and open practice of all religions shall be assured to all citizens of the Rumanian state, as also to foreigners, and no obstacle shall be placed in the way of the hierarchal organization of the various communions, or of their relations with their spiritual leaders. Citizens of all Powers, merchants and others, shall be treated in Rumania without distinction of religion, on a footing of perfect equality. [24]

The Rumanians were indignant. They considered this article a violation of their sovereignty. They remembered, however, that it was not only a violation but also a condition. Even so, among educated Rumanians, the imposition of Article XLIV was regarded as unequal treatment of their country in the comity of nations. After all, they argued, the powers had not intervened in Russia, where the situation of the Jews was far worse than in Rumania. This, of course, was a specious argument, for Russia was a great power and already sovereign in its territories. Such thoughts did not enter the minds of the illiterate masses, among whom outside support for the Jews served only to intensify anti-Semitism and to prompt new outbreaks of brutality and vandalism. The first victims of the peasant uprising in Moldavia during March 1907 were rural Jews. Atrocities took place regardless of the fact that in the meantime the conflict between Article XLIV of the Treaty of Berlin and Article VII of the Rumanian Constitution of 1866 had been solved. More than a quarter of a century had passed since October 18, 1879, when the Rumanian Parliament, by a vote of 133 to 9, removed Jewish disabilities by voting an amendment to Article VII to the effect that "difference of religious creed does not constitute an obstacle to the acquisition or exercise of civil and political rights." [25] In the long run, Jewish emancipation forced on Rumania by outside intervention in 1879 had about the same internal sociopolitical effect on the rise of local intolerance as the freeing of the Blacks in the American South by the North after the Civil War. Political anti-Semitism remained a virulent though legislatively controlled force in Rumania. But controls placed on it were wholly contingent on the continuation of a

European constellation of powers interested in the protection rather than sworn to the destruction of the Jews.

In Bohemia the Jewish community was the result of the *Drang nach Osten.* It had its roots in the early Middle Ages and is still noted by its architectural monuments, some of which—like the Old Synagogue in what used to be the Prague ghetto—date from the thirteenth century. The sixteenth-century Jewish legend of the Golem —the destroying monster created of clay and then cabalistically infused with life by Rabbi Löw of Prague—is a forerunner and possibly a source of Mary Wollstonecraft Shelley's *Frankenstein.* During the nineteenth-century modernizing process the Jews of Bohemia chose cultural identification with the German rather than with the Czech ethnic group in their pluralistic environment. Their presence in Prague and in other Bohemian-Moravian cities remained distinct, however, by its avoidance of other than linguistic-cultural assimilation to the Austro-Germans. It was due to this cultural orientation in Prague that Franz Kafka's (1883-1924) novels, written in German, became classics in world literature. Kafka's *The Castle,* is probably a surrealistic allegory of the frustrating reality of unaccepted Jewish presence.

With the exception of Croatia, where the late Habsburg Counter Reformation of the eighteenth century left a residue of anti-Semitism, the states below the Lower Danube had no Jewish problems before the First World War on which postwar Fascism could feed. The Jews of both Serbia and Bulgaria were predominantly of Sephardic origin. In Bulgaria the Sephardim retained their ethnic and cultural identity in undisturbed relations with their Orthodox Bulgarian neighbors.[26] In Serbia, its few Sephardim chose ethnic and religious assimilation to their Slav environment, gradually adopted Serbian patronymics, and soon melted into the national community.

This was the Jewish presence which acted as the matrix of Zionism through the early impressions it made on the mind and emotions of its founder. True, Theodor Herzl might never have worked out the Zionist program had it not been for his personal exposure in Paris to the Dreyfus case [27] during the 1890s. Still, it is of interest to note that the modern Moses of Zionism sprang from a land in the middle zone where the Jewish presence was then welcome and appreciated and not from an Eastern country where pogroms necessitated a choice between exodus and extermination.

19

The Coming of Socialism

The socialist idea and trade unionism were the last layers of the historical foundations on which the present-day middle zone was to rest. The formation of these final pre-1918 structural components was delayed by two factors. First, the process of substituting machines for muscle power [1] moved ahead more slowly in landlocked than in coastal Europe. Consequently, east of Prague and Vienna, labor remained tied to agricultural production longer than was the case in countries to the west. Second, after the rise of the Marxist doctrine during the 1860s and 1870s in Germany and in Russia, both German and Russian socialists remained strongly influenced by their brands of nationalism in analyzing the problems of the landlocked zone lying between them. The German socialists continued to see it as an area that must be brought within the German civilizational orbit by a peaceful *Drang nach Osten* before it could or should be successfully penetrated by scientific socialism. The Russian socialists, in their turn, were so much imbued with the Pan-Slav idea that, in their minds, the establishment of a vast Slav commonwealth under the tsar's leadership took priority over revolutionary plans of socioeconomic reorganization west of Russia.[2]

The upshot of all this was that socialism made a relatively late entry into the middle zone. It had begun in the agrarian sector during the 1840s; failed to see its objectives realized during the revolutions of 1848-1849; and then passed through a utopian phase during the 1850s and 1860s. After the rise of, first, Lassallean nonrevolutionary and then Marxist revolutionary socialism between 1865 and 1885, the spread of the doctrine and of the movement was slowed down at the start by the scarcity of an industrial proletariat and later by the fact that, when it came to the middle zone, its German and Russian propagators were not only socialists but also expansion-oriented nationalists.

A typical representative of the early agrarian-utopian phase was the Hungarian Mihaly Tancsics [3] (1799-1884), a self-taught pupil of Rousseau, Cabet, and Fourier, whose activity before and during the 1848-1849 revolution had a populist, pro-peasant character. In the early 1840s Tancsics was agitating for the liberation of the serfs on the basis of the most radical program: no indemnity to the landowners. In freeing him from his fortress prison and driving him through the city in triumph on March 15, 1848, the people of the Hungarian capital created one of the memorable spectacles of their revolution. During the revolution Tancsics became a proponent of land reform on the pattern set at the end of the French Revolution by Gracchus Babeuf (1760-1797): [4] a division of the holdings of both the nobles and the state among the peasants after a seizure of power in order to establish an egalitarian society. Following the suppression of the revolution, his underground literary production included such pamphlets as "What Is Socialism and What Is Communism?" and "Who Are the Red Republicans and What Do They Want?" It was due to Tancsics's socialist pamphleteering and partly to a politically provocative scene about utopian socialism in a contemporary theatrical production that a major polemic was raging in the Budapest press in 1862 about the merits and demerits of Fourier's phalansterian schemes. [5]

When more surplus agrarian workers began moving into the cities in the mid-sixties, Tancsics started shifting to socialist propaganda and organizational work in the industrial sphere. As a living memento of 1848 and a venerable patriarch of socialism, he was elected in 1869 president of the newly formed (1868) General Workers' Association. The name was a literal translation of Lassalle's Allgemeiner Deutscher Arbeitverein, founded in 1864. But the more up-to-date proletarian cadres of the GWA unceremoniously dumped him in a few years for his tactical blunder of applying to the government for financial subsidies. [6] He spent the last twenty years of his life in penury, feverishly pamphleteering. To the end he remained primarily an agrarian socialist, unable to update his utopian ideology to the new concepts of the class struggle and surplus value.

The revolutions of 1848-1849 in the middle zone were overwhelmingly nationalistic explosions with very limited socialist content. The anarchist Michael Bakunin (1814-1876), who was later responsible for the disintegration of Marx's First International (1864-1874), rushed to Prague in June 1848, not as a socialist to make common cause with the radical fringe of the Czech uprising, but rather as a Pan-Slav agitator. Bakunin was enthusiastic over the objectives of the All-Slav Congress held in the Bohemian capital a few weeks before the rebellious city was bombarded into submission by the Austrian army. Before reaching Prague he had stopped off in Paris and Berlin to organize revolutionary nationalist freedom fighters among the Polish refugees of 1831 for a return to the homeland as a vanguard of the coming Pan-Slav uprising against the Prussian and Austrian overlords. After the quick collapse of the Prague rebellion, the Austrians arrested and imprisoned Bakunin as a dangerous nationalist revolutionary. He was subsequently extradited to the Russians, who promptly exiled him to Siberia as a subversive socialist enemy of the established order.[7] Obviously he was *persona non grata* to both sides, though for different reasons.

Tancsics's and Bakunin's careers spanned the quarter-century interval in the development of socialist doctrine from the early agrarian and utopian phase to the rise of the internationals, starting in 1864. In the middle zone during this transitional period there was increasing pressure on the land by expanding rural populations. Industrialization was not progressing fast enough to absorb surplus agrarian workers. In the mid-sixties plant production on a large scale was just coming into existence in a few isolated middle-zone areas: the Warsaw–Lodz region, Russian-held Latvia, the Prague-Brno sector, and the environs of Buda and Pest. Discontent among workers in the difficult transitional stage from agricultural to industrial employment became not only widespread but also more articulated because of the expansion of literacy and the proliferation of the radical popular press. The failure of the last Polish uprising in 1864 and the seeming success of the Austro-Hungarian Compromise in 1867 both signalled a retreat from romanticism to realism and acted as powerful stimuli for a new era of modernization accompanied by industrialization.

This process was favorable to the expansion of socialist indoctrination and organization in the sense that the new Polish, Latvian, Bohemian, and Hungarian industrial centers began filling up with dispossessed rural populations conditioned by centuries of statically substandard existence to turn to radical solutions for haunting social and economic problems. The propagandizing of radical solutions and the organization of workers into class-interest groups was given an unexpected boost by the overthrow of the Paris Commune in 1871. Middle-zone ethnics who had played political roles or participated in the struggle against the troops of the Versailles government either died on the barricades, becoming martyrs to the cause among their countrymen, or fled France to escape retribution. Refugees either went to London to work with Marx, or returned to their homelands to enter the budding socialist and trade unionist movements as organizers.[8] The economic-cycle theory of capitalism seemed to play into their hands. In 1873 the gathering Europe-wide depression culminated in a catastrophic drop of prices on the Vienna stock exchange. The resulting panic brought on the mass closing of newly established credit banks, the bankruptcy of private-enterprise railroads financed by them and still being built, curtailment of production, and layoffs at the factories.[9] The ugly realities of unemployment, beggars, and seething social unrest made their appearance in an era which knew no unemployment relief, social security, or workmen's compensation. There was also a polarization between the noncomprehending upper classes at the top and the miserable masses at the bottom of the social scale. The climate was ideal for the spread of radical ideas.

Workers in agriculture, probably because of their larger numbers, proved to be a more fertile ground for "left" socialist propaganda than their comrades in industry. In the Hungarian central lowlands, the breadbasket of the Habsburg monarchy, spontaneously sprung and originally unco-ordinated movements of dispossessed peasant *"puszta-*seekers" (farmstead squatters) and "pasture-dividers" had begun during the late sixties to merge into "Democratic Circles." [10] Circle members absorbed theory during evening sessions from penny-sheet workers' newspapers and then translated theory into militant action in demonstrations, riots, and armed clashes with the rural gendarmerie. In 1868 the government closed the Democratic Circles after a particularly bloody encounter between peasants and gendarmes. But violence continued during the last quarter of the century and beyond. The peak was reached in the harvesters' strikes of 1897 and 1906, which ended in pitched battles, a large number of casualties, and mass trials in provincial towns. One of the famous trials of agrarian socialists was held in the Trans-Tisza town of Hodmezövasarhely in the mid-nineties. The leading defendant received a five-year prison sentence; his twenty-six lieutenants got off with shorter terms.[11] As compared with the outcome of similar trials held during the previous decade in Russian Poland, where the sentence passed on several defendants was death, the Habsburg courts were lenient enough. The Hungarian government banned agrarian socialist organizations, but the circles and cells continued to exist underground. Their secret members supplied a radicalizing leaven to the various local industrial workers' associations which began to mushroom in Czech, Polish, Hungarian, Croatian, and Slovak industrial and mining centers during the late 1860s.

This was the period of the First International (1864-1867), organized by Marx and Engels and eventually exploded by Bakunin. The two German socialists had set certain implicit strategic priorities for their revolutionary socialist program: England and Belgium first; the Russian and Habsburg lands last. Both Marx and Engels were strongly anti-Russian. Without actively encouraging German imperialism in the middle zone, they did not wish to impede what they considered the German civilizing mission in the east. Marx, for example, condemned the English for oppressing the Irish but looked benignly on the continuing German colonial penetration of Bohemia. As far as he was concerned, an independent Bohemia was out of the question because it would leave Germany looking like "a loaf gnawed by rats." [12] As early as 1851 Engels had expressed the opinion that Slav nationalism was a dangerous thing and that the completion of the German civilizing mission, a euphemism for the *Drang nach Osten,* had to precede the building of socialism in Eastern Europe. [13]

Both Marx and Engels strongly believed that socialist support for the "oppressed nationalities" would lead to a process of Balkanization, a multiplication of small and nonviable states, to decentralization instead of the centralization which they thought would work to the advantage of socialist expansionism. It was a leading tenet of the First International that socialist propaganda and organizational activity should be carried on primarily, if not exclusively, in large, independent, and rapidly industrializing states, [14] where the social revolution would first flare up between the capitalists and the proletariat because of the concentration of capital in fewer and fewer hands along with the widening of proletarian despair. From the coastal view of nineteenth-century industrializing Europe it seemed quite inconceivable that the social revolution to usher in the building of socialism would eventually start in the least rather than in the most industrialized European state.

Socialism and trade unionism thus came to the middle zone in spite rather than because of the early German and Russian socialists. One might make out a good case for French influences. Certainly, the Babouvian precedent and the French utopian models left perceptible traces before the turn of the century. After the crushing of the 1830-1831 Polish revolution, Louis Blanc (1811-1882) was the only socialist of European stature to show a sympathetic interest in the "oppressed nationalities" of the east. [15] After the last stand of the Paris communards in the Père Lachaise Cemetery, it was the memory of martyrs like the Polish Yaroslav Dombrowski (1836-1871) [16] and the unceasing work of refugees like Dombrowski's compatriot Valery Wroblewski (1836-1908) [17] and the Hungarian Leo Frankel (1844-1896) [18] that popularized French socialist models among their people, whether in exile or in the homeland. Both Wroblewski and Frankel collaborated with Marx and Engels; Frankel returned to engage in organizational work in the politically permissive atmosphere of post-Compromise Hungary.[19] The survivors of the Paris Commune thus helped lay the groundwork for social democratic parties and trade unions in the middle zone.

German socialist influences and models were strongest in Prussian Poland, in Bohemia, and subsequently in Hungary, Croatia, and Slovakia. In the western Polish areas under Hohenzollern rule it was the Polish migrant workers—the precursors of today's guest workers—who, having come into contact with socialist ideas and organizations in Westphalia and Silesia, started Polish unions on the German Social Democratic model after their return home.[20] In Bohemia and Hungary the establishment of the Social Democratic Party in Austria in 1888 and the launching of the Second International in 1889 proved to be portentous events. The Czech Social Democratic Party was organized in 1889 on the Austrian model. The Czech trade unions were sparked by Vaclav Klofac during the 1880s, became members of the Second International, and maintained liaison with socialists in other Slav countries.[21]

The founding congress of the Second International in Paris was attended by socialist delegates from the Habsburg lands and the Balkans. The congress entrusted the Austrian Social Democrats with the task of supporting socialist organization in the component units of the Dual Monarchy.[22] Strategically this was a continuation of the original Marxist concept: the promotion of socialism under centralized leadership in large, independent, industrializing countries. After a joint meeting between Austrian and Hungarian socialist leaders held in Pressburg immediately after the Paris congress, the Hungarian Social Democratic Party was established in 1890 with a platform calling for universal suffrage and for the socialization of the means of production.[23] In a letter from Engels read to the first Hungarian SDP congress, the founders were reminded of the international character of the workers' movements.[24] Accordingly, the new party styled itself not the Hungarian Social Democratic Party, but a "Social Democratic Party in Hungary."

Two other social democratic parties developed in the Hungarian half of the Dual Monarchy during the next decade, in Croatia and in Slovakia. The Croatian party was established in 1894 and received its guidance from Vienna rather than Budapest. Its membership was recruited from industrial workers, mostly printers, as well as from peasants. The leadership was "reformist" and concentrated more on the struggle to improve working conditions than on the socialization of the means of production.[25] In nearby Bosnia-Herzegovina the Austrian SDP also served as a model for local socialist and trade union organization, which began, especially among labor in the tobacco fields, after the occupation of 1878.[26]

In Slovakia, where the mining industry was strongly developed and labor unrest and strikes had been endemic since the sixteenth century, the Slovak Social Democratic Party was organized at the turn of the century with the assistance of its sister Czech party. Emanuel Lehoczky (1876-1930), a tailor by trade, was the acknowledged leader of the party and also the editor of its Slovak-language newspaper. In 1906 the Slovak party merged, probably against Lehoczky's better judgment, with the Hungarian SDP,[27] which, it will be recalled, operated under a charter as an SDP *in* Hungary and not as an ethnic Magyar organization. Before and after 1906, party as well as affiliated trade union membership had a strong Slovak coloring in Hungary. It was to the advantage of socialist and trade union organizing that, as a matter of curious coincidence, both the Second International and the Hungarian government were opposed, though for different reasons, to ethnic decentralization. During 1905-1906, when the Slovak SDP was absorbed in its Hungarian counterpart, the latter was under a moderate "reformist" leadership, fighting off attacks from its left-wing opposition for its "opportunistic, temporizing policies." [28] The charge of opportunism went back to the days of Tancsics and implied collaboration with the government on matters of domestic politics, including the bringing of the minorities into the "Hungarian political nation."

Elsewhere in the middle zone, in Russian Poland and in the Balkans, the socialist stimulus came from Russia. In those parts of Poland that became Russian between 1772 and 1795, Marxian socialism made its first appearance among Polish students returning from Russian universities who had read *Das Kapital* in its first Russian translation (1873).[29] The movement was soon driven underground. Trials of Polish socialists held in 1883-1885 resulted in Siberian exile and in at least seven executions.[30] The severity of the Russian authorities prompted a flight of Polish socialists to Austrian Poland, commonly known as Galicia, where the Polish Socialist Party

(PPS) became legal in 1890.[81] By 1900 there was even a separate Polish-Jewish radical socialist party in Galicia, the Bund, existing on the peripheries of Zionism.[82] The PPS participated in the elections and sent deputies to the Vienna Reichsrat, where the Polish socialists sat together with their Czech comrades.

In the meantime socialism and trade unionism had been making headway, under Russian influence, in the independent Balkan countries of Serbia, Bulgaria, and Rumania. In Serbia the Marxist Social Democratic Party with affiliated trade unions had developed by the 1890s. It followed the lead of the Second International and was represented in the Skupshtina, the Serbian parliament.[33] Especially strong was the revolutionary socialist current in Bulgaria. As in Russian Poland, the socialist ideology was imported by students returning from Russian universities. Toward the end of the century the outstanding Bulgarian revolutionary leader was Lyuben Karavelov, who had spent nearly ten years in Moscow (1857-1867) and was personally acquainted with Bakunin. The Social Democratic Party came into being during 1891 and soon split into two factions: the *tesni* or "narrows," who stood on a platform of strict class warfare; and the *shiroki* or "broads," who stood for co-operation with bourgeois parties. The Bulgarian SDP was also an affiliate of the Second International and sent deputies to the Bulgarian national assembly, the sobranje.[34] One of the *tesni* trade union leaders on the eve of the First World War was Georgi Dimitrov (1882-1949), of later fame as Secretary General of the Third International and as Communist Party leader of post-World War II Bulgaria.

The Rumanian SDP was founded in 1893 as a stage in socialist development which had begun in the 1870s under the influence of fugitive Russian revolutionaries crossing the Bessarabian border into Moldavia. The Rumanian Social Democrats were of the early "reformist" variety, stood for collaboration with bourgeois liberals, and took their cue from the Second International.[35] On the eve of World War I their up-and-coming leader was the Bulgarian-born Christian Georgyevich Rakovsky (1873-?), destined to play important roles during the Russian Revolution and to disappear in a Stalinist prison.

Events in Russia continued to influence the socialist parties in the eastern borderlands of the middle zone. At the turn of the century a break had taken place in Russian Poland between the left and right wings of the socialist movement. As the waning strength of the Romanov empire was being made visible to the world by its defeat in the Russo-Japanese War (1904-1905), by the daring of the protesting populace on Bloody Sunday (January 22, 1905), and by the concessions granted in the tsar's October Manifesto of that year, the Polish left-wing faction, among whose leaders was Rosa Luxemburg (1870?-1919), thought the hour had struck for revolutionary action. Early in November 1905 Rosa Luxemburg and her left-wing Polish socialists organized and held a mass demonstration under red flags in the center of Warsaw. As in St. Petersburg, the crowds were surrounded, fired upon, and charged by Cossack cavalry. Rosa Luxemburg was arrested and deported to Germany.[36] She died while under military arrest during the Spartacist uprising of 1919 in Berlin.

As repressive measures increased, the right wing under Joseph Pilsudski (1867-1935) began to resort to violent action also. One famous example was the great train robbery they pulled in 1908 at Bezdan, in which a considerable amount of money was seized for the coffers of the party.[37] But it was not safe to be a socialist in Russian Poland, and in 1911 Pilsudski fled (after serving a term in Siberia) to Austrian Poland. Not only was there a freer atmosphere for socialists under Habsburg rule than either in Russian or in Prussian Poland, but, additionally, as Austrian-Russian rivalry in the Balkans for the spoils of the Ottoman Empire gradually brought the middle zone to the brink of war, the Austrian government began to welcome the activities of such men as Pilsudski.[38] Vienna looked with favor on the organizing of Polish paramilitary units, which would fight against Russia in the event of hostilities.

While Polish socialists continued to flee across the border into Austrian territory, the social democratic parties in both Hungary and Austria were being called upon to play important political roles in the developing crisis of the dualistic Compromise. As early as 1899 the Brünn convention of the Austrian SDP, alarmed by the exacerbation of the monarchy's nationalities problem, proposed a transformation of Austria-Hungary into a "democratic federation of nationalities." [39] Such Austrian socialist critics as Karl Renner (1871-1905) and Otto Bauer (1882-1938) were outspoken in attributing the crisis of the existing system to an anachronistic Hungarian governmental resistance to even evolutionary change. Renner rejected dualism, held up Swiss "trialism" as an example, and in 1906 referred to the constitutional system that had been worked out by Deak and Beust in 1867 as a "corpse." [40]

There was some justification for this premature postmortem. The Hungarian elections of January 1905 had resulted in a resounding defeat of the ruling Liberal Party. In the ensuing parliamentary deadlock the Emperor-King Francis Joseph had to resort to the appointment of an extraconstitutional government in June 1905, which

Parliament refused to accept. During the political crisis, which lasted until April 1906, the emperor-king played his trump card by permitting the nonparliamentary government to enter into negotiations with the Hungarian SDP regarding the introduction of universal suffrage in Hungary.[41] This was a major point in the Hungarian SDP's platform but anathema to the traditional Hungarian establishment, which clung to a restricted franchise to keep the large masses of national minorities as well as Hungarian agricultural and industrial workers from the polls. The Hungarian Social Democrats made common cause with the Habsburgs against the recalcitrant Hungarian political elite. They were strange bedfellows indeed. Vienna threatened to introduce universal suffrage, already an accomplished fact in Austria, into Hungary. The SDP backed up the threat by raising the specter of a general strike. The strategy worked. The Hungarian establishment capitulated and agreed to form a parliamentary government. The status quo was thus upheld, though the conviction grew that it was tied to the life span of the aged emperor-king, who had been on the throne since 1848. His heir, Archduke Francis Ferdinand (1863-1914), was openly contemptuous of the dualistic system, and there was little doubt that on his accession to the throne he would institute the "trialism," under which the empire's Slavs would be brought into political power as equals of the Germans and Hungarians.

In the meantime, however, the political crisis of dualism was heightened by the widening of a new European depression. Layoffs, strikes, and violence in the streets and in the countryside became endemic. Radicalization was a natural side-effect of the political-economic crisis. Mass organization began beyond and outside the SDP. In 1906 a national association of "agrarian proletarians" and the "Independent Socialist Peasant Party in Hungary" were launched. The demands of the new radical groups included not only those of the moderate SDP but also a nationalization of large estates.[42]

The agrarian proletarians of the early twentieth century were demographic descendants of the malcontent heathens, heretics, and serfs of earlier epochs. Only they were more numerous, more literate, and, because of the spread of socialism and trade unionism, far better organized. They still suffered some casualties in their struggle against the establishment, but even in tsarist Russia contemporary standards of civilization saved their leaders from receiving the kind of treatment that had fallen to the lot of Dozsa and Nalivaiko. The organized agricultural and industrial workers' discontent thus added significantly to the centrifugal force of nationalism tearing at the seams of the Habsburg and Romanov empires. In the case of the latter, the power-drain started by the Japanese war in 1905 was so serious that the status quo was not likely to survive another military defeat. In the Habsburg lands the process of deterioration was less obvious, but observers, some of them objective foreigners, others alienated natives, were pessimistic about the impact of war on the antiquated dualistic structure.

When war finally came, first to the Balkans in 1912 and then to the rest of Europe in 1914-1916, the socialist parties and the trade unions of the middle zone were powerless to resist the sweep of the nationalistic current. The Second International took an antimilitaristic stand during the two Balkan Wars (1912-1913). These minor conflicts prompted antiwar protests by the Rumanian SDP and by the *tesni* faction of the sister Bulgarian party, though the *shiroki* group showed a preference for military patriotism rather than for socialist pacifism.[43] When the Great War of 1914 broke out, the majority of the social democratic parties identified themselves with their governments and voted war credits. This was the case with the SDP deputies represented in the Vienna Parliament. Elsewhere in the area, where the socialist parties had not yet become parts of the official establishment, there was opposition to the war. The Serbian SDP in 1914 and the Bulgarian party in 1915 refused to vote for war credits.[44] The Rumanian party declared itself against the war and staged large-scale antimilitaristic demonstrations by dockworkers in the Danubian port city of Galati.[45] Such demonstrations did, however, little more than stress points of socialist honor. What mattered was the early stability of support for the war effort by the socialist parties and by trade union membership in the territories of the major belligerents. However, the longer the war lasted and the more visibly the home establishment's power dwindled, the more openly socialist support for military operations was metamorphosed into bitter opposition.

20

The War—Reprieve
from Dependence

On June 28, 1914, the day Archduke Francis Ferdinand and his wife were shot in the Austrian-annexed Bosnian capital, five of the middle-zone states were fully independent: Albania, Bulgaria, Montenegro, Rumania, and Serbia. Hungary to the north was semi-independent, or rather interdependent with Austria. Croatia was interdependent with Hungary, as Hungary was with Austria. Farther to the north, Bohemia, Poland, and Lithuania were completely dependent, respectively, on Austria and Russia. Latvia, a medieval colonial offshoot of Lithuania, was part of Russia. Slovakia, which had no record as a state, although during the ninth century parts of it were included in the Moravian empire, spread over ten northern Hungarian counties. Subcarpathian Ruthenia, which had never known statehood or independence either, lay somnolent on the southeastern slopes of the Carpathian Bastion as a part of the Hungarian kingdom.

Five years later there were no dependent states left, only dependent populations. Albania, neutralized in 1913,[1] stayed out of the great world conflict, aloof as usual from its surroundings. Her neutral status did not keep Serbs, Austrians, French, and Italians out of Albania during the war. When hostilities were over, much of the country was under Italian and French occupation, nor were internationally recognized frontiers drawn until 1927. With Austro-Hungarian protection gone, it was merely a question of time as to when one of Albania's neighbors, whether one across the mountains or one across the sea, would reduce the land of the Shqipetars to a state of dependence.[2] Mussolini's Italians performed this historic deed on Good

Friday, 1939. Serbia had no choice. It was attacked by superior force
and fought, as was its wont, against overwhelming odds in a terrain
favoring the defender. Montenegro, the other sovereign Serb state,
was not attacked but declared its Slavic solidarity with its kinsmen
and fought on till victory. Bulgaria and Rumania considered the
possibilities and then entered the war, in 1915 and 1916 respectively,
on what they thought was going to be the winning side, Bulgaria
wrongly, Rumania rightly.

As far as Hungary was concerned, both of her nineteenth-century
nationalist leaders proved to be true prophets: Louis Kossuth in
predicting that, by making a compromise with Austria, the Magyars
would lose control over their political destinies; Francis Deak in fore-
telling that, in a conflict among the great powers, Hungary would
be "swallowed or dismembered" by her neighbors. Croatia became
interdependent with Serbia, as she had been with Hungary, but
hardly happier about it in spite of the Slavic blood ties. Bohemia,
Lithuania, and Latvia all appeared on the map as sovereign states.
Bohemia regained her historic frontiers in the west and obtained
ethnic ones in the south and in the east, to combine with Slovakia
and Ruthenia into the new sovereignty of Czechoslovakia. Poland
was resurrected among her ancient frontiers, which had not previously been seen since or before 1772, at the expense of both her
defeated and temporarily powerless neighbors, with a corridor
through Germany to the sea. The other new state on the map, the
one whose advent Austria-Hungary had been dreading, was Yugoslavia, the country of the South Slavs. The new state included not
only Serbia, Croatia, and Montenegro, but also Austrian, Hungarian,
and Albanian territories. Rumanian nationalist aspirations were more
than satisfied: Transylvania, Bessarabia, Bukovina, parts of the Banat
and of the Dobrudja were pulled together to unite all Rumanian-
inhabited lands with Wallachia and Moldavia. A complete cartographic revolution took place in the middle zone between 1914 and
1920.

All this became possible not just because of the Allied triumph
over the Central Powers but also because of the preliminary German
victory over Russia. The end result was the nearly simultaneous
collapse of the three great multinational empires of Austria-Hungary, Russia, and Germany. Of the three, Austria-Hungary fell to
pieces completely. It disappeared from the map, disintegrating in
defeat under the pull of centrifugal nationalisms. The other two
formerly dominant empires survived, but not as multinational states,

or—in the case of Russia—not as a European multinational state. Germany was relieved of her non-German populations both in the east and in the west.

The collapse of the three imperial powers and the contraction into a nation state of the Ottoman Empire produced a constellation of forces the middle zone had not observed since the fourteenth century: a concurrent depletion, both to the east and to the west, of the Great Powers' expansionist potential. The time was ripe once again, for the first time since the heyday of the Monarchy of the Three Seas, for the organization on a basis of self-determined independence of the vast continental area set off by the Baltic, the Adriatic, and the Black Sea. Only this time the power to organize the new status quo did not come from ambitious local dynasties but from the accumulated energies of nationalism assisted by distant coastal powers. It was not realized, however, at the dawn of this age that the change from dependence to independence would be only of very short duration. Strategic myopia prevented the state-builders from seeing that the political vacuum in which the new state system was being erected could last only as long as both Russia and Germany remained devoid of power. The new minor states, both Allied and formerly enemy, were certain to relapse into a state of dependence as soon as either Germany or Russia regained and reapplied an expansionist power potential that the coastal Allies were either unwilling or unable to match. Prospects were made even gloomier by the omission of both Germany and Russia from the establishment of the new status quo in their own backyards. The two defeated giants were ignored, even though the new order of things involved the erection of buffer states lying athwart the strategic east-west invasion routes by which Berlin could reach Moscow or Moscow could penetrate to Berlin.

The 1918-1920 reorganization of the middle zone was the second liberation of the area since the Ottoman rollback of 1683-1699. A third liberation followed in 1944-1945. Each of these three liberations had a distinct pattern of its own. The liberating agent was the main difference between the first and the second liberations. At the end of the seventeenth century Austria was on the liberated scene and immediately filled the vacuum created by Ottoman evacuation. This pattern was repeated in the third liberation, with Soviet power replacing German might in 1945, without leaving a temporary vacuum. Dissimilarly, at the end of the First World War the victory of the distant coastal Allies and of the United States acted as a vicarious and absent liberating agent without filling the power vacuum left by the collapse of the Habsburg, Hohenzollern, and Romanov empires. The first of these three defunct Great Powers had disappeared for good from the stage of history. The other two, however, were undergoing accelerated historical change, which soon turned them into far more powerfully expansionist powers than they had ever been in the course of their history.

There were also two similarities between the liberations of the seventeenth and of the early twentieth centuries. The centuries-old French political strategy of supporting small powers in the German rear was put to new use by the organization of the Little Entente—an alliance of Czechoslovakia, Rumania, and Yugoslavia—for the triple purpose of preventing the return of the Habsburgs, frustrating Hungarian aspirations to regain lost territories, and sandwiching Germany between allied states, great in the west, small in the east. A new gimmick was added to the traditional French strategy this time by using not only the Little Entente but the whole zone, including Poland and the defeated states of Hungary and Bulgaria, as a *cordon sanitaire,* a political-ideological quarantine area to prevent the westward spread of Communism from Russia.

The other similarity between the first and the second liberations was the price assessed on the liberated. The second liberation did not come at as high a price as the first. The victorious Allies fixed the amount of the liberation costs to be paid by Czechoslovakia, Poland, Rumania, and Yugoslavia at 1.5 billion gold francs, of which Czechoslovakia, the most prosperous of the new states, was to pay 750 million gold francs.[3] The defeated enemy states of Hungary, liberated from interdependence with Austria, and Bulgaria, which was not liberated from anyone though reduced in territory, had to pay reparations.

How exactly was dependence terminated and independence gained at the end of the First World War? In the case of countries already independent and not neutral under international law (Serbia, Montenegro, Bulgaria, and Rumania) the basic requirement was to emerge from the war on the winning side and then augment the national domain by the transfer of still dependent territories annexed from the three disintegrating empires. In the case of dependent peoples without catalytic states of their own (Czechs, Poles, Lithuanians, Latvians, Slovaks, and Ruthenians), the shift from dependence to independence called for the maintenance of quasidiplomatic relations with and participation in the war effort of the Allies.

By virtue of the Austrian attack on her national territory, Serbia found herself automatically a belligerent on the Allied side.[4] It took the invading Austro-Hungarian army more than a year (August 1914-December 1915) to overcome Serb and Montenegrin resistance, without destroying either of the defending armies. The Serbian army retreated across the Albanian mountains to the Adriatic coast and was evacuated by Allied naval units to the island of Corfu, from which groups of this tough fighting force were shipped to the western, eastern, and Salonika fronts to continue the fight against the Central Powers. The Montenegrins, after abandoning Cetinje, their capital, holed up in their inaccessible mountains. King Peter of Serbia and King Nikita of Montenegro found refuge, respectively, on Corfu and in Italy. A Serbian government in exile, was established on Corfu. A Yugoslav Committee of refugee Croatian and Dalmatian leaders from Austrian territories was organized in London. A declaration issued on Corfu in July 1918 called for the union of Serbs, Croats, and Slovenes in a united kingdom under the scepter of the Karageorgevich family. Within a few days of the capitulation in the autumn of 1918 of the Austro-Hungarian, Bulgarian, and Turkish armies, the Croatian National Assembly proclaimed the secession of Croatia-Slavonia from the Habsburg empire (October 20, 1918). A week before the German armistice in the west, the representatives of the Serb Government-in-Exile and of the London Yugoslav Committee met in Geneva (November 3, 1918) and agreed on the holding of a constituent assembly. This body laid the foundations of the new Kingdom of Serbs, Croats, and Slovenes. Almost simultaneously national councils of South Slavs in Austrian Dalmatia and the Hungarian Voyvodina proclaimed their union with the new kingdom. On November 26 the Montenegrins deposed their King Nikita of the ancient Njegosh rulers and merged their country with Serbia under the Karageorgevich dynasty. The following day the Croatian National Council dissolved itself and the Serb-Croat-Slovene kingdom (renamed Yugoslavia in 1929) was solemnly proclaimed in Belgrade on December 1, 1918.[5]

The national territory of the new South Slav state was recognized in a series of five international treaties and agreements. With Bulgaria at Neuilly (November 27, 1919), with Austria at St. Germain (September 10, 1919), with Hungary at Trianon (June 4, 1920), and with Italy at Rapallo (November 12, 1920) and Rome (January 24, 1924). Bulgaria agreed to minor frontier rectifications in favor of Yugoslavia along the Timok river in the north and in the Struma valley in the south. The Austrians and the Hungarians recognized the devolution to Belgrade of Croatia, Slovenia, Dalmatia, Bosnia-Herzegovina, the Sanjak of Novi Bazar, the Voyvodina, part of the

Banat, a slice of territory between the Drava and the Mura rivers, and the southeastern tip of the Hungarian county of Baranya.

It was more difficult to terminate South Slav dependence in the case of Austrian areas claimed by Italy, an Allied power. A secret agreement signed in London on April 26, 1915, between the Allies and then still nonbelligerent Italy [6] had provided for the transfer to Italy, as the price of her entry into the war against the Central Powers, the Slav-inhabited territories of the Istrian Peninsula with the cities of Trieste, Fiume, and Pola; Dalmatia; and certain Adriatic islands. The territorial bargaining at Rapallo and Rome between 1920 and 1924 (as well as the nationalist heroics of the Italian poet D'Annunzio) gained Italy possession of Istria with Pola, Trieste, and Fiume (without its eastern Sushak port area); Zadar on the Dalmatian coast; and a few islands. All South Slavs, except roughly 200,000 Croats and about 400,000 Slovenes, thus passed from a state of dependence to independence.[7] Yet the new Yugoslavia was still multinational, like the vanished Dual monarchy of the Habsburgs. Out of its total population in 1919 of about 12.5 million, over 1.8 million (16 per cent) were non-Slavs transferred from their previous state of independence or interdependence to dependence. These newly dependent populations included 1.5 million Austro-Germans, 467,000 Hungarians, 439,000 Albanians, 251,000 Rumanians, 150,000 Turks (descendants, for the most part, of Bogomil heretics), and 12,000 Italians.[8]

Bulgaria bet on the wrong horse. During the Sarajevo crisis of July 1914 the calculating disposition of King Ferdinand made him reluctant to take sides.[9] The reluctance to see Bulgaria join either camp was reciprocated by both. By August 2, Vienna, Berlin, and Petersburg all had urged Sofia to remain neutral. These urgings were motivated by the fear that Bulgarian belligerence might bring Turkey into the war against Russia or Rumania against the Central Powers. Accordingly, Bulgaria declared her neutrality on August 14 and maintained it until the following autumn, by which time the entry of Turkey into the war as one of the Central Powers had radically altered the strategic picture. During the ensuing twelve months Sofia was tempted by both camps with territorial offers in Thrace, Macedonia, and the Maritsa valley. Swayed by these territorial lures from Vienna and Berlin, enticed by a German-Austrian loan of 400 million Swiss francs, and misled by the failure of the British campaign to force the Dardanelles at Gallipoli (February-August 1915), Bulgaria finally entered the war on the side of the Central Powers in October 1915.[10]

Sofia's early military successes seemed to augur well for the re-establishment of the medieval Bulgarian empire. Yet, it was on the extended Bulgarian front that the great Allied offensive of September 1918 accomplished the breakthrough which sealed the doom of the Central Powers. When the Bulgarian front cracked at the end of September and Sofia sued for a ceasefire, the Turkish, Austrian, and German surrenders followed in quick succession. Bulgaria, victim of the Treaty of Berlin in 1878, felt itself victimized by the Treaty of Neuilly on November 27, 1919. Under the terms of the new peace Bulgaria lost her outlet to the Aegean, had to accept limitations on her armed forces, and had to undertake to pay the Allies $445 million in reparations.[11] The centuries-old rivalry between Serbs and Bulgarians for hegemony in the Balkans was thus decided, perhaps for several future centuries. The South Slavs of the peninsula—or most of them—were united under the successors of Stephen Dushan and not of Ivan Asen. In addition to the emergence of the long-awaited South Slav state around the catalytic Kingdom of Serbia rather than Bulgaria, the Yugoslav annexation of most of Macedonia (large sections of which the Bulgarian armies had conquered while Serb military fortunes were at their lowest ebb in 1915-1917) did not bode well for good neighborly relations between the two Slav nations during the interlude of independence during the next quarter of a century.

Rumania bet on the right horse but too early. She had to pay dearly for her haste until the bet could finally be paid off. The outbreak of the war found Bucharest in a deep quandary. A treaty of alliance had bound the country to Vienna since 1883. The sympathies of her Hohenzollern king naturally lay with Germany. Her two unredeemed provinces were Transylvania, under Hungarian rule, and Bessarabia, under Russian. Hungary and Russia were enemies. In the circumstances, she would be immediately invaded and overrun by Russia if she joined the Central Powers in the hope of winning Bessarabia; by the Central Powers, if she came in on the Allied side in response to promises of Transylvania as the price of her belligerence.[12]

Caught in this bind, Rumania remained neutral, without formally declaring her neutrality, until August 1916. But then the spectacular though ephemeral successes of the great Russian offensive under General Aleksei A. Brusilov convinced the Rumanian Government that a German-Austrian victory was no longer possible. Time proved this a correct conclusion. But in August 1916 this was a premature conclusion, made for the wrong reason. The defeat of the Central Powers, instead of being just around the corner, was still more than two years away. Consequently, when Rumania declared war on Austria-Hungary and invaded Transylvania at the end of August 1916, she was counterattacked and had to sue for an armistice in early December. Bucharest was occupied by the Germans. Peace was dictated in May 1917. Under its terms Rumania had to yield the Dobrudja to Bulgaria and the Carpathian passes leading into Transylvania to Austria-Hungary. There was one compensation, however. The Rumanian population of Bessarabia, emboldened by the collapse of the traditional order in Russia in 1917, proclaimed a "Moldavian Republic," which then joined Rumania.[13] Since the transfer of territory was at the expense of Russia, Germany and Austria-Hungary, at that moment in occupation of Bucharest, recognized the union. Russia never did. She reclaimed the lost province as soon as she was once again on her feet. Yet Rumanian policy was right even if it was implemented prematurely, because the defeat of the Central Powers was only postponed. When the debacle began in the autumn of 1918 with the Allied breakthrough on the Bulgarian front, Transylvania fell like a ripe fruit into the lap of resurgent Rumania. Thus what was impossible in 1914, the acquisition of both Bessarabia and Transylvania, became possible four years later upon the mutual destruction of the Russian and Austrian overlords.

In the treaties of St. Germain, Neuilly, and Trianon, all in the period from September 1919 to June 1920, the union of long-dependent and already independent Rumanians was recognized by both the victorious and defeated contracting parties. Bukovina was ceded by Austria; Transylvania, Maramaros, Crisana, the eastern fringe of the Banat, and the lowland Partium between Transylvania and Hungary proper, by Hungary; South Dobrudja, by Bulgaria. The shift of Rumanian populations from a state of dependence to independence did not terminate the typically multinational character of middle-zone statehood. In 1899, with large masses of Rumanians still dependent, the population of Rumania had been slightly less than six million. Of this total 92 per cent were Rumanians and 8 per cent non-Rumanians. During the first decade of independence following the peace treaties, the total population of Rumania rose to 18 million. Of this 14.5 million (80 per cent) were ethnic Rumanians; 3.5 million (20 per cent) non-Rumanians. The new minorities, transferred from independence, interdependence, and dependence to a new form of dependence, included 1.3 million Hungarians,

680,000 Germans, 536,000 Jews, 550,000 Ukrainians, 300,000 Bulgarians, 230,000 Turks and Tartars, 120,000 Russians, 48,000 Serbs, and 35,000 Poles.[14]

The new sovereignty dubbed Czechoslovakia in 1918 did not have to pick a winner in 1914. Unlike Yugoslavia, Bulgaria, and Rumania, it had no independent catalytic agent with diplomatic and military freedom of action when hostilities broke out. The ancient and highly civilized Kingdom of Bohemia had failed to get an interdependent status from Vienna in 1871 and had remained to all practical purposes a Habsburg province. Without the power to act as a sovereign state, the only opportune Czech means to independence was watchful waiting and delicately astute political maneuvering in preparation for a possible disintegration of the Dual Monarchy. The outbreak of war reactivated long-dormant separatist tendencies. The Czechs and Slovaks, of course, had nothing to gain from a German-Austrian-Hungarian victory and possibly everything to gain from an Allied triumph. As the war years progressed and the latter possibility gradually turned into a strong probability, official Czech and Slovak participation in the Habsburg war effort started diminishing toward zero, which was finally reached in the autumn of 1918. Concurrently, unofficial political and military co-operation with the Allies gained in intensity, until on September 3, 1918, topping recognition from the British and the French, the United States Government accepted the Czechoslovak National Council in exile as a *de facto* belligerent government.[15]

Czechoslovak *de facto* belligerence on the Allied side began as early as August 1914, when a Czech volunteer unit joined the Russian army to fight on the eastern front.[16] Before the end of 1914 the number of Czechs fighting on the Russian side was greatly increased by a steady stream of deserters from the Austro-Hungarian army. A Czechoslovak unit fought bravely at the Battle of Zborov in 1917 in the Russian ranks. The establishment of a Czechoslovak army had been negotiated with the Russian High Command. Then came the Russian revolution. The outbreak of hostilities between Czech armed units in Russia and the Russian Red Army in May 1918 complicated matters.[17] The Czechoslovak Legion fought its way across Siberia in the greatest Czech military effort since the Battle of the White Mountain in 1621 and was repatriated to its liberated homeland across the Pacific and the Atlantic.

This daring military exploit was, in fact, a part of the Allied intervention against the new Bolshevik government of Russia. It tied the emerging Czechoslovak state more firmly to the western Allied side. The Czechoslovak National Council sitting in Petrograd disappeared and the rival exile Council in Paris under Professors Masaryk and Benes emerged as the recognized *de facto* governing body of the Czechs and Slovaks. This exile organ maintained close connections with resistance groups led by national committees in Bohemia and Slovakia. After the disintegration of the Dual Monarchy, the council returned to Prague to assume authority. This was more easily said than done. In the chaotic conditions of 1918-1919, Czech military action was necessary to incorporate the Sudeten German areas of Bohemia. It took two clashes with the resisting Hungarians to occupy Slovakia. A show of force was made against the allied Poles to seize parts of disputed Teschen. A convincing ethnic-strategic argument was presented at the peace conference to obtain Subcarpathian Ruthenia. In 1919-1920 the treaties of St. Germain with Austria and Trianon with Hungary finally gave international recognition to independent though multinational Czechoslovakia. The census of 1921 showed the new state had a total population of 13.6 million. Of this 8.7 million (65 per cent) were Czechs and Slovaks; 4.9 million (35 per cent) minorities. The newly dependent populations included 3.1 million Germans, 745,000 Hungarians, 461,000 Ukrainians and Russians, 180,000 Jews, and 75,000 Poles.[18]

The pattern of Polish liberation resembled the Czechoslovak model. The objectives of national independence were attained by means of quasidiplomatic ties with the future liberators and by placing armed units at their disposal. There were, however, two significant differences. While the Czechoslovak military units fought with the Russians, Pilsudski's Polish legions fought against them. Czechoslovak national territory was spared the ravages of war. For nearly four years the eastern front lay across Polish territory, from the Gulf of Riga in the north to Czernowitz in the Carpathian foothills. Poland, however, was fortunate, even more than Rumania, in profiting from the concurrent defeats of her overlords. The three partitioning powers of Germany, Austria-Hungary, and Russia all bowed to the will of the victors and regurgitated their oppressed nationalities. The resurrection of Poland as a state was, therefore, almost automatic. Reconciliation and fusion of the Paris National Council under Roman Dmowski with the newly established Warsaw government under Joseph Pilsudski was not difficult.[19] Great difficulty lay, however, in the establishment of the new national frontiers in the wide-open Vistula plain, where the principles of historical possession and ethnic heterogeneity formed a Gordian knot of twisted contradictions. What complicated the situation beyond the hope of a permanent solution was the unsuccessful Ukraininan attempt to pass from dependent to independent status at the expense both of resurgent Poland and of disintegrating Russia. The frustrated Soviet attempt in 1920 to push the frontiers of the revolution west of Warsaw prolonged the birth pangs of the new state. The Poles fought on until 1920 in defense of their indefensible national territory. They fought not only against Germans and Russians, but also against their former Lithuanian associates in the north. They were on the verge of fighting against the Allied nation of Czechoslovakia in the south.

The treaties of Versailles and St. Germain in 1919 fixed the new Polish frontiers where it was easy: in the west and the south. The delineation of the difficult eastern boundary began with the elaborate process of drawing the so-called Curzon Line in December 1918.[20] This was a temporary border proposed to divide Poland from the Soviet Union on the basis of a compromise between ethnic and historical principles. The frontier which was finally agreed upon between the two neighbors was drawn by the Treaty of Riga in March 1921. The treaty was negotiated, after the abortive Russian invasion of Poland, in a moment of Soviet weakness. The new political boundary was drawn far to the east of a reasonable ethnic dividing line. Consequently, Poland emerged as a multinational state, resembling both in ethnic composition and in the indefensibility of her frontiers the old pre-1772 kingdom. Because of the independence of Lithuania and Latvia, Poland was again cut off from the Baltic coast, except at Danzig, which was made a free city, to which she was given a corridor through German territory. This anomalous arrangement sprang from President Wilson's Thirteenth Point. It was justifiable both on the grounds of historical precedent and of economic necessity, but certainly neither from the ethnic point of view nor from that of European security. When Poland's frontiers were finally recognized, out of her total population of 27.2 million in 1921 only 18.8 million (69 percent) were Poles. The remaining 31 per cent consisted of dependent minorities, which included 3.9 million Ukrainians, 2.1 million Jews, 1 million Germans, 1 million White Russians as well as Russians, Lithuanians, Czechs, and others in groups numbering less than a hundred thousand.[21]

Lithuanian nationalists were able, after five hundred years of dependence, to resurrect the ancient Grand Duchy of Lithuania though only as a small state.[22] Success was due, first, to German victory on the eastern front during the winter of 1917-1918; later, to the Allied policy of the *cordon sanitaire*, the quarantine designed to insulate Europe from Bolshevik contagion by a barrier of western-oriented states. The Lithuanian declaration of independence was issued during the German occupation in February 1918. Independence was successfully defended against disorganized attacks by both Communist Russians and anti-Communist Germans. For the moment the threat to newly won Lithuanian independence came not from the exhausted Russians and Germans (from whom the fledgling state was able to wrest the Memel territory in 1923) but from the resurgent Poles. The ancient Lithuanian capital Vilna (Wilno) was seized in 1919 and incorporated in 1922 by Poland. Surrounded by hostile neighbors, multinationality added to the woes of the small new republic. Of her population of approximately 2 million, 16 per cent were dependent minorities: Jews, 8 per cent; Poles, 3 per cent; Russians, 2.5 per cent; and others 2.5 per cent.[23]

To the north of Lithuania an independent Latvia appeared for the first time in history in the area of formerly Russian- and Swedish-dominated Livonia and Courland.[24] The emergence of the new state was due to the successful self-assertion of the forces of local nationalism during 1918-1919, at the moment of the nearly simultaneous exhaustion of Russian and German imperial power. The temporary German victory in the east brought about the liberation of the Letts from Russia. The Germans immediately filled the vacuum left by the Russians but retained it for less than a year. Seven days after the German surrender in the west, the full independence of Latvia was proclaimed in Riga on November 18, 1918. British and French naval units in the Baltic protected the Latvian government against both Germans and Russians until finally in October 1919 independence from both seemed to be assured. Like Lithuania to the south, Latvia was also multinational. Of her population of 1.6 million in 1920, which increased to 1.84 million by 1925, only 1.35 million were Lettish-speaking Latvians. The remaining 1.5 million consisted of Russians, Lithuanians, Germans, and Jews.[25]

As an exception to the prevalence of multinationality, an independent Hungary reappeared on the map, ethnically all but homogeneous among greatly restricted frontiers. Before and during the war the Hungarian government had the least maneuverability and also the least desire to maneuver. As constituted under the 1867 Compromise, Hungary had no ministry of foreign affairs, war, or finance. The government's principal war aim was the preservation of territorial integrity as reconstituted in 1867-1871. Opposition to the war in 1914 came from a pro-Allied parliamentary faction and associated intellectuals led by Michael Karolyi (1875-1955), a high-minded liberal aristocrat and inheritor of the Kossuth-Mocsary ideas of independence from Austria and understanding with the other Danubian nationalities. The outcome of the war proved equally wrong the policies of pro-German government and pro-Allied opposition. The official policy, inspired probably more by Hungarian admiration for Hohenzollern Germany than for Habsburg Austria, continued to be based on the likelihood of German victory. Up to the very eve of the collapse of the Central Powers, the German-dictated peace of Brest-Litovsk in the spring of 1918 seemed to confirm the correctness of the official policy.

The foreign policy of the Karolyi opposition compounded the basic error of official policy on several incorrigible counts. When the war began, Karolyi was on his way home from an American lecture tour. He was arrested and interned in France as an enemy national. Instead of remaining and openly declaring for the Allies, as did Masaryk, Benes, and others, Karolyi chose to return to Budapest and re-enter the parliamentary struggle.[26] His rather quixotic political objective at this time seems to have been to bring sufficient Hungarian pressure on Austria to detach her from Germany and make her conclude a separate peace.[27] When, after the abortive attempt of the new King-Emperor Charles (1916-1918) to negotiate a separate peace with the Allies, the defeat of the Austro-Hungarian army was formalized in the Padua armistice (November 3, 1918), Karolyi committed a second mistake. As the head of an independent pro-Allied Hungarian government, he asked for and obtained a separate Hungarian armistice at Belgrade on November 13, 1918. This armistice tacitly accepted French military authority over Hungarian territory, in contrast with the Padua armistice, which had made no provisions whatsoever regarding Hungary. During the ensuing four months Paris made use of its military prerogatives under the Belgrade armistice to permit Serbian, Rumanian, and Czech military advance into Hungarian territory to strategic lines of demarcation beyond justifiable ethnic boundaries.

Karolyi had come into power in October 1918 as a minority leader who had correctly bet on the Allies. His tenure of office rested on the forlorn hope that, when it came to a territorial settlement, the victorious Allies would restrain the appetites of their clients, Hungary's neighbors. When this illusion vanished with the handing to Karolyi of the famous Vyx Note [28] from Paris (March 20, 1919), ordering additional permanent cession of Hungarian territory, he resigned. He did so in the conviction that, his pro-Allied policy having failed, the only possible remaining Hungarian foreign policy orientation was toward Moscow. To effect this reorientation, he handed power to the Social Democrats, not knowing that these had already agreed with the Communist leader Bela Kun on proclaiming the dictatorship of the proletariat.[29]

The ensuing Hungarian Communist attempt at a military reconquest of Slovakia and Transylvania was frustrated by the Allies.[30] With the rise of the Hungarian Soviet Republic in the spring of 1919 the local problem of making territorial arrangements among the new states of the middle zone had risen to the magnitude of primary Allied concern: that of the *cordon sanitaire* policy to stop the westward spread of Soviet power. Whereas before Bela Kun the Allies had simply favored the claims of friendly states against defeated Hungary too lately converted to their cause, with Kun in power, Paris and London proceeded to apply their anti-Bolshevik interventionist policy to Hungary. Accordingly the Rumanian army received Allied approval to dislodge the Hungarian Soviets from Budapest. This was done. A Hungarian nationalist, anti-Communist regime under Admiral Nicholas Horthy (1868-1957) was then permitted to fill the political vacuum thus created. What followed was a reversal to the peculiar Hungarian state of affairs extending back to the Luxemburg and Habsburg king-emperors: the political dominance, superimposed on a modern parliamentary structure, of a landed elite (containing pseudo-gentry and German assimilant elements) in a kingless and sealess kingdom.

The Hungarians thus finally got the independence from Austria they had vainly fought for during four centuries and then compromised in 1867. The price of independence, in addition to annual reparations payments of 10 to 13.5 million gold crowns for forty years,[31] was the cession of two-thirds of their population and three-fourths of their territory. As constituted by the Treaty of Trianon (1920), Hungary retained in its central plains a population of 7.9 million, among whom the proportion of the Hungarian ethnic element rose, due to the loss of the multinational peripheries, from 51 per cent in 1910 to 90 per cent in 1920. Only two dependent groups, Germans and Slovaks, numbered more than 100,000 each.[32]

The foregoing analysis of how the postwar state system of predominantly multinational countries came into existence should end with an appraisal of the socialist role in establishing the new status quo. As hostilities seemingly progressed interminably, the socialist stance gradually shifted from approval, expressed by voting war credits in 1914, to bitter opposition toward the end by affiliates of the Second International. In April 1915 a conference of SDP leaders in Germany, Austria, and Hungary issued a patriotic communi-

qué stating that "the Social Democratic Parties of the belligerent states
are acting in defense of their countries." [33] When the next socialist
meeting was held in the Swiss village of Zimmerwald during September 1915 (it was attended mostly by left-wing socialists), the majority condemned the official establishments which had brought about
the war and called for peace as soon as possible.[34] Six months later,
in the spring of 1916, an international socialist congress meeting at
Kienthal stopped just short of recommending revolutionary methods in the coming struggle to end the war.[35] At the Stockholm socialist conference during June-July 1917, the consensus of the participants was for peace without delay.[36]

By this time, differences between socialist opponents and defenders of the existing state system were coming out in the open.
While the memorandum of the Hungarian SDP at Stockholm asked
for a peace settlement which would leave intact the Dual Monarchy's
and Hungary's territorial integrity, the document submitted by the
Czech SDP demanded the establishment of an independent Czechoslovak state within a Danubian confederation.[37] The gap between
the socialists of the future victorious and vanquished countries was
thus becoming apparent. On May 1, 1918, the Slovak Social Democrats celebrated international Labor Day with a permit from the
Hungarian police and demanded the "unconditional right of self-
determination" for their dependent nationality.[38] A year later, after
the Slovaks had seceded from Hungary, the Hungarian Red Army
invaded and occupied eastern Slovakia and stayed to protect a newly
proclaimed Slovak Soviet Republic until it was ordered to withdraw
by the Allied War Council in Paris.[39] (This also was an application
of the policy of the *cordon sanitaire*.) It would seem, therefore, that
in shifting their stance on the war from approval to opposition, the
middle-zone socialists remained as wedded to their brands of nationalism at the end of the war as they had been at its outbreak.
They continued resolutely to uphold the right of their nationalities
to statehood regardless of which multinational model was to be the
norm: the Austro-Hungarian or the Czechoslovak. Socialism as well
as nationalism must consequently be recognized as a creative force
partly responsible for filling the middle zone with independent states
at the end of the war.

Adding in 1918-1920 five more independent states (Czechoslovakia, Hungary, Latvia, Lithuania, and Poland) to the five already in
existence in 1914 (Albania, Bulgaria, Montenegro, Rumania, and
Serbia) [40] was essentially an extension from the south to the north
of the Danube of the process of Balkanization. The treaties signed in

the Paris suburbs during 1919-1920 followed the precedent set by the Treaty of Berlin in 1878 in erecting small states on the ruins of a large empire by territorially satisfying competing nationalisms. There was, however, more diplomatic wisdom at Berlin in 1878 than around Paris in 1919-1920. In 1878 the concert of the powers saw to it that the independence of the new Balkan states would be consonant with the interests of all of its members, including Russia, Germany, and the Dual Monarchy. By 1918 the concert of European powers was only a memory. Paris and London no longer cared about the effects of state-making on Great Power interests traditionally pursued by Berlin and Moscow, not to speak of Vienna. In consequence, while the process of Balkanization was being geographically extended from the Aegean to the Baltic, the political foundations of the extended system were laid in apparent oblivion to the fact that sooner or later Berlin and Moscow would resume their traditional great-power interests with a vengeance. The victors of 1918 failed to realize that they were granting their allies only a reprieve from dependence.

Epilogue

The independent states of the middle zone were born at the end of the first great war into a world without precedent. The European state system had been broken [1] in the struggle between the coastal and inland powers; it would remain in a state of fragmentation for at least half a century. Socialism, for the first time in history, had found a sovereign power base in this broken world and was organizing in one country for expansion into others. Anti-Semitism, previously a sociological aberration manipulated by demagogues reaching for power, was becoming in several countries part of the political platform of factions and parties ruling or getting ready to rule. European structural fission, power-based socialism, and officially programmed anti-Semitism were thus circumstantially dominant factors at the historical moment the long-frustrated nationalisms of most of the middle-zone peoples finally found gratification.

Had the two immediately preceding attempts at middle-zone state-making succeeded, even temporarily, during the structural flux and political turmoil that accompanied the French Revolution and the 1848-1849 uprisings, a shift from dependent to independent status could not have been sustained permanently. In an unbroken European state system new small states could not have survived—in fact, did not survive—in violation of great-power interests, any great power's interests, maintained by a concert of the dominant countries. Nor could such countries, emerging between 1795 and 1849, have been affected and molded by the yet nonexistent forces of power-based socialism or officially programmed anti-Semitism. Historically the impossibility of state-making in the middle zone from the late eighteenth to the middle of the nineteenth century—except on Ottoman ruins in the Balkans—is attested by the tragedy of the Polish and Hungarian Jacobins, the quick extinction of the Duchy of Warsaw, the futility of Napoleon's call for an independent Hungary, and the universal fiasco of all revolutionary attempts north of the Danube between 1830 and 1865.

Austria and Russia, acting in concert, put an end to the ephemerally independent Hungarian state in 1849. By 1919 there was no imperial Austria, and Russia had become a socialist outcast. There was therefore no immediately available countervailing power left in existence to snuff out independence. The succession states filling the void left by the dissolved empires could thus go on existing. But their newly won independence was not only for home use. It was strategically utilized for two extraneous purposes by the victorious coastal powers, which had created and supported the new status quo. One purpose was to prevent German or Austrian imperial resurgence. The other strategic objective was to erect an impassable barrier to keep Russian Communism from spilling over into Western Europe. Only one-half of the first objective was reached: there .was, indeed, no Austrian imperial restoration after 1918. But the barriers against Germany and Russia collapsed like a house of cards.

As for socialism, it first triumphed not in England, as had been predicted, but unexpectedly on the eastern fringes of the middle zone, in Russia. Consequently, during the twenties and the thirties proximity to the homeland of the brewing world revolution brought about in most of the middle-zone countries anti-Communist tension resembling a permanent state of siege. The uneasy neighborhood widened the dangerous schism inside the new sovereignties between the top and bottom social strata, between those who had everything to lose and those who could only gain from a westward spread of Communism. Such enhanced internal divisiveness was compounded by enmity between allies and former enemies of the coastal victors. Yugoslavia, Rumania, and Czechoslovakia had benefited from the new status quo. The allies of vanquished Germany—Hungary, and Bulgaria—had suffered from it. Additional cleavages appeared between the allies of the victors: between Czechoslovakia and Poland, between Poland and Lithuania. It was perhaps inevitable that the middle zone, stretching through the center of a broken world, should itself be broken.

Cleavages, rifts, and schisms within the middle zone facilitated outside penetration originating in three power centers. Penetration came first from Paris, during the immediate postwar era, and had as its aim the diplomatic organization of the new countries in accordance with traditional French strategic concepts. The main result of this diplomatic penetration was the creation of the Little Entente of Czechoslovakia, Rumania, and Yugoslavia to serve the objectives of French foreign policy. During the middle thirties, however, Paris-centered penetration was replaced by intrusion from anti-status quo Rome and Berlin, which started to construct a system of counter-alliances. The new alignment, known as the Axis, had objectives attractive to the anti-status-quo small powers of Hungary and Bulgaria. When Nazi Germany finally took the lead over Fascist Italy and resumed the *Drang nach Osten* in the most dynamic and violent form ever attempted, the middle zone gained paramount importance for the Third Reich by virtue of its geographical position athwart all the east-west invasion routes. When the German bid for European hegemony failed the second time in a century and these invasion routes were once again used for westward retreat and pursuit of the invader, the countries through which they ran were turned by military reality from previous western or German to present eastern alliance. From an antieastern exposure they were reversed to an antiwestern defensive position. Unlike the cannon of the Maginot Line defending France from Germany on the eve of the Second World War, the *cordon sanitaire* proved capable of being turned around 180 degrees.

Nazi penetration of the middle zone had been made easier by the existence of political anti-Semitism, which started making inroads into this area before Hitler's rise to prominence. Following the Padua armistice in November 1918, returning soldiers of the Austro-Hungarian army were reported to be looting and attacking Jewish shops as well as aristocratic manor houses in the provinces.[2] An ill-supplied armed mob is a menace to an even moderately propertied group, especially in times of adversity. Defeat at the end of the war aggravated this basic behavior pattern into disorganized violence against a minority reinforced by waves of fairly recent immigration, dynamically pursuing the local advantages of social mobility. As the historical level continued to rise, with the masses exerting an increasingly strong effect on political dynamics, age-old prejudices surfaced from the depths of society with Ortega's "vertical barbarians."[3] Semieducated demagogues and cashiered subalterns, smarting under military defeat, appealed to these prejudices by focusing on the participation of Jewish intellectuals in the bourgeois and Communist revolutions of 1918-1919. Reds and Jews were identified. The counter-revolutions that followed the revolutions were steeped in anti-Semitism. In the mid-twenties there was a brief return to constitutional normality and the rule of moderate rightists. Yet, as Keynes had predicted,[4] the economic consequences of the peace were already opening the floodgates to a rising tide of misery. In the middle zone, as well as in Germany, the world depression that began in the late twenties produced an economically sinking but politically rising lower middle class. The local cadres for private armies wearing shirts of varying hues were provided by the unemployed and the unemployable of this emerging and disoriented group. During the late thirties rival quislings, encouraged by early Nazi diplomatic and military successes, and their local storm troopers were offering to rule the middle-zone countries as dependencies of the Third Reich.

The Germans moved into this divided area with the greatest of ease, encountering armed resistance only from the romantic Poles and from intransigent, mountain-dwelling Yugoslavs. The Nazis retained the post-Versailles territorial status quo though they gradually adjusted it to totalitarian German interests. Bohemia-Moravia, Western Poland, Lithuania, and Latvia came under direct German rule. Independence under Nazi quislings was bestowed on Croatia and Slovakia. Transylvania was divided between Rumania and Hungary. Before being taken over completely, Poland and Hungary were allowed to participate in the dismemberment of Czechoslovakia. Exodus and holocaustal extermination cut the Jewish presence back to its eighteenth-century low. The waiting quislings got their chance at once in conquered countries with fallen prowestern governments. In the originally Axis-oriented states they were helped into power only after the apparent decline of German military fortunes prompted secret feelers of separate peace by the collaborating old regimes.

At the end of the Second World War the Russians fought their way into the area against the combined resistance of retreating German and satellite forces. The vacuum left by the expelled Nazis was immediately filled by Soviet power, though the imposition of Communist ideology was accomplished only gradually. Changes made by the Germans in the territorial system were naturally cancelled. Friendly governments, evolving from monarchic to Soviet in character, were substituted for the quisling regimes. The *cordon sanitaire* was reversed not only to insulate the USSR from the west but to turn it into a forward military defense zone to protect the western Soviet frontiers. As formerly Russian territories, Lithuania, Latvia, and Bessarabia were reannexed outright. Poland was moved several hundred miles to the west by means of Soviet annexations of Polish territory in the east, compensated by Polish annexations of German territory in the west. Strategic East Prussia and Subcarpathian Ruthenia were also annexed; the former from defeated Germany, the latter from allied Czechoslovakia.

The extent of these Soviet territorial gains, unprecedented in Russian history or in the middle-zone past, proved socialism supported by nationalism a more powerful ideology than Pan-Slavism in bringing to fulfillment the mystic prophecies about the Third Rome: Moscow as the third imperial city ruling a universal empire in succession to Rome and Byzantium. Indeed, a new socialist commonwealth, much larger than its Byzantine Balkan prototype, came into existence with a control center in Moscow. The organization of the commonwealth showed certain striking similarities (as well as dissimilarities) to the model established by the 1867 Austro-Hungarian Compromise. National autonomy within national boundaries under trusted ruling groups was granted, but control over foreign affairs, defense, and the economy became supranational.

Some of the other changes in the middle zone after 1938 and 1945 were also unrecognized historical continuity. The Third Reich and after its collapse the Soviet Union became contemporary additions to the unceasing succession of controlling empires: Roman, Byzantine, Carolingian, Holy Roman, Habsburg, Hohenzollern, and Romanov. As during the War of the Spanish Succession, the Adriatic coast of the Balkan peninsula was recognized, but not utilized, as a strategic point of penetration to retain independence. On liberating the area from the occupying Nazi forces, the Soviet armies followed the example set by the Austrians in driving out the Turks at the end of the seventeenth century. They permitted no delay in replacing defeated power with victorious power. Geography again saved the Greeks in the south and the Finns in the north from being taken over. As usual, the Yugoslavs were able to hold out against both conquerors and liberators. True to form, the Albanians remained aloof from their neighbors and found a distant protector in China. Multinationality remained a strong area characteristic, in spite of frontier adjustments and drastic population transfers. Revolutionary movements for self-determination again failed in Poland, Hungary, and Czechoslovakia. Concessions to the defeated rebels established a *modus vivendi* and to some gave illusions of independence. As before, with the indefinite prolongation of dependence, patterns of collaboration replaced those of resistance. Swarms of politically apprehensive or undesirable populations were emitted to use their inbred energies and talents for civilization-building in other countries and on other continents. The clashing nationalisms of the countries these émigré swarms abandoned were restrained by the imposition of a *pax russica*. The age-old economic problem of integrating the area as a favored give-and-take partner in world commerce remained acute but unsolved. A new, historically amnesic generation, born after the interlude of independence between the two wars, ceased to look for liberation and adjusted its biological existence to the political condition of dependence. Would future generations also prove to be so forgetful?

Genealogical Tables

Dynastic marriages strongly affected the course of middle-zone history from the fourteenth to the twentieth century. By virtue of their descent in the female line from the extinct Arpad dynasty, the Neapolitan Anjous (TABLE I) were able to ascend the Hungarian throne early in the fourteenth century. By intermarrying with the Polish Piasts, about to become extinguished, and with the Bosnian-Serb Nemanya-Kotromanoviches (TABLE I), the Anjous of Hungary came into possession of hereditary claims to extend their domains northward into Poland and southward into the Balkans. At the end of the fourteenth century, through the marriages of two Anjou-Nemanya-Piast sister princesses, Maria to Sigismund of the House of Luxemburg (on his descent see TABLE II) and Jadwiga to Vladislas of Jagiello (TABLE I), the middle-zone dynastic confederation came to include Bohemia and Lithuania. This was the zenith of the Monarchy of the Three Seas in the triangle of the Adriatic, Black, and Baltic Seas. The marriage of Sigismund of Luxemburg's daughter Elizabeth (on the House of Luxemburg see TABLE III) to Albert of Habsburg (TABLES I AND II) in the early fifteenth century first placed the Habsburg family on the thrones of Hungary and Bohemia. The Austro-Hungarian-Bohemian dynastic ties were once again established early in the sixteenth century by two parallel Habsburg-Jagiello marriages: the last of the Jagiellos, Louis II of Hungary and Bohemia married Maria of Habsburg, sister of Emperor Charles V and Archduke (later King-Emperor) Ferdinand I; this latter Habsburg scion took to wife Anne of Jagiello, sister of Louis II of Hungary-Bohemia (TABLE IV). The last Jagiello's sudden death in battle in 1526 left both the Hungarian and Bohemian thrones vacant for the related Habsburgs, who mounted these thrones and remained on them until 1918 (TABLE IV).

Table I
DESCENDANTS OF THE HOUSE OF ARPAD
(ANJOUS, LUXEMBURGS, JAGIELLOS, HABSBURGS)

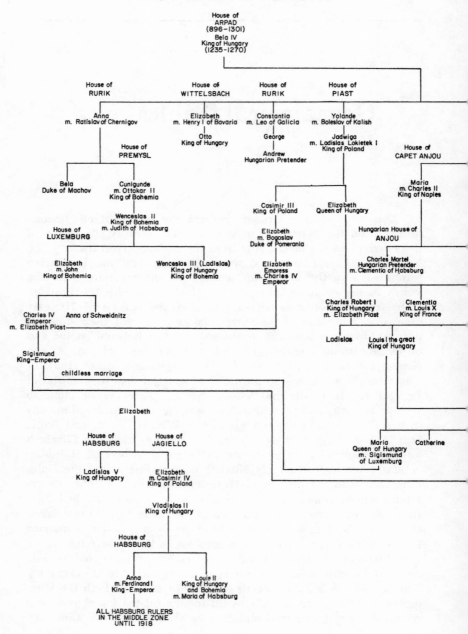

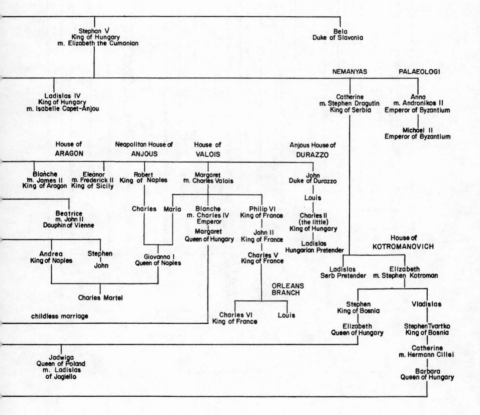

Table II
ANCESTRY OF SIGISMUND OF LUXEMBURG
HOLY ROMAN EMPEROR
KING OF HUNGARY
KING OF BOHEMIA
896-1437

FAMILY NAME

Sigismund
1437

Elizabeth

Charles IV
Holy Roman Emperor
King of Bohemia

John
King of Bohemia

Margaret

Henry VII
Emperor

Elizabeth

Wenceslas I
King of Bohemia

Casimir III
King of Poland

Ladislas I

Elizabeth

Anna — Gedimin, Duke of Lithuania

Boguslav, Prince of Pomerania

Margaret

John

Mathilde — BETHUNE

Guido {
Margaret – Baldwin I, Emperor of Constantinople — FLANDERS
William, Count of Flanders — DAMPIERRE
}

Alix {
Yolanda – Robert, Count of Dreux
Hugh IV, Duke of Burgundy — CAPET
}

Henry {
Maria
Henry II, Duke of Brabant — HOHENSTAUFEN / BRABANT
}

Beatrice

Felicity — COUCY

Baldwin {
Margaret–Baldwin I, Emperor of Constantinople — FLANDERS
2 Brothers
Burchard, Count of Avesnes — D'AVESNES
}

Henry

Margaret

Henry {
Ermesinde — Henry, Count of Luxemburg — DE BAR
Waleram, Count of Arlon — NAMUR / ARLON
}

Judith

Anna

Hedwig {
Anna – Conrad-Berthold, Duke of Carinthia — HOHENBERG
Ulrich — ZÄHRINGEN / KYBURG
}

Albert {
Rudolph, Count of Habsburg — HABSBURG
Agnes — HOHENSTAUFEN
}

Rudolph I
King of Germany

Ottokar II

Wenceslas {
Ottokar, King of Bohemia — PREMYSL
Constantia
Anna
Bela III, King of Hungary
}

Cunigunde

Cunigunde

Ratislav — Michael, Prince of Chernigov — CHÂTILLON / ARPAD / RURIK

Anna {
Maria
Anna – Emperor Alexius III — ANGELOS
Theodoros, Emperor of Nicaea — LASCARIS
}

Yolanda {
Bela IV, King of Hungary
Gertrude of Meran — ANDECHS
Andrew II, King of Hungary — ARPAD
}

Jadwiga

Boleslav, Prince of Kalish

Euphrosina, Duchess of Oppeln — PIAST

Casimir, Duke of Cujavia

JAGIELLO

POMERANIA

Table III

THE HOUSE OF
LUXEMBURG—LIMBURG
1136—1457

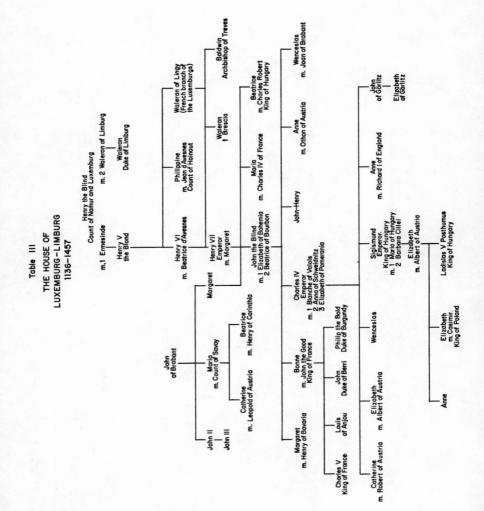

Table IV
THE HABSBURG DYNASTY

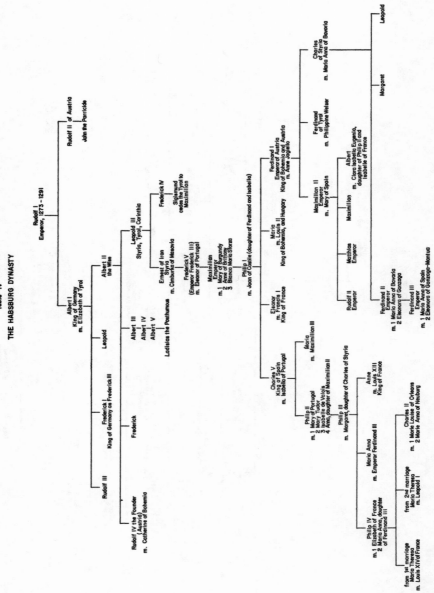

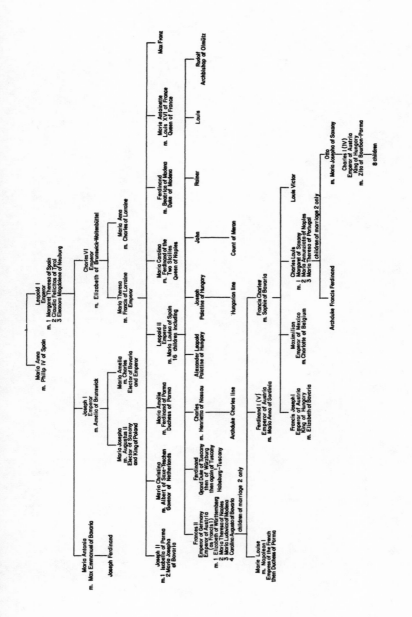

Notes

INTRODUCTION

1. Hersch Lauterpacht (ed.), *Oppenheim's International Law,* vol. I: (London, 1947), p. 256.
2. Ibid., p. 254.
3. See Chapter I below on the coming of the Romans.
4. See Chapter IX below on the Phanariots.
5. See Chapters IV and V on Transylvania.
6. Louis Eisenmann, *Le Compromis austro-hongrois* (Paris, 1904), p. 659.
7. See Chapter XVI below on the Austro-Hungarian Compromise.
8. Richard V. Burks, *East European History: An Ethnic Approach,* American Historical Association Pamphlets No. 425 (1973), p. 35. See also Francis Dvornik, *The Making of Central and Eastern Europe* (London, 1949).
9. J. H. Randall and G. Haines, "Controlling Assumptions in the Practice of American Historians," *Social Science Research Council Bulletin,* No. 46 (1946).

CHAPTER 1

1. W. W. Tarn, *Alexander the Great* (Boston, 1971), vol. I.
2. Carl Roebuck, *The World of Ancient Times* (New York, 1966), Map XIV, p. 404.
3. Colin McEvedy, *The Penguin Atlas of Ancient History* (Harmondsworth, Eng., 1968), map for 375 B.C., p. 55.
4. Alexander Marschack, *The Roots of Civilization* (New York, 1972), p. 393.
5. Alfonz Lengyel and George Radan, *Handbook of Pannonian Archeology* (to be published during 1976 by the University Press of Kentucky).

6. McEvedy, *Atlas* (1968), map for 50,000 B.C., pp. 16-17; Marschack, *Roots*, pp. 36-37; Lengyel and Radan, *Pannonian Archeology*.

7. Lengyel and Radan, *Pannonian Archeology*.

8. *The Encyclopedia Britannica,* XXII (1973), p. 269.

9. McEvedy, *Atlas*, Map for 1850 B.C., pp. 28-29.

10. Lengyel and Radan, *Pannonian Archeology*.

11. McEvedy, *Atlas*, map for 4500 B.C., pp. 20-21, 22-23.

12. Ibid., map for 1200 B.C., pp. 38-39.

13. Ibid., maps for 2250 and 1600 B.C., pp. 24-25, 30-31.

14. Ibid., maps for 1200 and 323 B.C., pp. 38-39, 58-59.

15. Ibid., map for 1300 B.C., pp. 32-33.

16. Ibid., pp. 32 and 50; *Britannica*, XXII, 269-270.

17. *Britannica*, XXII, 269-270.

18. McEvedy, *Atlas*, p. 50.

19. Ibid., maps for 375 and 323 B.C., pp. 52-53, 58-59.

20. Roebuck, *Ancient Times*, p. 366.

21. Ibid.

22. The Bretons, for example, crossed the Channel to the British Isles only to return to Brittany (Bretagne), driven by post-Roman Germanic invaders. The Celtic cross-channel movement (by the Hallstatt Celts) began in the fifth century B.C.

23. Lengyel-Radan, *Pannonian Archeology*.

24. R. W. Seton-Watson, *A History of the Roumanians* (Cambridge, 1963), p. 1.

25. McEvedy, *Atlas*, map for A.D. 138, pp. 80-81.

26. Lengyel-Radan, *Pannonian Archeology*.

27. Otto J. Maenchen-Helfen, *The World of the Huns* (Berkeley, Calif., 1973), pp. 18-23; Ferdinand Lot, *Les Invasions barbares* (Paris, 1937), II, 92-97.

28. Francis Dvornik, *Origins of Intelligence Services* (New Brunswick, N.J., 1974), pp. 129 ff.; Lot, *Invasions*, II, 99-101.

29. Dvornik, *Origins*, pp. 129 ff.; Lot, *Invasions*, I, 225 ff.

30. Erik Molnár, (ed.), *Magyarország története* (Budapest, 1964), I, 41-47; Bálint Hóman and Gyula Szekfü, *Magyar történet*, I (Budapest, 1928), 119-130.

31. Dvornik, *Origins*, pp. 129 ff.; Lot, *Invasions*, II, 108-110.

32. Antal Kampis, *The History of Art in Hungary* (London, 1966), p. 15.

33. Dvornik, *Origins*, pp. 272 ff.; Lot, *Invasions*, II, 110-111.

CHAPTER 2

1. *Richard II*, Act II, Scene 1.

2. Francis Dvornik, *The Slavs in European History and Civilization* (New Brunswick, N.J., 1962), pp. 3 ff.; Ferdinand Lot, *Les Invasions barbares* (Paris, 1937), I, 218-230.

3. Erik Molnár (ed.), *Magyarország története* (Budapest, 1964), I, 29-37;

Bálint Hóman and Gyula Szekfü, *Magyar történet,* I (Budapest, 1928), 9-92.
4. Alexander Marschack, *The Roots of Civilization* (New York, 1972), p. 393; Colin McEvedy, *The Penguin Atlas of Ancient History* (Harmondsworth, Eng., 1968), p. 24.
5. Cf. Richard V. Burks, *East European History: An Ethnic Approach,* American Historical Association Pamphlets 425 (1973), pp. 6 ff.; and Dimitri Obolensky, *Byzantine Commonwealth: Eastern Europe, 500-1453* (New York, 1971), pp. 5-41.
6. A Russian naval attack against Byzantium was beaten back in 860.
7. On the origins of the Luxemburg dynasty, see Paul Weber, *Histoire du Grand-Duché de Luxembourg* (Brussels, 1957).

CHAPTER 3

1. George A. Buttrick *et al.* (eds.), *The Interpreter's Bible,* XI (New York, 1955), 3-4.
2. George Radan, "Comments on the History of the Jews in Pannonia," *Acta Archaeologica Academiae Scientiarum Hungaricae* No. 25 (Budapest, 1973), pp. 265-278.
3. Alfonz Lengyel and George Radan, *Handbook of Pannonian Archeology* (to be published during 1976 by the University Press of Kentucky).
4. Ibid.
5. Dimitri Obolensky, *The Byzantine Commonwealth: Eastern Europe, 500-1453* (New York, 1971), p. 203.
6. Ibid., pp. 86 ff.
7. Ibid., pp. 93-94.
8. Ibid., p. 96; Roger Portal, *The Slavs* (New York, 1972), pp. 90-93.
9. Obolensky. *Byzantine Commonwealth,* p. 109.
10. Ibid., p. 132; Francis Dvornik, *The Slavs in European History and Civilization* (New Brunswick, N.J., 1962), p. 89; Portal, *Slavs,* p. 40.
11. Obolensky, *Byzantine Commonwealth,* pp. 243-247; Dvornik, *Slavs,* pp. 82-92; Portal, *Slavs,* p. 94.
12. Obolensky, *Byzantine Commonwealth,* pp. 97 ff.; Dvornik, *Slavs,* pp. 89 ff.; Portal, *Slavs,* pp. 103 ff.
13. Obolensky, *Byzantine Commonwealth,* illustration No. 76. (The author's comments are based on a personal examination of the crown and the coronation insignia.)
14. Ibid., illustration No. 75. (For both crowns, see also Gyula Moravcsik, *Byzantium and the Magyars* [Amsterdam, 1970]).
15. Obolensky, *Byzantine Commonwealth,* p. 155; Moravcsik, *Byzantium.*
16. Obolensky, *Byzantine Commonwealth,* p. 155.
17. Obolensky, *Byzantine Commonwealth,* pp. 11, 161; Moravcsik, *Byzantium.*
18. Obolensky, *Byzantine Commonwealth,* pp. 258-259.
19. Oscar Halecki, *Poland* (New York, 1966), pp. 8 ff.
20. Ibid., p. 14.

21. Oscar Halecki, *Borderlands of Western Civilization* (New York, 1952), p. 56.
22. Ibid., pp. 79-81.
23. Obolensky, *Byzantine Commonwealth*, pp. 81, 84.
24. Ibid., pp. 154, 155; Bálint Hóman and Gyula Szekfü, *Magyar történet*, I (Budapest, 1928), 90 ff.; Erik Molnár (ed.), *Magyarország története* (Budapest, 1964), I, 33.
25. Obolensky, *Byzantine Commonwealth*, pp. 72 ff.; Dvornik, *Slavs*, p. 43; Portal, *Slavs*, pp. 90 ff.
26. Obolensky, *Byzantine Commonwealth*, pp. 84-85 ff.
27. Ibid., pp. 93-94.
28. Obolensky, *Byzantine Commonwealth*, pp. 161-163; Moravcsik, *Byzantium*.
29. Obolensky, *Byzantine Commonwealth*, p. 163; Moravcsik, *Byzantium*.

CHAPTER 4

1. Dimitri Obolensky, *The Byzantine Commonwealth* (New York, 1971), p. 91.
2. Ibid., p. 118.
3. Ibid., pp. 57 ff.; Francis Dvornik, *The Slavs in European History* (New Brunswick, N.J., 1962), p. 42.
4. S. Harrison Thomson, *Czechoslovakia* (Hamden, Conn., 1965), p. 133; Roger Portal, *The Slavs* (New York, 1969), pp. 79-80; Oscar Halecki, *Borderlands of Western Civilization* (New York, 1952), p. 43; Bálint Hóman and Gyula Szekfü, *Magyar történet*, I (Budapest, 1928), 176-177.
5. Hóman and Szekfü, *Magyar történet*, I, 159-184; Eric Molnár (ed.), *Magyarország története* (Budapest, 1964), I, 50-51; Peter Gunst, *Magyar történelmi kronológia az östörténettöl 1966-ig* (Budapest, 1968), p. 20.
6. Hóman and Szekfü, *Magyar történet*, I, 239-286; Molnár, *Magyarország*, I, 56-57; Gunst, *Kronológia*, p. 22.
7. Molnár, *Magyarország*, I, 57; Gunst, *Kronológia*, p. 23.
8. Oscar Halecki, *Poland* (New York, 1966), pp. 11-12, 15, 26, 34; Molnár, *Magyarország*, I, 57.
9. The heathen Prussians belonged to the Baltic and not to the Germanic branch of the Indo-Europeans. Their name has been inherited by the modern Prussians, a people of Germanic speech and culture.
10. Halecki, *Poland*, pp. 67-68, and *Borderlands*, pp. 111-112; Obolensky, *Byzantine Commonwealth*, p. 263; Portal, *Slavs*, pp. 54-55; Dvornik, *Slavs*, p. 77.
11. Dvornik, *Slavs*, pp. 96 ff.; Obolensky, *Byzantine Commonwealth*, pp. 121 ff.; Portal, *Slavs*, pp. 93 ff.; Hóman and Szekfü, *Magyar történet*, I, 187; II, 8 ff.; III, 61 ff.
12. Obolensky, *Byzantine Commonwealth*, p. 215.
13. Ibid., pp. 121-127.
14. Ibid., pp. 124, 126.

15. Alojz Benac and Oto Bihalji-Merin, *Bogomil Sculpture* (New York, 1963).
16. Ibid., xvii.
17. Obolensky, *Byzantine Commonwealth*, p. 126, and Stephen Runciman, *A History of the Crusades*, Vol. III (New York, 1954), accept the possibility of a link between the Bogomils and Albigensians. So does Louis Bayle, *Procès de l'Occitanisme* (Toulon, 1975). Norman F. Cantor, *Medieval History* (London, 1969), pp. 417-420, 453-454, rejects it.
18. Howard Kaminsky, *A History of the Hussite Revolution* (Berkeley, Calif., 1967).
19. Ibid., pp. 1 ff.; Dvornik, *Slavs*, pp. 189 ff.
20. Kaminsky, *Hussite Revolution*, p. 339; Dvornik, *Slavs*, p. 201; Portal, *Slavs*, p. 87.
21. Dvornik, *Slavs*, pp. 336 ff.; Portal, *Slavs*, p. 87.
22. Dvornik, *Slavs*, pp. 3 ff.; Portal, *Slavs*, p. 88.
23. Dvornik, Slavs, p. 406; Thomson, *Czechoslovakia*, pp. 109-110.

CHAPTER 5

1. Norman F. Cantor, *Medieval History* (London, 1969), p. 107; Colin McEvedy, *The Penguin Atlas of Medieval History* (Harmondsworth, Eng., 1967), map for A.D. 362, pp. 14-15.
2. W. L. Langer, *An Encyclopedia of World History* (Boston, 1972), p. 169; see also A. W. A. Leeper, *A History of Medieval Austria* (Oxford, Eng., 1941).
3. S. Harrison Thomson, *Czechoslovakia* (Hamden, Conn., 1965), p. 19.
4. Ibid., pp. 24 ff.
5. Peter Gunst, *Magyar történelmi kronológia az östörténettöl 1966-ig* (Budapest, 1968), pp. 21 ff.
6. Eric Molnár (ed.), *Magyarország története* (Budapest, 1964), I, 57; Bálint Hóman and Gyula Szekfü, *Magyar történet*, I (Budapest, 1928), 266.
7. Molnár, *Magyarország*, I, 70; Hóman and Szekfü, *Magyar történet*, I, 331-390.
8. Oscar Halecki, *Poland* (New York, 1966), pp. 32-33.
9. Ibid., p. 36.
10. Thomson, *Czechoslovakia*, pp. 132 ff.
11. Stephen Runciman, *A History of the Crusades* (Cambridge, 1951), I, 140-141, 147-148; Gunst, *Kronológia*, pp. 26, 32.
12. Hóman and Szekfü, *Magyar történet*, I, 123-124.
13. Ibid., pp. 403-404.
14. Molnár, *Magyarország*, I, 64 ff., 100.
15. Hóman and Szekfü, *Magyar történet*, II (1930), 32, 357; Francis Dvornik, *The Slavs in European History* (New Brunswick, N.J., 1962), p. 14.
16. For the geographical location of the Barcza fief, see Molnár, *Magyarország*, I, 128, map No. 5, 46° northern latitude, 25° eastern longitude.
17. Gunst, *Kronológia*, p. 35.
18. Halecki, *Poland*, pp. 34-36; Dvornik, *Slavs*, p. 14.

244 *A History of Middle Europe*

19. Halecki, *Poland*, p. 35.
20. McEvedy, *Atlas of Medieval History*, map for A.D. 1401, pp. 80-81.
21. Dvornik, *Slavs*, pp. 13 ff.; Halecki, *Poland*, pp. 76 ff.
22. Halecki, *Poland*, pp. 53-54.
23. Emile G. Léonard, *Les Angevins de Naples* (Paris, 1934), map No. 1, preceding preface.

CHAPTER 6

1. For the origins and rise of the Anjou (Angevin) dynasty, see Emile G. Léonard, *Les Angevins de Naples* (Paris, 1954), pp. 1-50.
2. Ibid., p. 344.
3. Eric Molnár (ed.), *Magyarország története* (Budapest, 1964), I, 98.
4. Bálint Hóman and Gyula Szekfü, *Magyar történet*, III (Budapest, 1934), 8-9.
5. On the origins and rise of the Luxemburg dynasty, see Paul Weber, *Histoire du Grand-Duché du Luxembourg* (Brussels, 1957). On Sigismund and the Hussites, see Howard Kaminsky, *A History of the Hussite Revolution* (Berkeley, Calif., 1967), pp. 3 ff.
6. Oscar Halecki, *Poland* (New York, 1966), p. 65.
7. Ibid., pp. 53-57; Peter Gunst, *Magyar történelmi kronológia az östörténettöl 1966-ig* (Budapest, 1968), p. 53.
8. Francis Dvornik, *The Slavs in European History* (New Brunswick, N.J., 1962), p. 135.
9. Léonard, *Les Angevins*, pp. 301-302.
10. Oscar Halecki, *Borderlands of Western Civilization* (New York, 1952), p. 100.
11. Marcel de Vos, *Histoire de la Yougoslavie*, 2nd ed. (Paris, 1965), pp. 44-45; Hóman and Szekfü, *Magyar történet*, III, 198-199.
12. Halecki, *Poland*, pp. 75 ff., 118 ff.
13. Ibid., pp. 65-74.
14. Dvornik, *Slavs*, p. 75.
15. Ibid., p. 78.
16. Halecki, *Borderlands*, p. 99; Molnár, *Magyarország*, p. 107; Hóman and Szekfü, *Magyar történet*, III, 68.
17. Gunst, *Kronológia*, p. 57.
18. All nobles, great and small, "shall enjoy one and the same freedom" (*sub una et eadem libertate gratulentur*). Hóman and Szekfü, *Magyar történet*, III, 121; Molnár, *Magyarország*, I, 106.
19. Léonard, *Les Angevins*, p. 476.
20. Hóman and Szekfü, *Magyar történet*, III, 184.
21. Ibid., p. 202.
22. Ibid., pp. 205-206.
23. See Kaminsky, *Hussite Revolution*.
24. Hóman and Szekfü, *Magyar történet*, III, 261-266.

CHAPTER 7

1. Erik Molnár (ed.), *Magyarország története* (Budapest, 1964), I, 118-120.
2. Roger Portal, *The Slavs* (New York, 1969), p. 87.
3. Henri Pirenne, *Medieval Cities: The Origins and Revival of Trade* (Princeton, N.J., 1952), pp. 76-105, 115.
4. The phrase was coined by Immanuel Wallerstein, and is used in his *Modern World System: Capitalist Agriculture and the Origins of the European World Economy* (New York, 1974).
5. Molnár, *Magyarország*, I, 120-121.
6. Ibid., p. 148.
7. Ibid., pp. 120 ff.
8. This was the first Pope John XXIII (1410-1415), Baldassare Cardinal Cosa before his election to succeed Pope Alexander V. See *Annuario Pontificio* (Vatican City, 1974).
9. Gyula Szekfü, "A Magyar Renaissance" (in Bálint Hóman and Gyula Szekfü, *Magyar történet*, III [Budapest, 1934], p. 399); Eric Molnár (ed.), *Magyarország története*, I (Budapest, 1964), 120; Peter Gunst, *Magyar történelmi kronológia az östörténettöl 1966-ig* (Budapest, 1968), p. 64.
10. Szekfü, "A Magyar Renaissance," p. 123; Molnár, *Magyarország*, I, 120-121; Gunst, *Kronológia*, p. 64.
11. *Chronicle of Gáspár Heltai*, a Transylvanian Saxon, cited by Molnár in *Magyarország*, I, 123.
12. Molnár, *Magyarország*, I, 157.
13. Szekfü, "A Magyar Renaissance," pp. 136 ff.; Molnár, *Magyarország*, I, 148.
14. János Bak, "Quincentennial of the Birth of György Székely Dózsa: A Report on the State of Research," *East Central Europe—L'Europe du Centre-Est*, I. 2 (1974), 153-167.
15. Ibid.; Molnár, *Magyarország*, I, 149-154; Szekfü, "A Magyar Renaissance," pp. 429-430, 480; Gunst, *Kronológia*, pp. 80-81.
16. Same references as in N. 15, above.
17. Bak, "Dózsa," p. 163.
18. Molnár, *Magyarország*, I, 155; Szekfü, "A Magyar Renaissance," pp. 431-434; Gunst, *Kronológia*, p. 81.

CHAPTER 8

1. Francis Dvornik, *The Slavs in European History and Civilization* (New Brunswick, 1962), pp. 291-296.
2. Dvornik, *Slavs*, p. 297.
3. Antal Kampis, *The History of Art in Hungary* (London, 1966), p. 123.
4. Dvornik, *Slavs*, p. 296.
5. Ibid., pp. 305-306.
6. Oscar Halecki, *Poland* (New York, 1966), pp. 89-90; Erik Molnár (ed.), *Magyarország története* (Budapest, 1964), I, 127-128; Gyula Szekfü, "A

Magyar Renaissance" (in Bálint Hóman and Gyula Szekfü, *Magyar történet*, III [Budapest, 1934], 279-280); Peter Gunst, *Magyar történelmi kronológia az östörténettöl 1966-ig* (Budapest, 1968), p. 67.

7. Stephen Runciman, *The Fall of Constantinople, 1453* (Cambridge, Eng., 1969).

8. Molnár, *Magyarország*, I, 129-130; Marcel de Vos, *Histoire de Yougoslavie* (Paris, 1965), p. 46; Gunst, *Kronológia*, p. 70; Szekfü, "A Magyar Renaissance," pp. 313-314.

9. Szekfü, "A Magyar Renaissance," pp. 285-286.

10. Oscar Halecki, *Borderlands of Western Civilization* (New York, 1952), p. 142; Robert L. Wolff, *The Balkans in Our Time* (Cambridge, Mass., 1967), pp. 26, 58; Molnár, *Magyarország*, I, 127-130; Szekfü, "A Magyar Renaissance," p. 467.

11. Dvornik, *Slavs*, pp. 205 ff.; S. Harrison Thomson, *Czechoslovakia* (Hamden, Conn., 1965), pp. 37 ff.; Molnár, *Magyarország*, I, 131-142; Szekfü, "A Magyar Renaissance," pp. 322-419 ff.

12. Dvornik, *Slavs*, pp. 205 ff.; Thomson, *Czechoslovakia*, pp. 37 ff.; Halecki, *Borderlands*, pp. 138-140; Roger Portal, *The Slavs* (New York, 1969), pp. 232-233.

13. Szekfü, "A Magyar Renaissance," pp. 340-341.

14. M. Izzedin, "Djem Sultan," *Orient*, No. 30, 2e trimestre (1964), pp. 79-99.

15. Szekfü, "A Magyar Renaissance," pp. 340 ff.

16. *The Buda Castle* (Budapest, 1971), p. 46; Alfonz Lengyel, "The Italian Quattrocento in the Court of King Matthias Corvinus in Buda," to be published in *Renaissance Studies* in 1976.

17. Szekfü, "A Magyar Renaissance," p. 286.

18. Halecki, *Poland*, p. 90.

19. Ibid., p. 110.

20. R. W. Seton-Watson, *A History of the Roumanians* (Cambridge, 1963), p. 43.

21. Ibid., pp. 50 ff.

22. Roger B. Merriman, *Suleiman the Magnificent* (New York, 1966).

23. Bálint Hóman and Gyula Szekfü, *Magyar történet*, IV (Budapest, 1928), 16.

24. Gyula Szekfü, "A Magyar Renaissance," p. 441.

25. Ibid., p. 446; Molnár, *Magyarország*, pp. 156-158.

26. Károly Kisfaludy (1788-1830), "Mohács," an elegy in distichs, in *Hét Évszázad Magyar Versei* (Budapest, 1966), I, 939-941.

CHAPTER 9

1. Robert Mantran, *Histoire de la Turquie* (Paris, 1968), p. 33.

2. Peter Gunst, *Magyar történelmi kronológia az östörténettöl 1966-ig* (Budapest, 1968), p. 56.

3. Fernand Braudel, *La Méditerranée et le monde méditerranéen à l'époque de Philippe II* (Paris, 1966), II, 13 ff.

4. Leonard Bloomfield, *Language* (New York, 1933), pp. 68 ff.; Mantran, *Histoire*, p. 6.
5. Cyril D. Darlington, *The Evolution of Man and Society* (New York, 1971), p. 381.
6. Mantran, *Turquie*, pp. 15 ff.
7. Roger B. Merriman, *Suleiman the Magnificant* (New York, 1966).
8. Darlington, *Evolution of Man*, pp. 382-383.
9. Mantran, *Turquie*, p. 46; Stephen Runciman, *The Fall of Constantinople, 1453* (Cambridge, 1969); Darlington, *Evolution of Man*, p. 382.
10. Darlington, *Evolution of Man*, p. 382.
11. Ibid.
12. R. W. Seton-Watson, *History of the Roumanians* (Cambridge, 1963), p. 129.
13. Ibid., p. 60.
14. Ibid., p. 78.
15. Braudel, *La Méditerranée*, II, 410, 419; R. W. Seton-Watson, *Roumanians*, p. 78. See also G. K. Chesterton's poem, "Lepanto."
16. R. W. Seton-Watson, *Roumanians*, p. 77.
17. Ibid., pp. 87 ff.
18. Ibid., p. 99.
19. Ibid., p. 159.
20. Ibid., p. 100. A somewhat different account (strangling instead of beheading) of the execution is given in *La Nouvelle Biographie générale depuis les temps les plus reculés jusqu'à 1850-1860* (Paris, 1863), IV, 698.
21. R. W. Seton-Watson, *Roumanians*, p. 159.
22. Bálint Hóman and Gyula Szekfü, *Magyar történet*, IV (Budapest, 1928), 23.
23. Ibid., pp. 26-28 ff.
24. Ibid., pp. 224 ff.; V (1929), 63 ff.
25. Ibid., III, 327.
26. Darlington, *Evolution of Man*, p. 383.
27. Roger Portal, *The Slavs* (New York, 1969), p. 242; Darlington, *Evolution of Man*, p. 382.
28. Erik Molnár (ed.), *Magyarország története* (Budapest, 1964), I, 181.
29. Darlington, *Evolution of Man*, pp. 382, 384 n.; Mantran, *Turquie*, p. 62.
30. Mantran, *Turquie*, p. 59.
31. Darlington, *Evolution of Man*, pp. 382-383.
32. Mantran, *Turquie*, p. 57.
33. Darlington, *Evolution of Man*, pp. 387-388.
34. Portal, *Slavs*, p. 246.
35. Molnár, *Magyarország*, I, 217-230; Gunst, *Kronológia*, pp. 104-109; Hóman and Szekfü, *Magyar történet*, IV, 383-386.
36. Gunst, *Kronológia*, p. 106.
37. Ibid., p. 88.
38. Ibid., p. 98; Molnár, *Magyarország*, I, 204-205.
39. Gunst, *Kronológia*, p. 98; Molnár, *Magyarország*, I, 206.

40. Molnár, *Magyarország*, I, 202-203.
41. Ibid.
42. Braudel, *La Méditerranée*, I, 174-176; Molnár, *Magyarország*, I, 202-204.
43. Merriman, *Suleiman*, pp. 289-290; Gunst, *Kronológia*, p. 95.
44. Hóman and Szekfü, *Magyar történet*, IV, 142-145.
45. Ibid., p. 123.

CHAPTER 10

1. Imre Lukinich (ed.), *Sources of Hungary's History under the Turks: Diaries and Memoires* (Budapest, 1923), cited by Bálint Hóman and Gyula Szekfü, *Magyar történet*, V (Budapest, 1929), 18-19.
2. Hóman and Szekfü, *Magyar történet*, V, 19.
3. Roger Portal, *The Slavs* (New York, 1969), p. 247.
4. Marcel de Vos, *Histoire de la Yougoslavie*, 2nd ed. (Paris, 1965), p. 53.
5. Francis Dvornik, *The Slavs in European History and Civilization* (New Brunswick, 1962), pp. 94 ff.
6. Loránd Benkö (ed.), *A magyar nyelv története* (Budapest, 1967), p. 284.
7. Abdulah Shaljič, *Turcizmi u srpskohrvatskom jeziku* (Sarajevo, 1966), p. 23.
8. Alf Grannes, *Etude sur les turcismes en bulgare* (Oslo, 1970), p. 11.
9. "Les Archives de Raguse," in Fernand Braudel, *La Méditerranée et le monde méditerranéen à l'époque de Philippe II* (Paris, 1966), II, 533; De Vos, *Yougoslavie*, pp. 48-49; Portal, *Slavs*, pp. 243-244; Braudel, *La Méditerranée*, I, 29 ff., and II, 69 ff.
10. De Vos, *Yougoslavie*, pp. 49-52.
11. Ibid.
12. Ibid.
13. Ibid.
14. Portal, *Slavs*, p. 246.
15. *Magyar Irodalmi Lexikon* (Budapest, 1965), Vol. III.
16. Ibid.
17. Ibid., Vol. I.
18. "Protestant Schools and Printing Presses in Hungary during the XVIth Century," in Erik Molnár (ed.), *Magyarország története* (Budapest, 1964), I, 200 (map).
19. See Paul Coles, *The Ottoman Impact on Europe* (New York, 1968).
20. Jules Bloch, *Les Tsiganes* (Paris, 1969), p. 11.
21. Ibid., p. 34; Peter Gunst, *Magyar történelmi kronológia az östörténettöl 1966-ig* (Budapest, 1968), p. 154; Robert Mantran, *Histoire de la Turquie* (Paris, 1968), p. 75.
22. Bloch, *Les Tsiganes*, pp. 14-15.
23. Hans J. Hillerbrand, *The World of the Reformation* (New York, 1973), pp. 107-108.
24. Ibid., p. 212; Owen Chadwick, *The Reformation* (Harmondsworth, Eng., 1972), pp. 444-445.

25. Bálint Hóman and Gyula Szekfü, *Magyar történet,* IV (Budapest, 1928), 145.
26. John Hesselink, "Contemporary Dutch Theology," *Reformed Review,* XXVI.2 (Winter, 1973), 67. Prior to the organization of the new church, its so-called Belgic Confession had been adopted in Antwerp in 1566. See Pieter Geyl, *Geschiedenis van de Nederlandse Stam* (Amsterdam, 1948), I, 205 ff.
27. Gunst, *Kronológia,* p. 97; Imre Révész, *Magyar református egyháztörténet* (Debrecen, Hung., 1938), pp. 193-194.
28. Molnár, *Magyarország,* I, 196-197.
29. *Magyar Irodalmi Lexikon,* Vol. I; Hóman and Szekfü, *Magyar történet,* V, 74-75.
30. Sándor Petöfi, *Összes Költeményei* (Budapest, n.d.), p. 176. After sampling the various vintages in the wine cellar of the pastor preparatory to a drinking bout, the theological student leaves his host holding the palm of his hand on the bunghole of a huge cask of wine from which a faulty spigot had to be removed. The pastor entrusts the student with the task of finding a new spigot to replace the old one. While searching for a replacement in the parsonage, the seminarian is invited to a wedding next door, where the sound of music and the bouquet of freely flowing wine make him forget about his friend the pastor, who is left indefinitely with his palm planted on the bunghole, with infernal expletives as his only recourse.
31. Bálint Hóman and Gyula Szekfü, *Magyar történet,* IV (Budapest, 1928), 231-288; Molnár, *Magyarország,* I, 196 ff.
32. Hóman and Szekfü, *Magyar történet,* IV, 251.
33. Ibid.
34. On the bibliography of Luther and the Turks, see ibid., p. 409.
35. Braudel, *La Méditerranée,* II, 226 ff.
36. Portal, *Slavs,* p. 246.
37. Leland Miles (ed.), *St. Thomas More: A Dialogue of Comfort against Tribulation* (Bloomington, Ind., 1965), pp. 9-10.
38. Cicely V. Wedgwood, *The Thirty Years War* (London, 1968), pp. 69-102.

CHAPTER 11

1. Cicely V. Wedgwood, *The Thirty Years War* (London, 1968), pp. 94, 95 ff. Erik Molnár (ed.), *Magyarország története* (Budapest, 1964), I, 226-230.
2. Wedgwood, *The Thirty Years War,* pp. 69-102.
3. Francis Dvornik, *The Slavs in European History and Civilization* (New Brunswick, N.J., 1962), pp. 398 ff.; S. Harrison Thomson, *Czechoslovakia in European History* (Hamden, Conn., 1965), pp. 102 ff.
4. Oscar Halecki, *A History of Poland* (New York, 1966), pp. 123-125.
5. *Cambridge History of Poland* (**CHP**), I (1950), 329, 344, 346, 397.
6. Ibid.
7. Ibid., pp. 336, 344-345.

8. Ibid., pp. 345-347, 410-411; Halecki, *Poland,* pp. 123-125. The history of anti-Trinitarian Unitarianism in Poland is fascinating, from its appearance in 1551 under its apostle Lello Sozzini or Socinus (1525-1552), with his followers fleeing persecution in Italy, through the experiment of the Unitarian religious community in the city of Racau and the open Protestant schism with the Calvinists in 1562, until the banishment of the faithful and their flight in 1658 from Poland to Transylvania, where Unitarianism had been one of the four accepted and recognized religions since 1571.

9. Halecki, *Poland,* pp. 123-125.

10. Dvornik, *Slavs,* pp. 242 ff.; Roger Portal, *The Slavs* (New York, 1969), p. 200; Halecki, *Poland,* pp. 114 ff.

11. *CHP,* I, 410 ff.

12. Ibid., pp. 270, 343, 344, 422, 429.

13. Michael Hrushevsky, *History of Ukraine* (New Haven, Conn., 1941), pp. 151 ff., 162, 174, 222. "Registered" meant bearing arms for the king of Poland.

14. Ibid.

15. Ibid.

16. *CHP,* I, 359-368; Dvornik, *Slavs,* p. 471; Halecki, *Poland,* pp. 117-127.

17. *CHP,* I, 359-368.

18. Ibid., p. 459; Portal, *Slavs,* pp. 211-212; Halecki, *Poland,* p. 139; Dvornik, *Slavs,* p. 473.

19. Dvornik, *Slavs,* p. 473.

20. Peter Gunst, *Magyar történelmi kronológia az östörténettöl 1966-ig* (Budapest, 1968), p. 81 and index.

21. Hrushevsky, *Ukraine,* pp. 187-193.

22. Dvornik, *Slavs,* pp. 471-472.

23. Halecki, *Poland,* p. 146; Dvornik, *Slavs,* pp. 242-244 ff.

24. Halecki, *Poland,* p. 149.

25. Ibid., p. 162.

26. Hrushevsky, *Ukraine,* pp. 277-318; *CHP,* I, 511-517; Halecki, *Poland,* pp. 155-157; Dvornik, *Slavs,* pp. 475-477; Portal, *Slavs,* p. 206.

27. Halecki. *Poland,* pp. 172-174.

28. *CHP,* I, 458.

29. Halecki, *Poland,* pp. 167-170; *CHP,* I, 546.

30. *CHP,* I, 547-548.

CHAPTER 12

1. *Cambridge History of Poland* (**CHP**), I (1950), 547-548; Oscar Halecki, *A History of Poland* (New York, 1966), p. 171.

2. Roger Portal, *The Slavs* (New York, 1969), p. 247.

3. Peter Gunst, *Magyar történelmi kronológia az östörténettöl 1966-ig* (Budapest, 1968), p. 134.

4. Halecki, *Poland,* pp. 172, 174.
5. *CHP,* I, 517 ff.
6. Ibid., pp. 520 ff.
7. Ibid., p. 546.
8. Ministère des Affaires Etrangères, *Recueil des instructions données aux ambassadeurs et ministres de France depuis les traités de Westphalie jusqu'à la révolution française:* XXIX. *Turquie* (Paris, 1969), pp. 149-151.
9. A. de Boislisle (ed.), *Mémoires du Duc de Saint-Simon* (Paris, 1893), XVI, 200-201.
10. Robert Mantran, *Histoire de la Turquie* (Paris, 1968), p. 68.
11. Béla Köpeczi, *A Rákóczi-szabadságharc és Franciaország* (Budapest, 1966).
12. Ibid., p. 163.
13. Ibid., pp. 24, 26, 46, 76, 414, 417.
14. Ibid., pp. 13 ff.
15. Ibid., p. 62, nn. 46 ff.
16. The Rákóczi insurrection in Hungary had a side effect on the development of warfare in the west. The form of light cavalry known as hussars, which played an important tactical role during the wars of the French Revolution and Napoleon, was developed in the French army on an expanding scale after the Hungarian surrender in 1711. The early French hussar regiments were formed and organized from refugee *kuruc* cavalry units, trained by Ladislas-Ignace de Bercheny (1689-1778), son of Rákóczi's second-in-command Nicholas Berchényi (1665-1725). The younger Bercheny rose to the rank of marshal of France (1758). [See *Dictionnaire de biographie française* V (1951), 1481-1482.]
17. Erik Molnár (ed.), *Magyarország története* (Budapest, 1964), I, 285-286.
18. Ibid., p. 291.
19. Victor L. Tapié, *The Rise and Fall of the Habsburg Monarchy* (New York, 1971), p. 154; Molnár, *Magyarország,* I, 290-294.
20. Molnár, *Magyarország,* I, 292.
21. Ibid., p. 293.
22. Ibid., p. 288.
23. *Buda Castle* (Budapest, 1971), p. 57.
24. Molnár, *Magyarország,* I, 286-288; Bálint Hóman and Gyula Szekfü, *Magyar történet,* V (Budapest, 1929), 385.
25. Molnár, *Magyarország,* I, 286; Hóman and Szekfü, *Magyar történet,* V, 385.
26. *"Faciam Hungariam captivam, postea mendicam, deinde Catholicam!"* This statement has been attributed both to Bishop Kollonich and to King-Emperor Ferdinand II (b. 1578-d. 1637).
27. Molnár, *Magyarország,* I, 290.
28. Bálint Hóman and Gyula Szekfü, *Magyar történet,* VI (Budapest, 1931), 17; Gunst, *Kronológia,* p. 156.
29. Molnár, *Magyarország,* I, 290-291; Gunst, *Kronológia,* p. 133.
30. Gunst, *Kronológia,* pp. 147-149.

31. Molnár, *Magyarország*, I, 288, 292; Hóman and Szekfü, *Magyar történet*, V, 388; Gunst, *Kronológia*, pp. 132-134.

32. Molnár, *Magyarország*, I, 328; Gunst, *Kronológia*, p. 157.

CHAPTER 13

1. On the Pragmatic Sanction see Victor L. Tapié, *The Rise and Fall of the Habsburg Monarchy* (New York, 1971); Robert A. Kann, *The Habsburg Empire* (New York, 1957); Arthur J. May, *The Hapsburg Monarchy* (Cambridge, Mass., 1951); Oscar Jászi, *The Dissolution of the Habsburg Monarchy* (Chicago, 1929); and Bálint Hóman and Gyula Szekfü, *Magyar történet*, VI (Budapest, 1931), 100-104.

2. Kann, *The Habsburg Empire*, p. 74.

3. *Cambridge History of Poland* (**CHP**), Vol. 1 (1950).

4. Ibid.; Oscar Halecki, *A History of Poland* (New York, 1966), pp. 163, 200.

5. *CHP*, I.

6. There is disagreement among Polish historians concerning the first use of the *liberum veto*. Professor M. Korduba (*CHP*, I, 514) wrote: "for the first time, in 1652, a single member broke up Parliament." In the same authoritative work (I, 500), Professor W. Czaplinski remarked: "The *Seym* of 1645 . . . owing to an individual veto, failed to vote the funds for war." Halecki, *Poland*, p. 163, may have been the arbiter in declaring: "it is not accurate to date it [the *liberum veto*] from the Diet of 1652."

7. At the beginning of the eighteenth century Poland was the second largest European state, exceeded in size of territory only by Russia, but inhabited by only about twelve million people, about half the population of France at that time with a much smaller state area. About 1 per cent of the Polish population, or roughly 120,000 souls, formed the nobility, who alone had the right to sit in the Diet. The great landowning aristocrats or magnates—the Czartoryski, Potocki, Lubomirski, Radziwill, Sapieha, etc.—numbered about fifty to sixty thousand persons. These great families—the Czartoryski were known as "The Family"—some Polish, others Lithuanian, owned hundreds of thousands of acres, thousands of villages, and hundreds of towns. The rest of the nobility, also numbering about fifty to sixty thousand souls but divided into thousands of families, were the penniless petty nobility, whose social, economic, and intellectual level was hardly distinguishable from their peasant neighbors. In modern American terms the social relationship between the *szlachta* and the serfs may be best explained by reference to the behavioral pattern of the "poor white trash" in the deep South. The relationship between the *szlachta* and the magnates was ambivalent. On the one hand, the impecunious country gentry fancied itself as being in a state of social equality with the magnates in the Republic and used the parliamentary device of the *liberum veto*, the decision-making or -unmaking single noble voice, to advertise the existence of *una et eadem libertas* (one and the same liberty), in other words, complete social equality among the nobles, whether

owners of hundreds of thousands of acres or of none. On the other hand, poverty-ridden members of the *szlachta* tended to become hangers-on of the magnates, living as parasites in the courts and on the estates of the great families, forgetting about social equality in acting as stewards and straw bosses for their princely and baronial masters. From the point of view of the oligarchs the *quid pro quo* for this sort of social symbiosis lay in the political utility of the *szlachta* in providing a bargainable bloc of votes in the Diet and an army of feudal retainers in a possible confederation. (Some of the points discussed in the foregoing are mentioned and illustrated in Roger Portal, *The Slavs* (New York, 1969), pp. 212-213.

8. *CHP*, I.

9. For parliamentary statistics on the use of the *liberum veto* see *CHP*, I, under *liberum veto*, and Portal, *Slavs*, p. 214.

10. Portal, *Slavs*, p. 214. *CHP*, II (1941), 85, states: "From [1763] there were no more exploded Diets."

11. *CHP*, II, 85.

12. *CHP*, II, 55. Under the Saxon kings during the first half of the eighteenth century, the number of deputies in the *Seym* or Lower Chamber of the legislature reached the highest total of 182, not counting the deputies from Prussia.

13. Portal, *Slavs*, p. 214.

14. Ibid.

15. *CHP*, II, 61.

16. Portal, *Slavs*, pp. 215, 220; Halecki, *Poland*, p. 191.

17. *CHP*, II, 18; Portal, *Slavs*, pp. 210-211.

18. *CHP*, II, 67; Portal, *Slavs*, p. 211.

19. *CHP*, II, 133-135, 147-148.

20. Leszczynski was an enlightened philosopher-king and did marvels in the Duchy of Lorraine, where he ruled as duke after his exile from Poland. His statue still stands in the center of the city of Nancy, inscribed with a list of his political reforms. He was a forceful political writer, who dared to criticize the *liberum veto* (*CHP*, II, 179). He presented his ideas for an ideal commonwealth in his *Kingdom of Dumocla*, published in French in 1752.

21. Portal, *Slavs*, pp. 209-210.

22. *CHP*, II, 75-76, 78-79, 101.

23. Ibid.

24. Ibid.

25. Ibid.

26. Ministère des Affaires Etrangères, *Recueil des instructions données aux ambassadeurs et ministres de France depuis les traités de Westphalie jusqu'à la Révolution française: XXIX. Turquie* (Paris, 1969), for 1967-1968.

27. *CHP*, II, the First Partition.

28. Ibid., the Second Partition.

29. Ibid., the Third Partition.

30. Jean Jacques Rousseau, *Considérations sur le gouvernment de Pologne,* in his *Oeuvres complètes* (Paris, 1885), V, 237-302. See also Alfred Cobban, *Rousseau and the Modern State* (London, 1964) and Charles E. Vaughan (ed.), *Political Writings of Rousseau* (Cambridge, 1915), 2 vols.

CHAPTER 14

1. Tibor Vágvölgyi, *A magyar jakobinusok* (Budapest, 1968); Denes Silagi, *Jakobiner in der Habsburger-Monarchie* (Vienna, 1962) and *Aktenstücke zur Gesschichte des Ignaz von Martinovics* (Vienna, 1962), pp. 246-259.
2. Vágvölgyi, *Jakobinusok,* pp. 7-9, 10.
3. John G. Gagliardo, *Enlightened Despotism* (New York, 1967).
4. Victor L. Tapié, *The Rise and Fall of the Habsburg Monarchy* (New York, 1971), pp. 162-164; Erik Molnár (ed.), *Magyarország története* (Budapest, 1964), I, 333.
5. Bálint Hóman and Gyula Szekfü, *Magyar történet,* VI (Budapest, 1931), 289-292 ff; Molnár, *Magyarország,* I, 362; Peter Gunst, *Magyar történelmi kronológia az östörténettöl 1966-ig* (Budapest, 1968), pp. 163-164.
6. R. W. Seton-Watson, *History of the Roumanians* (Cambridge, 1963), p. 186; Molnár, *Magyarország,* I, 388-390; Gunst, *Kronológia,* p. 168.
7. Vágvölgyi, *Jakobinusok,* p. 104.
8. Ibid., pp. 118 ff.
9. Ibid., pp. 118-119.
10. Ibid., p. 120.
11. Kálmán Benda, *A magyar jakobinusok iratai* (Budapest, 1957), 3 vols.; Eric J. Hobsbawm. *The Age of Revolutions, 1789-1848* (Cleveland, Ohio, 1962), p. 79.
12. Vágvölgyi, *Jakobinusok,* p. 131.
13. Benda, *Jakobinusok iratai,* vols. I-III.

CHAPTER 15

1. See Endre Arató, *Kelet-Európa története a 19. század elsö felében* (Budapest, 1971), pp. 1-598.
2. The survival of these lost tribes as a linguistic unit speaking the same language as the Danubian Hungarians was reported by Friar Julian in 1236, sole surviving member of an expedition of four Dominicans dispatched by Andrew II in search of *"magna Hungaria"* on the eve of the Mongolian invasions of the thirteenth century.
3. Howard Kaminsky, *A History of the Hussite Revolution* (Berkeley, 1967), pp. 57 ff.
4. Bálint Hóman and Gyula Szekfü, *Magyar történet,* IV (Budapest, 1928), 9, 10, 399.
5. *Cambridge History of Poland* (CHP), I, (1950), 557.
6. Roger Portal, *The Slavs* (New York, 1969), pp. 364-365, 367, 379.

7. Peter Gunst, *Magyar történelmi kronológia az östörténettöl 1966-ig* (Budapest, 1968), pp. 159-165; Portal, *Slavs,* pp. 368-369.

8. Marcel de Vos, *Histoire de la Yougoslavie* (Paris, 1965), pp. 51-52.

9. For the origins and cartographically depicted evolution of the Military Guard Territories, see Gunther E. Rothenberg, *The Military Border in Croatia, 1740-1881* (Chicago, 1966), and his *The Austrian Military Border in Croatia, 1522-1747* (Urbana, Ill., 1960); and Gyula Székfü, *Magyar történet,* VI (Budapest, 1931), 97.

10. Ede Wertheimer, *Julius Andrássy* (Budapest, 1910), III, 475-501.

11. Georges Lefebvre, *Napoleon: From Tilsit to Waterloo, 1807-1815* (New York, 1970), pp. 226-229.

12. De Vos, *Yougoslavie,* pp. 57-58.

13. Lefebvre, *Napoleon,* pp. 154-155.

14. De Vos, *Yougoslavie,* pp. 58-59.

15. Ibid., p. 50; Portal, *Slavs,* pp. 369-371.

16. R. W. Seton-Watson, *History of the Roumanians* (Cambridge, 1963), pp. 192-219.

17. Ibid., pp. 243-246, 247 n. 1.

18. Oscar Halecki, *A History of Poland* (New York, 1966), p. 232.

19. The Hungarian uprising of October 1956 evolved from popular demonstrations at the statues of General Bem and the poet Petöfi. See Ferenc A. Váli, *Rift and Revolt in Hungary* (Cambridge, Mass., 1961), pp. 158, 266-267.

20. George Barany, *Széchenyi and Hungarian Nationalism* (Princeton, N.J., 1969).

21. Kossuth was a descendant of a Lutheran family of petty nobles, assimilated through generations to Hungarian nationality from originally Slovak ethnicity. As an assimilant and an extreme nationalist he resembled Kosciuszko, a product of generations-long assimilation from Ruthenian to Polish culture. Petöfi, the spellbinding poet of the nationalist revolution, a Lutheran turned Calvinist, was a more recent assimilant of nonnoble origins, the son of a father with a Serbian and a mother with a Slovak name. On Kossuth see J. H. Komlos, *Louis Kossuth* (Buffalo, 1973); on Petöfi, A. Nyerges, *Petöfi* (Buffalo, 1973).

22. Bálint Hóman and Gyula Szekfü, *Magyar történet,* VII (Budapest, 1933), 268. See also Leslie C. Tihany, "Hungarian Struggle for Independence," *Documents and State Papers,* U.S. Department of State, I. 5 (Washington, D.C., August, 1948), pp. 323-339.

23. Halecki, *Poland,* pp. 232-234.

24. Ibid., pp. 239-240.

25. Seton-Watson, *Roumanians,* pp. 195-198.

26. Erik Molnár (ed.), *Magyarország története* (Budapest, 1964), I, 493, 497; · Hóman and Szekfü, *Magyar történet,* VII, 20, 227, 339, 358.

27. Gunst, *Kronológia,* p. 235; Molnár, *Magyarország,* I, 543. There were 9.6 million serfs in Hungary and Transylvania as 1848 opened. In 1853, five

years after emancipation, there were still 7.2 million former serfs and other agricultural laborers landless in the same two areas. See E. Niederhauser, *Jobbágyfelszabadítás* (Budapest, 1962), pp. 141-150.
28. *CHP*, II, (1941), 378, 383.
29. Erzsébet Andics, *1848-49* (Budapest, 1968), pp. 221-224.
30. Ibid.
31. Ibid.
32. *CHP*, II, (1941), 349, 380.
33. Halecki, *Poland*, p. 239.
34. Ibid.

CHAPTER 16

1. Manó Kónyi (ed.), *Deák Ferenc beszédei* (Budapest, 1898), V, 321.
2. Ibid., p. 322.
3. Ibid., VI, 153.
4. For details of the Compromise see the standard works listed in note 1, Chapter 13, of this book (Tapié, Kann, May, Jászi, and Szekfü) and also two recent articles: George Barany, "Hungary: The Uncompromising Compromise," *Austrian History Yearbook*, III.1 (1967), pp. 234-259, and Leslie C. Tihany, "The Austro-Hungarian Compromise, 1867-1918: A Half Century of Diagnosis; Fifty Years of Post-Mortem," *Central European History*, II.2 (1969), pp. 114-138.
5. Ede Wertheimer, *Julius Andrássy* (Budapest, 1910), 3 vols.
6. Friedrich F. Beust, *Aus Drei Viertel-Jahrhunderten* (Vienna, 1887), II, 68, 142.
7. Ibid., pp. 142-143.
8. Ibid., pp. 157-159.
9. Woodrow Wilson, *The State* (New York, 1898), p. 336.
10. Bernard Auerbach, *Les Races et les nationalités en Autriche-Hongrie* (Paris, 1898), pp. 331-333.
11. Harold Larson, *Björnstjerne Björnson: A Study in Norwegian Nationalism* (New York, 1944), pp. 127-128, 154.
12. José Ortega y Gasset, *The Revolt of the Masses* (New York, 1932), pp. 21-29.
13. Gyula Szekfü, *Magyar történet*, VII (Budapest, 1933), 343.
14. Ibid., and Gyula Szekfü, *Három nemzedék* (Budapest, 1935), pp. 286-288.
15. Louis Kossuth, *Iratai* VIII (Budapest, 1900), 3-17.
16. See Tihany, "The Austro-Hungarian Compromise." p. 117.
17. Endre Kovács, *A Kossuth emigráció és az európai szabadságmozgalmak* (Budapest, 1967), pp. 402-417.
18. Oscar Jászi, *A nemzeti államok kialakulása és a nemzetiségi kérdés* (Budapest, 1912), p. 347.
19. György G. Kemény (ed.), *Mocsáry Lajos válogatott írásai* (Budapest, 1958), p. 55.
20. Ibid., pp. 103, 243-244.

21. Oscar Jászi, *Dissolution of the Habsburg Monarchy* (Chicago, 1929), p. 108.
22. Ibid., p. 105.

CHAPTER 17

1. Leslie C. Tihany, "Hungarian Struggle for Independence," *Documents and State Papers*, U.S. Department of State I. 5 (Washington, D.C., August, 1948), p. 333.
2. For the diplomatic history of the Eastern Question see William L. Langer, *European Alliances and Alignments* (New York, 1931). In the following pages the Eastern Question will be looked upon as the first instance since the Thirty Years War in the seventeenth century of a major interaction of middle-zone and coastal European history. The evolution of the Eastern Question will be treated in some detail as a process which, though completely beyond the control of the territorial inhabitants (see Lauterpacht I, 256—note 1, Introduction of this book), led to a reprieve from dependence and to a new middle-zone status quo.
3. Langer, *European Alliances,* pp. 66 ff.
4. Ibid.
5. Ibid., pp. 70-71.
6. See Delacroix's *Massacre of Scio* (1824) in the Louvre.
7. See Philip Magnus, *Gladstone* (London, 1954).
8. Robert Mantran, *Histoire de la Turquie* (Paris, 1968), pp. 100-102.
9. Langer, *European Alliances,* pp. 64 ff.
10. Ibid., p. 113; Gyula Hajdu (ed.), *Diplomáciai Lexikon* (Budapest, 1967), p. 142.
11. Hajdu, *Diplomáciai Lexikon,* p. 142.
12. See Rupert Furneaux, *The Breakfast War* (New York, 1958).
13. Langer, *European Alliances,* pp. 138 ff.; Mantran, *Turquie,* p. 102; Hajdu, *Diplomáciai Lexikon,* p. 755.
14. Langer, *European Alliances,* pp. 150 ff.; Mantran, *Turquie,* p. 102; Hajdu, *Diplomáciai Lexikon,* pp. 119-120.
15. Langer, *European Alliances,* p. 166.
16. Ibid., pp. 328-330.
17. Cyril E. Black, *Establishment of Constitutional Government in Bulgaria* (Princeton, N.J., 1943), pp. 19, 208.
18. See Philip G. Eidelberg, *The Great Rumanian Peasant Revolt of 1907: Origins of a Modern Jacquerie* (Leiden, 1974).
19. Edwin E. Ramsaur, *The Young Turks* (Princeton, N.J., 1957).
20. Bernadotte E. Schmitt, *The Annexation of Bosnia, 1908-09* (Cambridge, 1937).
21. For the final reduction of the Ottoman Empire from a multinational agglomerate to a nation state, see Harry N. Howard, *The Partition of Turkey: A Diplomatic History, 1913-1923* (Norman, Okla., 1931).

CHAPTER 18

1. Amos Elon, *Herzl* (New York, 1975), and Peter Lowenberg, "Theodor Herzl: A Psychoanalytic Study in Charismatic Political Leadership," in Benjamin B. Wolman (ed.), *The Psychoanalytic Interpretation of History* (New York, 1971), pp. 150-191.

2. George Radan, "Comments on the History of the Jews in Pannonia," *Acta Archeologica Academiae Scientiarum Hungaricae*, No. 23 (1973), pp. 265-278.

3. Oscar Halecki, *A History of Poland* (New York, 1966), p. 58.

4. Roger Portal, *The Slavs* (New York, 1969), p. 216.

5. Ibid.

6. Cecil Roth (ed.), *The World History of the Jewish People: The Dark Ages: Jews in Christian Europe, 711-1096* (New Brunswick, N.J., 1966), pp. 6 ff.

7. Fernand Braudel, *La Méditerranée et le monde méditerranéen à l'époque de Philippe II* (Paris, 1966), I, 121 ff., II, 13.

8. Ibid., I, 121 ff., II, 13.

9. Bálint Hóman and Gyula Szekfü, *Magyar történet*, V (Budapest, 1929), 375.

10. Roth, *The World History of the Jewish People*, pp. 10 ff.; Ferdinand Lot, *Les Invasions barbares* (Paris, 1937), II, 107; Bálint Hóman and Gyula Szekfü, *Magyar történet*, I (Budapest, 1928), 60-64.

11. Roth, *The World History of the Jewish People*, pp. 341 ff.; Hóman and Szekfü, *Magyar történet*, I, 60-64.

12. Leo Gershoy, *From Despotism to Revolution* (New York, 1944), p. 272.

13. Arthur J. May, *The Hapsburg Monarchy* (Cambridge, Mass., 1951); Victor L. Tapié, *The Rise and Fall of the Habsburg Monarchy* (New York, 1971); Erik Molnár (ed.), *Magyarország története* (Budapest, 1964), I, 382.

14. Molnar, *Magyarország*, I, 382.

15. Bálint Hóman and Gyula Szekfü, *Magyar történet*, VII (Budapest, 1933), 371-373.

16. Ibid., p. 373.

17. Lowenberg, "Theodor Herzl," p. 160.

18. Hóman and Szekfü, *Magyar történet*, VII, 372-373, 447.

19. Ibid., p. 372.

20. See Louis L. Snyder (ed.), *The Dreyfus Case: A Documentary History* (New Brunswick, N.J., 1973).

21. R. W. Seton-Watson, *History of the Roumanians* (Cambridge, 1963), pp. 220, 324, 347-353.

22. Ibid., pp. 220 ff.

23. Ibid., p. 347.

24. Ibid., p. 350.

25. Ibid., p. 352.

26. See Frederick B. Chary, *The Bulgarian Jews and the Final Solution* (Pittsburgh, Pa., 1972).
27. Lowenberg, "Theodor Herzl," pp. 162 ff.; Snyder, *Dreyfus Case*.

CHAPTER 19

1. T. K. Derry and Trevor I. Williams, *A Short History of Technology* (Oxford, 1970), pp. 275 ff.
2. David Caute, *The Left in Europe* (New York, 1966), pp. 205-206.
3. *Magyar Irodalmi Lexikon* (Budapest, 1965), III, 303-308.
4. See Maurice Dommanget, *Babeuf et la conjuration des égaux* (Paris, 1970); Colloque International de Stockholm, *Babeuf et les problèmes du babouvisme* (Paris, 1963); Claude Mazauric, *Babeuf et la conspiration pour l'égalité* (Paris, 1962).
5. *Magyar Irodalmi Lexikon*, II, 72.
6. Erik Molnár (ed.), *Magyarország története* (Budapest, 1964), II, 83-84.
7. E. H. Carr, *Michael Bakunin* (London, 1937); Francis Dvornik, *The Slavs in European History and Civilization* (New Brunswick, N.J., 1962), p. 553.
8. Caute, *The Left*, p. 207.
9. Peter Gunst, *Magyar történelmi kronológia az östörténettöl 1966-ig* (Budapest, 1968), p. 269.
10. Ibid., pp. 265 ff.
11. Molnár, *Magyarország*, II, 141; Gunst, *Kronológia*, p. 280.
12. Caute, *The Left*, pp. 204-207.
13. Ibid., p. 206.
14. Ibid., p. 205.
15. Ibid., p. 204.
16. *Bolshaya Sovietskaya Encyclopedia* (Moscow, 1952); B. Noël, *Dictionnaire de la Commune* (Paris, 1971); Stewart Edwards, *The Paris Commune* (Chicago, 1971), pp. 222 ff.
17. V. A. Dyakov, *Valery Wroblewski* (Moscow, 1968); Noël, *Dictionnaire de la Commune;* Edwards, *The Paris Commune*, pp. 233 ff.
18. *Bolshaya Sovietskaya Encyclopedia; Magyar Irodalmi Lexikon;* Noël, *Dictionnaire de la Commune;* Edwards, *The Paris Commune*, pp. 206 ff.
19. Molnár, *Magyarország*, II, 122-125.
20. *Cambridge History of Poland* (**CHP**), II (1941), 394.
21. S. Harrison Thompson, *Czechoslovakia in European History* (Hamden, Conn., 1965), p. 233.
22. Gunst, *Kronológia*, p. 276.
23. Ibid., pp. 276-277.
24. Ibid.
25. Robert E. Wolff, *The Balkans in Our Time* (Cambridge, Mass., 1967), p. 108.
26. Ibid., p. 109.
27. Victor S. Mamatey and Rademir Luža (eds.), *A History of the Czechoslo-*

vak Republic, 1918-1948 (Princeton, N.J., 1973), p. 10; Gunst, *Kronológia,* p. 291.

28. Gunst, *Kronológia,* p. 292.
29. *CHP,* II, 429.
30. Ibid., p. 456.
31. Ibid.
32. Ibid.
33. Wolff, *Balkans,* pp. 108-109.
34. Cyril E. Black, *The Establishment of Constitutional Government in Bulgaria* (Princeton, N.J., 1943), pp. 30-47; Wolff, *Balkans,* pp. 111-112.
35. Wolff, *Balkans,* pp. 114, 115-116; Franz Borkenau, *European Communism* (New York, 1953), p. 38.
36. *CHP,* II, 394, 429, 456, 458.
37. Ibid.
38. Ibid.
39. Leslie C. Tihany, "The Austro-Hungarian Compromise, 1867-1918: A Half Century of Diagnosis; Fifty Years of Post-Mortem," *Central European History,* II. 2 (1969), 127.
40. Karl Renner, *Grundlagen und Entwicklungsziele der Österreich-Ungarischen Monarchie* (Vienna, 1906), p. 165.
41. Gunst, *Kronológia,* pp. 290 ff.; Molnár, *Magyarország,* pp. 205 ff.
42. Gunst, *Kronológia,* p. 291.
43. Wolff, *Balkans,* p. 112.
44. Ibid., pp. 109 ff.
45. Ibid., pp. 115-116.

CHAPTER 20

1. Hersch Lauterpacht (ed.), *Oppenheim's International Law:* Vol. I. *Peace* (London, 1947), p. 231 n.
2. See Stavro Skendi (ed.), *Albania* (New York, 1956); E. P. Stickney, *Southern Albania or Northern Epirus, 1912-1923* (Stanford, Calif., 1926).
3. Victor S. Mamatey and Rademir Luža (eds.), *A History of the Czechoslovak Republic, 1918-1948* (Princeton, N.J., 1973), p. 37.
4. Marcel de Vos, *Histoire de la Yougoslavie* (Paris, 1965), pp. 90 ff.
5. Ibid., pp. 93 ff.
6. Ibid., p. 95.
7. Ibid., p. 96.
8. Ibid.
9. Bernadotte E. Schmitt, *The Coming of the War, 1914* (New York, 1930), II, 440-449.
10. Ibid.
11. G. P. Genov, *Bulgaria and the Treaty of Neuilly* (Sofia, 1935).
12. Schmitt, *The Coming of the War,* II, 431.
13. R. W. Seton-Watson, *A History of the Roumanians* (Cambridge, 1963), pp. 501 ff.

Notes 261

14. Ibid., pp. 566-567.
15. Mamatey and Luža, *Czechoslovak Republic*, pp. 39-40.
16. Ibid.
17. Ibid.
18. Mamatey and Luža, *Czechoslovak Republic*, p. 40.
19. Hugh Seton-Watson, *Eastern Europe between the Wars* (Cambridge, 1946), p. 159.
20. Oscar Halecki, *A History of Poland* (New York, 1966), pp. 285, 311, 322.
21. Seton-Watson, *Eastern Europe*, p. 430.
22. The standard work on the resurrection of Lithuania is Alfred E. Senn, *Modern Lithuania* (Leiden, 1966).
23. League of Nations, *Health Organisation Handbook Series No. 6, Official Vital Statistics of the Scandinavian Countries and the Baltic Republics* (Geneva, 1926), p. 106.
24. The standard work on the establishment of Latvia is Adolf Spekke, *History of Latvia* (Stockholm, 1951).
25. League of Nations, *Health Organisation Handbook*, pp. 104-105.
26. See Michael Károlyi's own version of his activities and motivation in *Az egész világ ellen* (Budapest, 1965).
27. Mme Michael Károlyi, *Együtt a forradalomban* (Budapest, 1967), pp. 177-179.
28. P. Pastor, "The Vix Mission in Hungary," *Slavic Review* XIX (September 1970), pp. 481-498; Mme Károlyi, *Együtt* (1967), pp. 465-466.
29. Mme Károlyi, *Együtt*, pp. 303-305, 466.
30. Mamatey and Luža, *Czechoslovak Republic*, pp. 30-33.
31. C. A. Macartney, *Hungary and Her Successors: The Treaty of Trianon and Its Consequences* (Oxford, 1937), pp. 463, 465, 469.
32. Francis Deák, *Hungary at the Paris Peace Conference* (New York, 1942), pp. 277-281, 548.
33. Franz Borkenau, *European Communism* (New York, 1953), pp. 32-33; Peter Gunst (ed.), *Magyar történelmi kronológia* (Budapest, 1968), pp. 304-308.
34. Gunst, *Kronológia*, pp. 304-308.
35. Ibid.
36. Ibid.
37. Mamatey and Luža, *Czechoslovak Republic*, p. 17.
38. Ibid., p. 26.
39. Rudolf L. Tökés, *Béla Kun and the Hungarian Soviet Republic* (New York, 1967), pp. 175, 184, 189, 191.
40. By merging to form Yugoslavia (originally the Kingdom of Serbs, Croats, and Slovenes), Serbia and Montenegro acted to reduce the number of the earliest independent states from five to four.

EPILOGUE

1. The term comes from the title of a play, *Le Monde cassé*, by the French existentialist playwright and philosopher Gabriel Marcel, written in 1933.

It was first used for historical writing by Raymond J. Sontag in his *Broken World* (New York, 1971).
2. Mme Michael Károlyi, *Együtt a forradalomban* (Budapest, 1967), p. 290.
3. José Ortega y Gasset, *The Revolt of the Masses* (New York, 1932), p. 89.
4. John M. Keynes, *The Economic Consequences of the Peace* (London, 1919), pp. 80 ff.

Bibliographic Guide

The most up-to-date summary of works in English on the entire middle zone is in R. V. Burks' *East European History: An Ethnic Approach,* American Historical Association Pamphlets No. 425 (Washington, 1973). For recent works on the principal East European countries in other Western languages one should consult J.-B Duroselle's *L'Europe de 1815 à nos jours,* Nouvelle Clio 38 (Paris, Presses Universitaires, 1970). For Slavic Europe covering the pre-1918 period the standard bibliographic guide is still R. J. Kerner's *Slavic Europe: A Selected Bibliography in the Western European Languages* (Cambridge, Massachusetts, 1918). For a specialized Balkans bibliography, more post- than antebellum, see R. W. Wolff's *The Balkans in our Time* (Cambridge, Massachusetts, 1967), pp. 588-596. For Hungary and Rumania the historical sections of the respective national Academies of Sciences list pertinent recent publications in western languages.

Such periodicals as *East Central Europe* (University of Pittsburgh), *The Journal of Central European Affairs* (Boulder, Colorado), *Central European History* (Emory University), *Austrian History Yearbook* (Rice University), *The Slavic and East European Journal* (University of Wisconsin), *The Slavic Review* (University of Washington, Seattle, Washington—formerly *The American Slavic and East European Review,* Menasha, Wisconsin), *Speculum* (Medieval Academy of America, Cambridge, Massachusetts), and the *Publications of the Program in East European and Slavic Studies* (State University of New York College at Buffalo) are helpful in providing on a quarterly or annual basis guides to recent articles, monographs, and book reviews in English (and also in other languages) dealing with antebellum middle-zone history.

As chronological aids William L. Langer's *Encyclopedia of World History* (Boston, 1971) and Neville Williams' *Chronology of the Modern World: 1763 to the Present Time* (New York, 1967) are highly useful. Péter Gunst's *Magyar Történelmi Kronológia* (Budapest, 1968) covers the early history of all middle-zone territories from Dalmatia to Galicia that were once under Hungarian sovereignty, as well as the comparative history of the other middle-zone countries, but is unfortunately in Hungarian.

Footnotes, bibliographies, and other references in Father Francis Dvornik's *The Slavs in European History and Civilization* (Rutgers University Press, 1962), Gyula Moravcsik, *Byzantium and the Magyars* (Amsterdam, 1970), Dimitri Obolensky, *The Byzantine Commonwealth: Eastern Europe, 500-1453* (New York, 1971), and in the present book list works basic to the pre-World War phases of middle-zone history, published up to 1975.

Index

Blenheim, battle (1704) of, 123
Bloody Sunday (January 22, 1905), 204
Bocskai, Stephen, 89-90, 105
Bodrogkeresztur, Hungary, 8, 18
Bogomils, 38-40, 42, 60, 65, 84, 96, 178; Albigensian heresy and, 39, 243n17
Bohemia, 11, 15, 21, 30, 68, 72, 108; Germanic eastward expansion and, 44, 45, 47-48, 51, 104, 105, 107, 153, 196, 201; Holy Roman imperial claims in, 105-106, 107, 117, 130, 163, 216; Hungarian alliance, 76, 77, 80, 105; Hussite movement in, 40-42, 48, 65, 73, 103, 108; Jews of, 20, 56, 57, 58, 59, 74; nationalist movement (nineteenth century) in, 159, 170-71, 199, 201; pagan revolts in, 35-36; Polish claims of, 51, 76; Renaissance in, 72, 73; serfdom in, 71; socialism in, 202; trade duties and, 55; in World War I, 208, 209, 212, 216-17; World War II and, 227. *See also* Czechoslovakia
Bohemian Brethren, 108, 109
Boii people, 11
Boleslav I, king of Poland, 28, 37
Bolshevik Party, 216, 218
Bona Sforza, queen of Poland, 110
Boris I, khan of Bulgaria, 24, 25, 30, 35
Boris II, tsar of Bulgaria, 25
Boris of Saxe-Coburg, prince of Bulgaria, 7, 184
Bosnia, Yugoslavia, 11, 60, 177; Austrian sphere of influence (1870's) in, 179, 181, 182, 185; Bogomilism in, 39-40, 84, 96; Hungarian conquest of, 62, 77; Hunyadi victories in, 75; socialism in, 203; Turkish government of, 178, 179, 180-81; World War I and, 208
Bosporus, The, 20, 177
Bourbon dynasty, 132, 149
bourgeoisie, 48, 110; nationalist movements (nineteenth century) and, 162, 172-73, 174; peasant revolts and, 68; Protestantism and, 99, 105; socialist tenets and, 204, 226; trade interests of, 55, 56, 57, 140
boyars, 34, 35
Brahms, Johannes, 99
Brancoveanu, Constantine, 85-86

Brandenburg, margraviate of, 51
Brandenburg Prussia, *see* Prussia
Brankovich dynasty, 75
Brashov (Kronstadt), Transylvania, 98, 100
Bratislava (Pozsony, Pressburg), Czechoslovakia, 46, 87, 94, 101, 171; as Hungarian capital, 105; Social Democratic Party in, 202
Brest, Union (1595) of, 112, 137
Brest-Litovsk, White Russia, 142
Brest-Litovsk, Peace (1918) of, 220
Brittany, France, 240n22
Brno (Brünn), Czechoslovakia, 18, 57, 199; Austrian Social Democratic Party in, 205
Brusilov, Aleksei A., 214
Brutus, 12
Bucharest, Rumania, 185
Bucharest, Treaty (1812) of, 156
Bucharest, Treaty (1913) of, 186-87
Buczacz, Treaty (1672) of, 116
Buda, Hungary, 20, 46, 57, 67, 78, 80; Christian recapture (1686) of, 92, 118, 125, 126, 127, 189; coronation of Francis Joseph in, 169; peasant revolt (1439), 68; revolutionary efforts (1795) in, 144; Tancsics in, 198
Budapest (post-1872), Hungary, 9, 12, 18, 126; Herzl in, 188; industrialization in, 199; Jewish population (twentieth century) of, 192; statue of St. Gellert in, 37
Bug River, 57
Bukovina, Rumania, 209, 215
Bulcsu, tribal chieftain, 27
Bulgaria, 11, 12, 16, 20, 142, 150; Alexander and, 8; attacks on Byzantium by, 25-26, 29, 31, 36; Balkan Wars (1912-1913) and, 186-87; Christian schism and, 23-25, 26, 30; Hungarian conquest of, 62; Hunyadi victories in, 75; independence (1908), 185, 208, 216, 222; Islamic conversions in, 84, 96; Jews of, 188, 196; nationalist movement (nineteenth century) of, 157, 178-79, 183-84; Ottoman victories in, 58-59, 119; pagan uprisings in, 35, 38-39; revolt (1875), 178-79; Russian sphere of influence in, 179, 182, 184; San

Maps

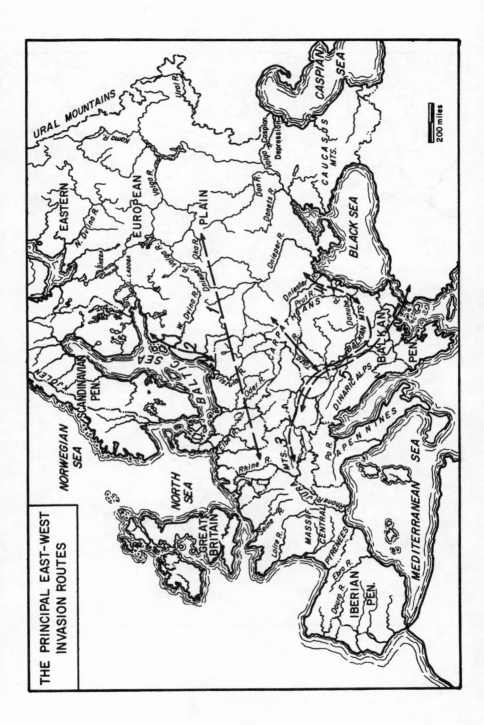

THE PRINCIPAL EAST-WEST
INVASION ROUTES

KEY EAST-WEST LINES OF MOVEMENT SOUTH OF THE VISTULA PLAIN

1 ODER GAP
2 ELBE RIVER GATE
3 MORAVIAN GATE
4 DANUBIAN BASIN
5 FIUME GATE TO HUNGARIAN PLAIN
6 ALBANIAN GAP (DRIN RIVER)
7 VARDAR-MORAVA VALLEY

THE GERMAN SLAV BORDERLANDS
13th to 15th CENTURIES

SCALE

50 0 50 100 Miles
50 0 50 100 150 Km.

BALTIC SEA

POLISH FIEF 1466

Königsberg

DUCHY OF PRUSSIA
1525

HOLSTEIN

Rügen

Danzig

Elbing VARMIA
Marienburg

Kolberg

P O M E R A N I A

ROYAL
TO POLAND
1466

TEUTONIC ORDER

x Grunwald

Tannenberg

Hamburg

MECKLENBURG

Stettin

PRUSSIA

GREAT

KUJAVIA

Dobrzyn

M A Z O V I A

B R A N D E N B U R G

Berlin

Küstrin

LUXEMBURG
1373-1415

P O L A N D

Poznań Gniezno

Warsaw

Magdeburg

LOWER
1368
LUSATIA

POLAND

S A X O N Y

Elbe

Leipzig

Meissen
Dresden

UPPER LUSATIA
Budissin

S I L E S I A N

D U C H I E S

Breslau

Sandomierz

GERMANY

TO BOHEMIA
1266

Eger
(Cheb)

Prague

Pilzeñ

Kutna Hora

Olomouc

POLAND
1457

Cracow

LITTLE

POLAND

UPPER
1353-73
PALATINATE

Nuremberg

B O H E M I A

KARLŠTÝN
LUXEMBURG
1310

Tabor

Budějovices

M O R A V I A

Brno

LUXEMBURG
1310

UPPER

HUNGARY

TO POLAND
ZIPS
1412

Danube

River

BAVARIA

Munich

A U S T R I A

Marchfeld

Vienna

TO BOHEMIA 1251

Bratislava
(Poszony)
(Pressburg)

Trnava

Nitra

H U N G A R Y

LUXEMBURG 1386

Salzburg

Innsbruck

S T Y R I A

TO BOHEMIA
1254

Graz

Gran (Esztergom)

Budapest

TYROL

1335-41 LUXEMBURG
1342-63 BAVARIAN
1353 HABSBURG

CARINTHIA
1269

CILLI
OT 1269
Cilli

VENETIAN

Ljubljana

REPUBLIC

CARNIOLA
1269

Trieste

Zagreb

ITALY

Venice

ISTRIA

CROATIA

FRONTIER OF THE EMPIRE 1378

FRONTIER OF THE EMPIRE 1466

DOMINIONS OF PREMYSL OTAKAR II
BEFORE 1282. DATES ARE THOSE
OF ACQUISITION.

DOMINIONS OF THE HOUSE OF LUXEMBURG
WITH DATES OF ACQUISITION

HABSBURG DOMINIONS IN THE 14th and
15th CENTURIES

X BATTLE

m.e.olrok 1967

Deg. E. Long. 14 20

Deg. N. Lat.

54

48

Deg. N. Lat.

54

48

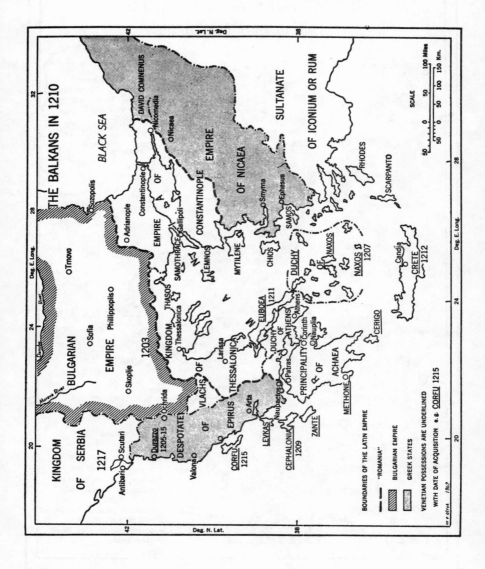

THE BALKANS IN 1210

Deg. N. Lat.

BLACK SEA

DAVID COMNENUS
Nicomedia
Nicaea

EMPIRE OF

CONSTANTINOPLE EMPIRE

Constantinople
Adrianople
Sozopolis

Trnovo

BULGARIAN

EMPIRE

Sofia

Phillipoplis

Skoplje

Danube River

KINGDOM OF SERBIA
1217

Scutari
Antibari
Durazzo 1205-15
Ochrida
Valona

DESPOTATE
OF VLACHS

EPIRUS
Arta
DESPOTATE
OF

Naupactus
LEVKAS
CORFU 1215
CEPHALONIA 1209
ZANTE

Larissa

KINGDOM OF
THESSALONICA
Thessalonica

THASOS
SAMOTHRACE
LEMNOS
MYTILENE

Gallipoli
Smyrna
Ephesus
SAMOS
CHIOS

EMPIRE

OF NICAEA

SULTANATE

OF ICONIUM OR RUM

EUBOEA 1211
DUCHY OF ATHENS
Athens
Corinth
Nauplia
PRINCIPALITY OF ACHAEA
Patras
METHONE
CERIGO

DUCHY OF
NAXOS 1207

Candia
CRETE 1212

RHODES

SCARPANTO

SCALE
50   0   50   100   150 Km.
50   0   50   100 Miles

BOUNDARIES OF THE LATIN EMPIRE
"ROMANIA"
BULGARIAN EMPIRE
GREEK STATES

VENETIAN POSSESSIONS ARE UNDERLINED
WITH DATE OF ACQUISITION e.g. CORFU 1215

w e alrok 1967

Deg. E. Long.

Deg. N. Lat.

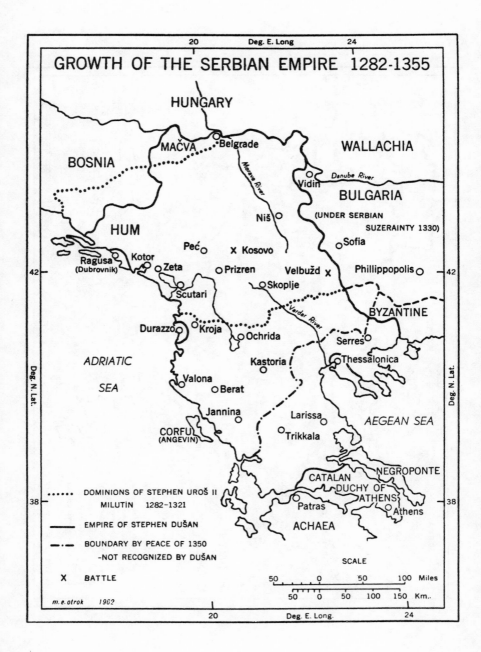

GROWTH OF THE SERBIAN EMPIRE 1282-1355

Deg. E. Long

HUNGARY

BOSNIA

MAČVA   Belgrade

WALLACHIA

Morava River

Vidin   Danube River

BULGARIA

Niš

(UNDER SERBIAN
SUZERAINTY 1330)

HUM

Peć   X Kosovo   Sofia

Ragusa
(Dubrovnik)   Kotor   Zeta   Prizren   Velbužd X   Phillippopolis

Scutari   Skoplje

BYZANTINE

Vardar River

Durazzo   Kroja   Ochrida

Serres

ADRIATIC   Kastoria   Thessalonica

SEA

Valona   Berat

Jannina   Larissa   AEGEAN SEA

CORFU
(ANGEVIN)   Trikkala

NEGROPONTE

CATALAN
DUCHY OF
ATHENS

●●●●●● DOMINIONS OF STEPHEN UROŠ II
        MILUTIN   1282-1321

Patras   Athens

———— EMPIRE OF STEPHEN DUŠAN

ACHAEA

—·—· BOUNDARY BY PEACE OF 1350
        -NOT RECOGNIZED BY DUŠAN

X   BATTLE

SCALE

m.e.otrok   1962

50   0   50   100 Miles

50   0   50   100   150 Km.

Deg. E. Long.

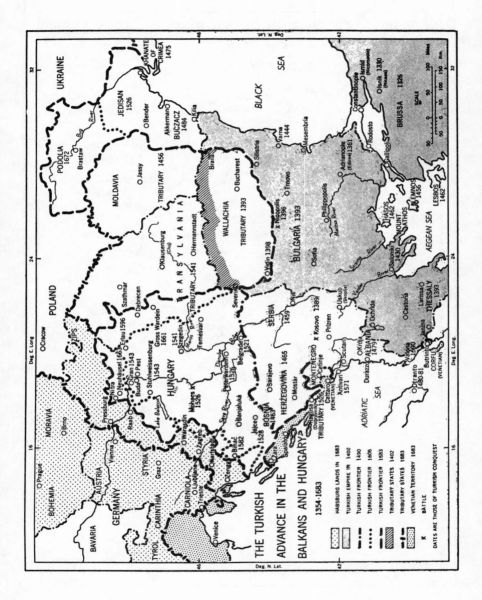

THE TURKISH
ADVANCE IN THE
BALKANS AND HUNGARY
1354-1683

HABSBURG LANDS IN 1683
TURKISH EMPIRE IN 1402
TURKISH FRONTIER 1490
TURKISH FRONTIER 1606
TURKISH FRONTIER 1683
TRIBUTARY STATES 1402
TRIBUTARY STATES 1683
VENETIAN TERRITORY 1683
BATTLE

DATES ARE THOSE OF TURKISH CONQUEST

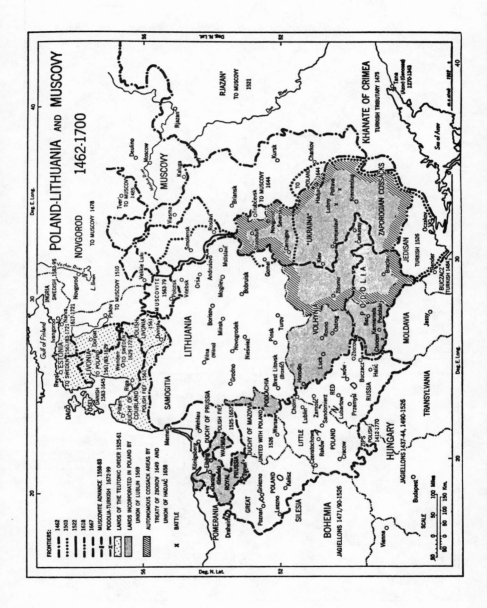

POLAND-LITHUANIA AND MUSCOVY 1462-1700

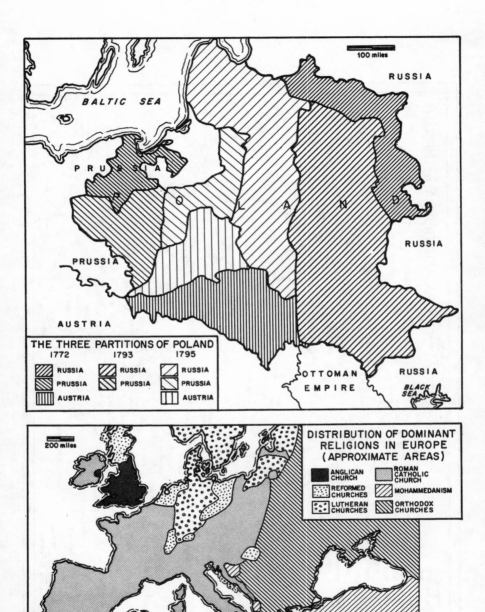

THE THREE PARTITIONS OF POLAND
1772   1793   1795
RUSSIA   RUSSIA   RUSSIA
PRUSSIA   PRUSSIA   PRUSSIA
AUSTRIA   AUSTRIA

DISTRIBUTION OF DOMINANT
RELIGIONS IN EUROPE
(APPROXIMATE AREAS)
ANGLICAN CHURCH   ROMAN CATHOLIC CHURCH
REFORMED CHURCHES   MOHAMMEDANISM
LUTHERAN CHURCHES   ORTHODOX CHURCHES

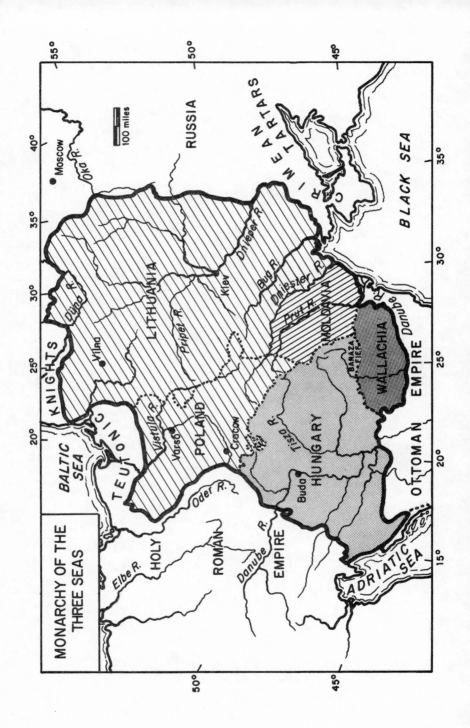

MONARCHY OF THE THREE SEAS

About the Author

A native Hungarian, Leslie C. Tihany emigrated to the United States as an exchange student from the Reformed (Calvinist) Church in his country. He graduated from Franklin and Marshall College and earned a Ph.D. degree from Northwestern University in English and another from the University of Chicago in history. He received two postdoctoral Sheldon Fellowships in comparative philology from Harvard University, where he has also served as a Teaching Fellow. During World War II, he rose to the rank of lieutenant colonel in the U.S. Army. His assignments as a career diplomat in the American Foreign Service for twenty-nine years carried him around the world, to four continents. Since his retirement as American Consul General in Belgium, he has been engaged in research, writing, and lecturing.